# Only Connect

## Shaping networks and knowledge for the new millennium

# Only Connect

## Shaping networks and knowledge for the new millennium

**British Library Cataloguing in Publication Data**
A catalogue record for this title is available from the British Library

**Library of Congress Cataloging-in-Publication Data**
A catalog record for this book is available from the Library of Congress

Published by Bowker-Saur
East Grinstead House, Windsor Court
East Grinstead, West Sussex RH19 1XA, UK
Tel: +44(0)1342 326972  Fax: +44(0)1342 335612
Email: lis@bowker-saur.co.uk
Internet Website: www.bowker-saur.co.uk

Bowker-Saur is part of REED BUSINESS INFORMATION LIMITED.

ISBN 1-85739-2167

Cover design by Wiremill Design
Typesetting by The Florence Group, Stoodleigh, Devon
Printed on acid-free paper
Printed and bound in Great Britain by Antony Rowe Ltd, Chippenham, Wiltshire

## Dedication

For George William Haywood, 1915–1998
gone but remembered.
For Wong Wai-lam, seen once and then lost.
For Primo Levi, gone but not lost.

# Contents

# Abbreviations

| | |
|---|---|
| CEO | Chief Executive Officer |
| EDI | Electronic data interchange |
| EPOS | Electronic point of sale |
| EU | The European Union |
| GDP | gross domestic product |
| ICT | information and communication technology |
| ICTs | information and communication technologies |
| IP | Internet protocol |
| IT | information technology |
| MIS | management information system |
| Net | Internet |
| NetPC | networked computer |
| OECD | The Organization For Economic Cooperation and Development |
| PC | personal computer |
| UK | United Kingdom |
| UN | The United Nations |
| UNESCO | United Nations Educational and Scientific and Cultural Organization |
| US | United States of America |
| WHO | The World Health Organization |
| W3/Web | The World Wide Web |

# Preface

'Only connect! That was the whole of her sermon. Only connect the prose and the passion, and both would be exalted, and human love will be seen at its highest.' E.M. Forster's now famous words from Chapter one of *Howard's End*[1] were written ninety years ago and have been used as a handy metaphor in many domains since. For me 'Only connect' represents the frustration that we all feel at some time or other when seeking to understand or to be understood. As we reach the end of a century that has seen the widespread adoption of mass education and the proliferation of so many different forms of communication we are perhaps startled to find that these frustrations, far from being diminished, have multiplied. Some of the old villains – class, poverty, cultural differences, abuse of power and racial hatred – are still active while the new saviours – the rule of law, universal franchise and network technology – have, in varying degrees, separated as many as they have brought together. This book explores some of the forces at work in the way we connect to share information and knowledge.

The context of the terms used in the text should illuminate their particular meaning but for those who prefer a little more precision I offer the following 'internal' definitions. By 'connect' I mean all the ways that we communicate and transact and all the environments, real and virtual, that we construct to do these things. By 'knowledge' I mean all the ways that we process information to build, grow and construct knowledge within formal and informal domains and via all the media that technology makes available. By 'network' I mean all the ways we use our intelligence to connect with institutions and with each other, and by 'electronic networks' I mean all the information and communication technologies (ICTs) that we use to access or give information and knowledge for pleasure, commerce and education.

Exploring how we connect embraces a seemingly infinite tapestry of possibilities. Just a few of them are explored here, some obvious, some not so obvious. The intersection of diverse influences on us at any one

time is always fascinating, particularly the coincidence of seemingly unrelated elements to create new kinds of empathy, connectivity, synergy and
commerce. Information technology offers the prospect of such coincidence and interaction in spades and well deserves the attention that
it gets. However the emotional and social context is still where we live,
it is still the driver of all the things that we value, and this book is as
much about that context as about the tools we use to connect and
communicate with each other. Humanity has many things in common. A
common ancestry that moved out of Africa around a 100 000 years ago,
a common interest in peace, happiness and prosperity and a common
inquisitiveness about our environment. We share a common desire to
grow knowledge about the world and ourselves and we share a history
of seeking to connect with each other that goes back at least 50 000
years. Yet, despite this long learning curve we each have too many stories
of our failure to connect effectively to be able to say with confidence that
we have reached, or are even approaching, a state of sang-froid in this
dimension of our lives. Sometimes this is because all the old reasons
for not wanting to connect – envy, greed, power, violence, personal
aggrandizement – are as alive and well as we near the end of the twentieth century as they were at the beginning. Some might even argue that
we have refined many more strains of the darker side of our hopes and
desires as we master the limits of space and time. But other failures are
just as often due to incompetence, lack of understanding, the velocity of
change or the failure of just one small part of a complex system. The
more complex the technology perhaps the grander our failures when we
get things wrong. The freer the markets the more intelligent the regulation needed. The more information available the more 'quality' time we
need to evaluate it.

These are conundrums that lie at the very heart of our connected
world. The canvas is wide and I would not claim to cover all the angles.
I have selected just some of the issues that face us today and a few that
might face us in the future. We have embraced many new tools to aid us
in making connections with each other and we will embrace many more.
It is always interesting to speculate on how these may or may not alter
our behaviour. There are lots of questions to ask. How will the promised
'nervous system' of ICTs impact on the things that we say we value? How
will it impact on some of the big issues that have been with us since the
beginning? What will the gains and losses be? How will it change the way

that we connect at work? Is the face-to-face contact that we have regarded as crucial for all our serious transactions really necessary in a wired society? What scope is there for spiritual nourishment in our increasingly material world? I would tend to emphasize how slow a lot of change really is, how we accommodate change incrementally and how we should practise finding the time to put the ICTs that will emerge over the next few years into a clear perspective with regard to our personal hopes and dreams. In accommodating technological change I believe that we should cultivate wisdoms of sceptical welcoming. Sceptical because the richest parts of our lives, what I would call the 'defining moments', often owe nothing to technological progress. The birth of our children, the love of family and friends, the discovery of insights among unlikely people and in unlikely places, the self-revelation that comes from deep introspection – these 'defining moments', though sometimes helped by technology, rarely owe their genesis to a wire in a wall. We may be able to predict the number of microprocessors that we will be able to get on a silicon chip or the number of servers 'living' on the Internet by the year 2010 but we can rarely predict what people will do with them. Sceptical also because the common good, although often a beneficiary, is rarely the primary aim of those that bring new technologies to market. Welcoming because, after assessing and testing how technological change might re-define the value and purpose of our lives, we should employ it as effectively as we can in helping to solve our problems and in adopting richer ways of connecting with each other.

The mechanics of convenience within our lives will be changed immeasurably by these technologies, as will our facility to mine more of the world's information that was once closed or inaccessible to us. As always the outcomes will be mixed. We can take the time to select, evaluate and juggle the novel opportunities that science and technology will bring or we can drown in the new uncertainties that knowing more always brings. Books like this one can be no more than a well-intentioned pebble dropped into the sea of the eternal debate about coincidence and convergence in social, economic, political and technological change. Over our history we have seen these factors collide and mix with each other in so many unpredictable ways that we have come to embrace paradox as a way of life and I make no apology for the regular references to irony and paradox in the chapters that follow. My chosen area is one that is redolent of both as in an event or circumstance that reverses human intentions and where the truth of a matter often looks absurd or contradictory. One paradox, common among many of us, is that we like some change in our lives but we also like stability. Unfortunately we are rarely in control of the mix and when it's not to our liking we often attempt to cope with change by seeking out oases of certainty. We want to control all the environments that we inhabit but we also like adventure and, on occasion, actively seek out situations where we are not in control.

Science and technology seek to reduce unpredictability and yet it is the unforeseen, serendipitous discovery that often pleases us most. It is chastening to remember that many of the 'great' events that have at one time or another dominated the world stage often took us all by surprise. Even the expensive intelligence services maintained by rich governments often failed to detect the signs that would have revealed the possibility of many of them. In 1914 the British press assumed that the year would be dominated by the crisis in Ulster, Gavrilo Princip lurking in Sarejevo could have been a horse running at Ascot. In 1929 the *New York Times* ran the Wall Street crash only as its second lead. Peter Drucker claims to have made his last prediction later that same year when he forecast a quick recovery for the stock market, thereby inoculating himself against the folly of making any similar predictions. The Berlin Wall came down to the surprise of all of us in November 1989 closely followed by the 'shock' release of Nelson Mandela in February 1990. In 1990 Saddam Hussain surprised everyone by his attack on Kuwait just as General Galteri had done in his invasion of the Falklands in 1982.

In a 'connected' world many of the distant events that we observe as interesting items of news on TV may now affect us directly within quite a short time. An Asian, Russian or South American 'Crisis' causes ripples across the globe impacting on financial markets, oil prices, employment and currency values in places seemingly far removed from the source of the problem. The 'source' may be geographically distant but the myriad of connections which countries now have with each other, including the almost invisible ones via inward investment and other arrangements, brings the impact of its behaviour much closer. Confidence, always a fickle sentiment, can now rush in and out of a nation, company or market in the blink of an eye via electronic networks. Many of the newly developed nations in the Far East have only recently seen how disruptive confidence trickling away down a wire can be.

In looking toward the future, even a few years hence, it is humbling to recall that most prophecy has a poor track record. Nonetheless the instinct to look ahead is profoundly human and I will be doing a little bit of it here. Due to the extensive media coverage that new technologies attract, we have shown a tendency to overestimate what might happen in the near future but to underestimate the changes that will affect us in, say, ten years' time. Some of the technologies that we will use in the future are already taking shape as ideas, research projects and secrets in the minds of many innovators scattered around the globe. Social and political change is much harder to predict as are the many, as yet, undetected geophysical forces that are grumbling away around our planet. The way that we connect with each other will continue to be the source of our greatest joys and our worst nightmares, as will the technologies that we use to facilitate it. Armed with a few precepts and defining some core values that we are determined to hang on to we stand more chance of maximizing the joy while leaving the nightmares to 'Elm Street'.

1.    We must always, however difficult it seems at time, seek to be the drivers of technology rather than the driven. This old cliché is generally appreciated at the Hollywood disaster movie level of 'we must not let the machines take over' but to be effective at a deeper level it requires some active involvement in the choices we make with regard to the way we spend our time. New, often superficial, definitions of urgency are squeezing us into relations with technology that both give and take time, energy and convenience. Developing a personal strategy to get the balance right, although sounding like a classroom/academic exercise, is something we must attend to if we are to preserve a sense of wellbeing, fulfilment and comfort among all the frustrations.

2.    Somnambulance is the disease of the remote control. We must continue to use all our senses to access and give meaning to the world rather than taking chunks of it shrink-wrapped for us by the many mediators that the ICTs throw up. We must not endow any technology with the curse of infallibility.

3.    We must fine-tune our grasp of when it matters to spend time growing 'thick' rather than 'thin' knowledge. We are becoming addicted to a skimming culture, trading attention span for quick response times and temporary fixes. A lot of the time this doesn't matter: we don't read the manual but we get the computer/

video/camera to work or we skim some of the detail in the letter but it's only asking about the dog. At other times 'skimming' can leave us exposed, frustrated and vulnerable. Knowing when and when not to bother to immerse oneself in the many different packages of information to which we are now exposed poses heightened challenges of selection. Skimming or misunderstanding some of the side effects of new technologies can be time-consuming, embarrassing and sometimes lethal.

4.   We must set a high price on the things and the people that we value, keeping them to the fore when evaluating 'new' ways of living, '. . . do not dull thy palm with entertainment of each new-hatch'd, unfledged comrade'.[2]

In reflecting on the range of issues covered here I am reminded of the last lines of George Cukor's 1933 comedy film *Dinner at Eight*:

> **Kitty** (Jean Harlow): 'You know, the other day I read a book. It's all about civilization or something – a nutty kind of a book. Do you know that the guy said machinery is going to take the place of every profession?'
> **Carlotta** (Marie Dressler): 'Oh, my dear: that's something *you* need *never* worry about!'

One always finishes, even a 'nutty kind of a book', with a mixture of euphoria and disappointment. Euphoria because it is the end of a long journey and it will be nice now to move on to something else. Disappointment over those missed connections and insights which just stayed out of sight until after the final printing, or worse, that emerge a year later when there are no deadlines to meet. I hope you enjoy reading it as much as I have enjoyed putting it together.

# References

1.   Forster, E.M. (1910) *Howard's End*. Chapter Two

2.   Shakespeare, W. (1601) *Hamlet*, Act 1, Scene III, Polonius's advice to Laertes

Trevor Haywood
February 1999

# Acknowledgements

A.J.P. Taylor, a flawed hero of mine, often said that when he wanted to find out about something he wrote a book about it. 'Writing books is a way of teaching myself and discovering ideas that I never thought of before.' And in writing about the often deserved criticism of himself as sometimes being 'slightly careless' he defended his approach by noting that 'if you wait until every detail is right, you will produce nothing.'[1] I feel much the same way in that everything I write becomes a personal voyage of discovery and self-illumination, some of which I hope to pass on to the reader. Waiting to get every detail right, if indeed there is such a thing in my chosen area, would be a search for unicorns.

The references and the bibliography at the end of the book declare my indebtedness to a whole range of writers and commentators but some, who may not always be noted in the text, deserve a special mention: Stephen Jay Gould for his self-confidence, breadth of knowledge, his unabashed self-congratulation, his fecundity and his joyous addiction to connection making. His collections of essays, first published in *Natural History* magazine, every month, since January 1974, and published in seven volumes up until now (two more are expected by 2001) are an inspiration for anyone seeking to explore 'the marriage of alluring detail with instructive generality'; A.J.P. Taylor for his audacity, his fallibility, his great gifts of communicating complex connections to wide audiences and his studious indifference to the manifold charges of popularism to which he was subjected by those of his contemporaries who preferred the cloister and the cell; Donald MacKenzie for his assiduous and scholarly studies of men interacting with machines; Henry J. Mintzberg for his iconoclasm and piercing common sense in the area of organizational management; Steve Graham, Simon Marvin, Mark Hepworth and others at the Centre For Urban Technology and the Department of Town and Country Planning, University of Newcastle. Their work on the role of telecommunications and the city embraces many important themes and issues concerning the role of new technologies in urban spaces; Primo Levi whose writings expose a luminous humanity and rationality in the face of inexplicable suffering has always been an inspiration; *The Economist* for its up-to-date statistics on everything, for its BigMac index and its regular and intelligent discussion of so many of the issues touched on here. I owe it a debt for providing me with so much of the data that I would have had to look for in a hundred different places if it did not exist.

My thanks also to my old friend Paul Embley at UCE in Birmingham whose conversations, occasional envelopes of cuttings and Web site references have always been a great help. Thanks also to Linda Hajdukiewicz of Bowker-Saur. Given the unhappy job of keeping an eye on me, and reminding me of the impending millennium, she accomplished it with tact and skill.

# Reference

1. Sisman, A. (1994) *A.J.P. Taylor: a biography*. London: Sinclair Stevenson, pp. 361–362.

# A selected chronology – media, computing and communications

Scribes were employed in Egypt in **2600 BC**.

The oldest existing document written on papyrus has been dated at **2200 BC**.

**Between 131 and 140 BC** the Chinese invented paper to use as a packing material, for clothing and for personal hygiene but not for writing. The invention of writing paper is generally credited to the Chinese eunuch Tsai Lun in **AD 105** and the first books are thought to have been printed in China at around **AD 600**. Picture books were available in Japan by **AD 765** and folded books appeared in China around **AD 950**.

Johannes Gutenberg started to use metal plates for printing in **1453**.

## 1896

Sears, Roebuck, and Company issues its first general catalogue offering low prices and a money back guarantee to the farmers who were Sears's principal customers. Its famous general catalogue was discontinued in 1990 but one hundred years after it inaugurated selling over distance to those who couldn't easily make it to a shop some of the first Internet catalogues appeared and online purchase using bytes rather than atoms became a reality.

## 1914

National Cash Register's star salesman, 40-year-old Thomas J. Watson leaves the company to rescue the flagging Computing-Tabulating-Recording Company. He aggressively markets C-T-R's Hollerith machine (a punch card tabulator) including supplying tabulators to the US government during World War I, tripling C-T-R's revenues to almost $15 million by 1920.

## 1924

Watson changes his company name to International Business Machines (IBM). The company soon dominates the market for tabulators, time clocks and electric typewriters, becoming the US's largest office machinery firm by 1940 with sales approaching $50 million.

## 1943

Tommy Flower, a UK Post Office telephone engineer, makes Colossus, an electronic machine built with 1500 valves to help in breaking the enciphered teleprinter code used between Hitler and his generals. This was the first practical application of a large scale program-controlled computer. Watson opines that the world market probably had room for about four or five computers.

## 1945

A US warplane drops atomic bombs on the Japanese cities of Hiroshima and Nagasaki.

The Science Fiction writer Arthur C. Clarke proposes a system of communication satellites in an orbit 35 900 km/22 300 miles above the equator all circling the earth in exactly 24 hours so as to appear fixed in the sky.

## 1947

December: The transistor (ancestor of the microchip and the modern $150 billion semi-conductor industry that has emerged around it) is invented at the Bell Telephone Laboratories in Murray Hill, New Jersey.

## 1948

Williams and Kilburn execute the world's first stored programme on the Mark 1 computer at Manchester University.

## 1951

Remington Rand's commercial computer (the UNIVAC) begins replacing IBM machines. IBM quickly responds using its superior research and development and marketing to build market share.

## 1952

IBM introduces its first commercial computer, the 701.

## 1953

IBM unveils its huge Type 650 Magnetic Drum Calculator designed to make a profit if 50 machines were sold. With about as much computing power as today's video cassette recorder it sold in many thousands by the time it was withdrawn in 1962, making this primitive machine the first mass-produced computer.

## 1957

September: eight engineers, including Gordon Moore and Jay Last resign en masse from William Shockley's Palo Alto company to found the Fairchild Semiconductor Company, the first truly successful semi-conductor company in what was to become known as Silicon Valley.

4 October: the USSR successfully launches the first 'Sputnik' leaving the US anxious about its place in the space race and plunging the US into a cold-war sweat that the USSR had gained a technological and military edge. Spurred on by cold-war paranoia the US begins to pour vast amounts of money into the arms race, the space race and high technology projects of every kind.

IBM introduces the FORTRAN programming language.

## 1958

The Advanced Projects Research Agency (APRA) is founded by the US government to finance hi-tech research. One area on which it focused was the (then extraordinary) notion of computer-to-computer communication. The idea was pioneered by Leonard Kleinrock to enable researchers to transfer the capability of other machines to their APRA machines via a network. Contrary to popular opinion this first electronic network was not constructed to help protect the US from a nuclear attack.

## 1959

Jack Kilby of Texas Instruments and Robert Noyce of Fairchild Semi conductor Company invent the integrated circuit.

## 1961

Yuri Gagarin makes the first orbit of the earth in a spacecraft reaching a height of 188 miles and spending nearly one and a half hours in space.

Alan Shepard became the first American to fly in space, albeit for only five minutes, 23 days after Yuri Gagarin made the first space flight. His fifteen minute sub-orbital flight (only five of these in space) reached a maximum height of 115 miles and restored American self confidence which had been badly shaken by the Russian coup and spurred on the US to be the first to reach the moon.

## 1962

Telstar, the first communications satellite, is launched.

John Glenn is launched into space inside a Mercury spacecraft perched on an Atlas missile rocket for a five-hour round trip. The city of Perth in Australia lights up so that he could see it from his orbit.

## 1963

People around the world are able to watch the funeral of President John F. Kennedy live via pictures bounced from Telstar.

## 1965

Gordon Moore forecasts that computing power will double every eighteen months to two years as engineers found ways to squeeze more integrated circuits of transistors onto silicon chips. Known as 'Moore's Law' this doubling of chip capacity has proved true for three decades and Intel continue to forecast that by 2006 chips will be one thousand times as powerful as today's products and yet cost the same.

## 1968

Intel, short for Integrated Electronics, is founded by Gordon Moore, Robert Noyce and Andrew Groves. Sales in the first financial year are $2672.

## 1969

APRANET project team is commissioned by the US Department of Defence to facilitate research into networking.

BBN develop the Information Message Processor (IMP) using a Honeywell 516 mini computer and 12 Kb of memory.

On Labour Day in the US two computers, one at UCLA and one at Stanford Research Institute, talk (briefly) to each other for the first time using 'packet-switching' (PS) software. PS was an important breakthrough in resource sharing as it only uses the connection when you are sending data. Data traffic tends to be highly 'bursted' – you send some, think a bit, then send some more; when you are not sending data it is possible for someone else to use that line rather than have them queuing up to wait for you to finish. PS also takes long messages and chops them up into little pieces with each travelling the network independently. Each 'packet' has an address saying where it wants to go and the network's switches check out each of these as they come in, they identify the address and send it one way; another packet may get sent another route due to the switch recognizing busy or broken lines. Packets of data thus meander around the network being routed intelligently toward their destination. At the destination they are all re-assembled again to be delivered as a complete picture or file.

At the end of 1969 there are 4 host computers linked to (what will become) the Internet.

# 1971

Apollo 14 moon flight (the third lunar landing mission) is launched commanded by Alan Shepard, the fifth man to walk on the moon and one of only twelve ever to do so.

Ted Hoff, an engineer at Intel, then a three-year-old manufacturer of computer memory chips, invents the microprocessor. Intel produced the 4004 microprocessor (with 2300 transistors) capable of executing (what at the time seemed an amazing) 60 000 instructions per second.

IBM introduces the floppy disk for storing programmes and data.

At the end of 1971 there are 23 host computers linked to the Internet.

# 1973

The first international connections to APRANET come online with connections to University College London and the Royal Radar Establishment in Norway.

# 1974

At the end of 1974 there are 62 host computers linked to the Internet.

# 1976

Two college dropouts, Steve Jobs and Stephen Wozniak, found Apple in the Santa Clara Valley. Their original plan to sell circuit boards changed to selling fully assembled microcomputers after Jobs' first sales call bought an order for 50 completed units. They built Apple 1 in Jobs's garage and sold it without a monitor, keyboard or casing.

# 1977

Wozniak substantially improves Apple 1 in his new Apple II by adding a keyboard, colour monitor and eight slots for peripheral devices that inspired numerous third party add-on devices and software programmes.

## 1980

Over 130 000 Apple II units had been sold by now. Revenues rose from just $7.8 million in 1978 to $117 million in 1980, the year in which Apple went public.

Intel's 8088 microprocessor now contains 30 000 transistors and runs at ten times the speed of the 4004.

There is a US nuclear alert when a computer error indicates a missile attack by the USSR.

Sony launches the 'Walkman', a small portable personal tape recorder.

Intelsat 5 communication satellite is launched capable of relaying 12 000 telephone calls and two television channels.

Tim Berners-Lee writes Enquire (short for Enquire Within Upon Everything) a software program to help him organize his research notes.

## 1981

Rupert Murdoch buys *The Times* and *Sunday Times* newspapers in Britain. The IBM Company launches its personal computer system using the Intel 8088 processor and the Microsoft disk-operating system (MS-DOS). The latter was a polished up version of Seattle Computer Products' operating system which Bill Gates bought (he had no operating system to sell at that time) on receiving an invitation from IBM to provide an operating system for its forthcoming PC.

The IBM PC with Intel (inside) and MS-DOS becomes the industry standard.

IBM's failure (it saw PCs as a bit of a sideline at the time) to secure exclusive rights to either Intel's chips or Microsoft's operating software paved the way for the clones that would eventually reduce IBM PC's share of the market from 100 per cent to less than 10 per cent today.

## 1982

*Time* magazine declares the computer to be 1982 'Man' of the year. It is interesting to note that the editorial accompanying this declaration, although mentioning several computer manufacturers like IBM, Apple, Texas Instruments, Commodore and Atari and some online services like MEDLINE, did not mention Bill Gates, Microsoft or MS-DOS, something that would be unthinkable 17 years on.

Compact disc (CD) players go on sale.

The first 'clone' of an IBM PC is produced using the same operating system as the IBM PC.

Annual turnover of Intel passes $1 billion

February 19th sees the first Flight of the Boeing 757.

The first issue is published of *USA Today*, an all-colour national newspaper. Many commentators gave it no chance of securing a national audience in so big and fragmented a market. They were wrong.

## 1984

Apple launch the Macintosh (incorporating a graphical user interface inspired by Xerox's Alto computer) via an intriguing TV commercial aired only once during the Super Bowl that challenged chief rival IBM by offering the computer 'For The Rest Of Us'.

AT&T is broken up into seven regional telephone systems (the 'Baby bells'), a research company and a residual corporation (still called AT&T) dealing with long-distance connections.

In the UK British Telecom is privatized and Mercury attempts to compete.

The Reuters news agency is floated on the UK stock market.

Robert Maxwell buys the Mirror Group of newspapers.

JANET (Joint Academic Network) is established to link university computer hosts in the UK.

William Gibson publishes *Neuromancer* and invents the term 'cyberspace'.

IBM sets the record for the most money every made by any firm in a single year clocking up $6.6 billion in profit.

The number of computer hosts linked to the Internet breaks through the

1000 mark.

## 1985

Cinema audiences in the UK rise by 33 per cent to 70 million.

United Newspapers buy UK Express Newspapers.

In March Capital Cities Communication buys the US television company ABC.

In April Rupert Murdoch buys 50 per cent of Twentieth Century Fox film company in the USA.

In May Rupert Murdoch buys most of Metromedia's television stations in order to form Fox Television, Inc.

In September Rupert Murdoch becomes a US citizen in order to comply with US law prohibiting aliens from owning television stations in the USA.

In December Canadian Conrad Black takes control of UK Telegraph Newspapers.

Intel ends memory chip production.

Steve Jobs leaves Apple, after a noisy power struggle within the company, to form NeXT with five former Apple employees.

The CD-ROM becomes available.

## 1986

Apple moves into the office market with the Mac Plus and the LaserWriter printer, a combination that ushers in the desk-top publishing revolution.

## 1987

The number of computer hosts linked to the Internet exceeds 10 000.

## 1988

2nd November, 7pm Eastern Standard Time, a lone college graduate, using just 3000 lines of code, released the Internet worm causing havoc among many government and academic computer networks, including 6000 military computers across the US.

PanAmSat, the first privately owned commercial international (as opposed to domestic) satellite is launched.

The first transatlantic optical fibre telephone cable to enter service links the US, the UK and France. It can handle 40 000 simultaneous conversations – almost five times more than a conventional copper cable.

## 1989

Toshiba of Japan produces the first commercial samples of 4-megabit DRAM computer chips.

Intel launches the 486 chip.

Lloyds of London develops a new insurance policy to cover losses caused by computer viruses. It excludes the US due to the proliferation of viruses there.

130 000 host computers are connected to the Internet.

## 1990

APRANET is closed down.

Microsoft launches Windows 3.0.

Mitch Kapor founds the Electronic Frontier Foundation (EFF).

300 000 host computers are connected to the Internet.

## 1991

Tim Berners-Lee completes the World Wide Web software (a wide-area hypermedia information retrieval initiative aimed at giving universal access to a large universe of documents) at the European Laboratory for Particle Physics (CERN), on which he has been working since 1989 and which is later placed in the public domain.

## 1992

Apple loses a key ruling in its suit against Microsoft and Hewlett Packard after claiming copyright protection for the 'look and feel' of the Macintosh user interface.

Intel's annual profits exceeds $1 billion.

1 100 000 host computers are connected to the Internet.

## 1993

Intel launches the Pentium processor.

IBM is in trouble. Having posted losses of more than $15 billion over the last three years and burdened by a bloated bureaucracy that was slow to react to downsizing and networking trends in the computer industry it saw sales of its lucrative mainframe and minicomputer business evaporate. CEO Lou Gerstner cuts staffing costs, shuts plants, cuts R&D, sells real estate and begins to re-focus on networking, client/server systems, PCs and software to boost sales.

University of Illinois releases the Mosaic Web browser developed by Marc Andreessen and others.

## 1994

The number of commercial computers connected to the Internet exceeds those of academic and research institutions.

Jim Clark and Marc Andreessen form Netscape Communications and place the first free version of their Navigator/browser on the Internet.

The first shopping malls appear on the Internet including food suppliers like Pizza Hut.

Microsoft launches Windows 95.

## 1995

Sun Microsystems formally announces Java and HotJava at SunWorld 1995, threatening the Windows/Intel hegemony by incorporating the Java Virtual machine (JVM). This allows programs to be processor-independent and distributed so that parts of them can be in different places. By hiding all the machine-specific code in the VM, a Java applet (application) or pro-gramme can (in theory) run on any computer where the JVM has been implemented – the origin of Sun's famous 'write once, run anywhere' mantra.

Intel launches the Pentium Pro.

December: Sun and Netscape announce JavaScript, a scripting language based on Java and accessible to non-programmers. IBM and Adobe announce a licensing agreement with Sun for the use of Java. Microsoft announces plans to license Java while announcing a suite of Internet prod-ucts, including Visual Basic script.

6 600 000 host computers are connected to the Internet.

## 1996

Intel form an alliance with Microsoft to develop the NetPC, a low-cost response to network computers under development by rivals.

The US 1996 Telecommunications Act replaces the 'creaky' Act of 1934 with the aim of promoting more competition in both local and long distance telephony.

WorldCom takes over MFS including its UU-Net Internet service.

Bell Atlantic takes over NYNEX.

SBC takes over Pacific Telesis.

12 800 000 host computers are connected to the Internet.

## 1997

The World Trade Organisation (WTO) announces an agreement between 69 countries to open their telecommunications markets to competition by 1998.

Intel launches the Pentium II.

BT still has 85 per cent of the domestic UK telephony market 13 years after privatization and de-regulation and more than half of US telephone subscribers still use AT&T, unfazed by the fact that it charges more than its rivals.

BT seeks to re-negotiate the terms of its merger with MCI. Later WorldCom makes a bigger all-paper bid for MCI. GTE makes a strong cash bid for MCI but WorldCom's offer succeeds.

Sun sues Microsoft alleging that it has violated Sun's Java licence by shipping an incompatible (improperly modified) version of Java in its Internet browser, Explorer 4, which fails to pass Sun's compatibility tests.

With 95 000 books published in the UK alone this year reports on the death of the book look wildly exaggerated.

19 800 000 host computers are connected to the Internet.

## 1998

1st January the EU Directive requiring the opening of all telecommunications among member countries to competition takes place.

US Telecoms Company SBC (already having acquired Pacific Telesis in 1996) acquires Ameritech. This alliance re-unites three of the seven 'Baby Bell' companies that AT&T was forced to spin off in 1984 and creates a $135 billion (by market capitalization) company.

AT&T takes over Teleport.

The number of commercial W3 sites is now around 750 000 and growing fast.

AT&T announces that it is acquiring Telecommunications Incorporated (TCI), the largest cable operator in the US, for $48 billion. This is the first time that AT&T has owned (rather than paying local operators for their services) local telephone lines since 1984.

AT&T and the UK's BT announce a joint venture to pool their international operations which is expected to generate an initial turnover of $10 billion and handle 25 billion minutes of telecommunications traffic annually.

Bell Atlantic and GTE, both local telecommunication groups in the US, agree an all-stock merger to create a $120 billion (by market capitalization) company with 63 million access lines, making it the largest US local exchange carrier.

Disney Corporation buys a 48 per cent stake in Infoseek.

The US Army selects Internet Security Systems intrusion detection technology 'RealSecure' to protect critical networked information in the first true enterprise-wide deployment by a Federal Government Agency of a commercial intrusion detection system.

Microsoft faces charges from the US Justice Department and the attorney generals of a number of states that it is 'engaging in anti-competitive and exclusionary practices designed to maintain its monopoly in PC operating systems and attempting to extend that monopoly to Internet browser software'. The precedent for this anti-trust action is the 1907 judgement against John D. Rockefeller's Standard Oil which led to the eventual break up of that company in 1911.

Microsoft launch Windows 98.

The US House of Representatives uses the Internet to disseminate the Starr Report which called for the impeachment of President Clinton on the grounds of perjury, witness tampering and abuse of power.

Apple launches their new iMac computer.

BSkyB is first to enter the race to provide digital television in the UK closely followed by terrestrial supplier OnDigital. The UK cable TV companies wait to see how things turn out before launching their own digital offerings sometime in 1999.

77-year-old John Glenn returns to space in the Space Shuttle Discovery mission of October 1998 for an eight day and twenty two hour round trip. The city of Perth was illuminated again in his honour.

It is estimated that there are now around 2000 satellites circling the earth supporting weather research and telephone and television communication.

AOL buys Netscape.

Dixon's, an electrical retailer in the UK, provides free access to the Internet and is closely followed by W.H. Smith, Tesco, 'Toys   Us' and BT, and opens the floodgates to a range of branded free ISP/Portal services.

## 1999

@Home buys Excite.

USA Networks (home shopping and retail operations) buys search engine/portal Lycos for $6 billion.

Cisco and Motorola announce a joint venture to develop mobile Internet products.

BT and Microsoft announce a partnership to create Internet and corporate data communications services for BT's 13 million mobile phone users spread across 10 countries.

Compaq spins off search engine/portal Alta Vista as a separate company.

Intel launches the Pentium III.

Intel settle 'out of court' with the US Federal Trade Commission regarding the charge that it denied certain of its customers access to prototype microchips and technical information.

Olivetti made a hostile bid for Telecom Italia, which retaliated by agreeing a merger with Germany's Deutsche Telecom (DT). The German government which still owns 74 per cent of DT assured the Italians of a 'hands off' approach to the new company which would otherwise look like a takeover by one country of another's principal telephone provider. Regulatory hurdles are likely to be fierce.

AT&T and BT each agreed to take a 15 per cent stake in Japan Telecom, Japan's third-biggest telecoms firm.

Cable and Wireless topped the bid by NTT to buy International Digital Communications Japan's second biggest telecoms company.

In a complex deal that avoided a bidding war and keeps friends all round AT&T and Comcast agreed to share the spoils of the US's fourth biggest cable company, MediaOne and involved Microsoft as both a $5 billion investor in AT&T and the owner of MediaOne's 30 per cent stake in UK cable company Telewest Communications. As part of the deal AT&T will increase the number of Windows CE based set top boxes that it takes from Microsoft from its current 5 million to nearly 10 million. Microsoft already has a 5 per cent interest in UK cable company NTL. If eventually approved this deal will make AT&T the US's largest cable company (just ahead of Time Warner) with 16 million cable subscribers. Together with earlier deals this one would give AT&T local access to over 60 per cent of US homes.

Microsoft reported a 43 per cent rise in profits to $1.92 billion for the first quarter of 1999 compared with the same period in 1998. The company also reorganized itself into five divisions to make it easier to respond to different groups of consumers.

BT bought a 20 per cent stake in China's mobile phone company SmarTone.

A former British Intelligence agent was alleged to have posted the names of more than 100 Secret Intelligence Agents, previously protected from Internet disclosures of this kind.

More than 30 000 000 host computers are estimated to be connected to the Internet.

**With thanks to:**

Hellemans, A. and Bunch, B. (1998) *The timetables of science: a chronology of the most important people and events in the history of science*. New York: Simon and Schuster

Grun, B. (1991) *The timetables of history*. New York: Touchstone

Zakon, Hobbes, R. *Hobbes' Internet timeline*, v. 3.3 at http://info.isoc.org/guest/zakon/Internet/History/HIT.html

CHAPTER ONE

# The context: a quick tour

'Each place has its advantages – Heaven for the climate and Hell for the society.'

Mark Twain

## Did we?

When we get beyond week one of the year 2000 what will we consider as the most formative events of the twentieth century? Just as in all the centuries before it, much of our communal intelligence was deployed to bridge those two dimensions that we believe inconvenience us the most, i.e. time and space. Our desire to connect with each other is one of our oldest desires and our effort to gain access to each other over the obstacles of time and space has been one of the most ubiquitous consumers of our ingenuity. The purposes to which we put this ingenuity have been many and various across a wide spectrum of good, bad, trivial and profound. Whatever the eventual value to us our determination to overcome the limitations of these two dimensions must certainly rank as one of the defining features of the twentieth century. All the technologies that we now use to overcome space and time enjoyed a mixed reception at birth but went on to revolutionize commerce and transform the way we connect with people and institutions beyond our normal ambulatory space. Initially accompanied by the ballyhoo of 'revolution' and 'transformation' they were also attended by the doomsayers and Jeremiahs who saw their investment in old certainties and old ways of life threatened.

# 2 Only Connect: Shaping Networks and Knowledge

Overcoming space and time easily and in comfort was a privilege once reserved for aristocrats but as populations grew, together with their spending power, so the impetus for mass solutions to take large populations of citizens beyond their small world also grew. The world is the same size as it's always been, but where once it was visited in representation as a picture in an atlas by most people it is now a real place that many of them can roam and communicate over with ease. Yet while much of the world's mystery has been explained to us and a small number of wheeler dealers can influence far-off financial markets overnight, most of us still live our lives and carry out our most important transactions in a quite specific and limited range of spaces. Through television, and more recently the Internet, we peer into peoples, spaces and cultures that books once described and photographs once froze for us. The great colonial projects of western nations always emphasized that the more we looked outward to the world the better we would understand it, and in understanding it the greater the good for those who looked and for those who were looked upon.

So what of our progress with regard to facilitating and improving that commonest, yet still that most capricious of connecting activities, the improvement of human relations? Did we carry on with our human relations, small scale and big scale, in ways that were much different from say the nineteenth century? Did we learn more tolerance towards each other? Did we come to appreciate peoples that we once didn't understand? We have grown accustomed to believing that wider access to knowledge reduces prejudice and improved understanding, so did our 'connected' world help us to understand better and accept cultural and ethnic differences or has its very fecundity overwhelmed and confused us? The following 'quick tour' around a selection of the highs and lows of the twentieth century is intended as a reminder of some of the movements and issues that occupied us in our increasingly connected world.

The twentieth century has been a pretty even mixture of great geopolitical forces, e.g. 'The US century', the 'Asian Century' or the 'Oil Century' and of great abstract movements, e.g. 'the neo-Darwinist', 'the Marxist', 'the Feminist', 'the Postmodernist' 'the Islamic' and 'the Information' century. Many great ideas, e.g. the feminist movement, were initially located in a particular space, i.e. the US; likewise the rise of Islamic fundamentalism, although spread unevenly around the middle and far east, can be dated from the return of the Ayatollah Hominy to Iran. Over the centuries one characteristic has always dominated human endeavour and the twentieth century saw some particularly stunning refinements to it. It was a century in which violence between and within nations affected more people, more times and with more devastating effect than ever before and it is war more than any other milestone that marked out the path we trod in the twentieth century.

## Legacies of war

The First World War shaped the century in many ways. It produced horrors and casualties on a scale that no war had done before. It produced the tank, the submarine and chemical weapons and put science at the centre of winning wars. Its aftermath produced the emancipation of women, the Russian Revolution and the rise of labour, trade unions and capital as the political influence of the landed aristocracy of Europe waned. Tragically the terms of its ending also sowed the seeds for a Second World War only twenty years later. The Holocaust and the radioactive mushroom clouds that rose over Nagasaki and Hiroshima in August 1945 at the end of that war became symbols of the damage that we could inflict on each other when we really applied ourselves to it. These two great acts of state violence have bequeathed to us both positive and negative legacies. To many they represent a horror that must not be repeated and through formal and informal channels they work for peace and the non-violent resolution of disputes. For others they represent a different kind of exemplar: they show what can be done in the name of winning and offer legitimacy to the genocide, ethnic cleansing and terrorism that they believe to be necessary to secure their own ends. Both legacies look destined to struggle just as hard with each other as we go into the next millennium as they did in the last century of the old one.

Our century saw the steady refinement of 'total war' where science and technology were used to ensure that war touched all the citizens of an enemy state rather than just the committed combatants. Large-scale civilian casualties were seen, not just as an unfortunate by-product of war, but as a legitimate war aim to help bring an enemy to its knees. Sherman's infamous march to the sea in 1864 during the American Civil War now seems small-scale in terms of the devastation it caused among a civilian population when compared with the violence that states are prepared to inflict on civilians now. We should also remember that all the 'smaller' wars since 1945, while perhaps not encompassing continents, were still 'world wars' to all those involved. The list of these is long and includes the Spanish Civil War, Korea, the Arab-Israeli wars, Northern Ireland, Vietnam, Cambodia, the Iran-Iraq War, the Falklands, Bosnia, Afghanistan, the Gulf War, Kosovo and all the wars and genocides across Africa in Sierra Leone, Angola, Mozambique, Liberia, Somalia, Congo and Rwanda.

Since the 1950s many of these wars have entered our homes via television, and the war journalist filing his or her report under fire or just a few steps away from the fighting has been one of the most ubiquitous images of the last half of the century. Reporting on wars has a long history. William Howard Russell brought a new 'realism' to the reporting of wars in his despatches from the Crimea to *The London Times* in 1854. There had been British armies in the past as badly led and supplied and as ravaged by disease as the army in the Crimea but none had had its blunders and inadequacies reported in such detail and with such accuracy as Russell took it on himself to report and his paper to print.

Today the satellite is so much mightier and faster than Russell's pen and our continued failure to resolve our differences by negotiation and agreement, other than after a war, is brought home to us by serial images of the war-torn and the ravaged. This is a clear testament of our failure to replace violence, that most animal of our human urges, by all the non-animal technology for connecting now at our disposal.

## Violence and the peace dividend

Whatever achievements we celebrate, and despite the widespread adoption of what we call 'civilization' and 'democracy' across the globe, it was a century where statistics representing horror, insecurity and fear were often measured in millions. It was a century that gave birth to the term 'crimes against humanity' and to messianic tyrants like Hitler, Stalin and Pol Pot who, although rising out of very different social and political systems, secured the right to inflict pain on large populations of 'others'. Many generals and politicians in South Africa, Chile, Iran, Iraq, Argentina, Serbia and elsewhere enthusiastically took up where they left off. The economic and human turmoil in Africa turned it into the great disaster area of the century as post-colonial tribalism and genocide, fuelled by indiscriminate arms supplies from both east and west, wreaked havoc in so many already destitute countries. Angola's grim claim to have more amputees per head of population than any other country – something like one in every 356 people – reminds us that this was as much the century of the land mine as of family battles over the TV remote control. The end of Apartheid in South Africa was one of the few beams of light across a continent that remained darkened by violence for peoples who have never enjoyed the day-to-day peace that most of us now take for granted. The much heralded peace dividend offered by the end of the cold war and the great deterrent competition has been squandered by the continued importance of arms manufacturing to the economies of rich countries alongside the growth in the sale of those arms to poor countries. Bloody civil wars and regional conflicts are more often than not fed by supplies of small arms that are difficult for international agencies to control. It is estimated that over 70 million of the simple (only six moving parts) but lethal Kalashnikov rifles have been made in the low-tech factories of Bulgaria, North Korea and Iraq to feed the seemingly insatiable demand of the dictators, urban terrorists and tribal warlords of the world. The aid agency Oxfam has estimated the global trade in small arms alone between 1990 and 1995 to be $22 billion and small arms proliferation in Africa is a major security issue at both national and regional levels. In September 1998 the North Koreans, with an estimated two million people dead from famine since 1995, launched a new, two-stage medium-range missile over the Sea of Japan. North Korea has previously sold missiles to Libya and Iran and many observers saw this as the demonstration of a new product to help bolster its sagging arms industry. Similarly the tragedy of India, with the largest number of poor people in the world, and Pakistan, both bleeding their economies to pay for arms and nuclear capability while having to submit to punitive conditions from international lending institutions, stands as testament to the limpet-like tenacity of the 'cold war' habit. The cold war turned into a cold peace. The old practices of re-equipping and modernizing defence forces, though modified in some of its detail, continue to be at the centre of the military–industrial–media complex.

It is an irony not lost on the foreign aid workers, doctors and nurses who attend the broken bodies of third world war victims that they often remove shrapnel and bullets made by their neighbours back home. One neighbour makes the bullet, the other comes to take it out. It's a curious way to connect with one's fellow humans but entirely compatible with the two-tier morality that conditions the way that business and governments in the west handle information and knowledge. We discover that eating too much sugar is bad for us so we export it to third world countries. We discover the carcinogenic properties of tobacco so we export our cigarettes to the third world. We have less use for land mines and other weapons so we export them to poor countries and we discover that humans can get all sorts of deadly side effects from using organophosphate fertilizers so guess whom we export these to?

## Oil! Still a factor

Other formative events were related to or interlinked with violence, including the growing importance of oil to the comfort, industry and mobility of industrialized countries. Most of the world's oil reserves are located outside Europe, East Asia and the US. Despite attempts by many nations to cut down on the use of oil-based products after the OPEC price rises of 1973, most notably by Japan, it remains a key strategic resource that will always command violent intervention when its supply is threatened. By the same token the human rights record of oil suppliers generally avoids much detailed scrutiny by the international community. Too much interference might interrupt the flow. Kuwait was never the most democratic of states, particularly in regard to the treatment of its huge band of foreign workers, and an obvious blind eye has been turned to the violence committed by 'oil' governments like Algeria and Nigeria. Given the capriciousness of the earth's geology the political choices involved in securing oil and energy supplies in the future are as likely to lie between Scylla and Charybdis as between more comfortable options. The US's tacit backing of the Pax Taliban in Afghanistan, in the hope that they would allow a US company to build a pipeline to bring Central Asia's energy reserves out via Afghanistan rather than through the territory of its old enemy Iran, is typical of the equivocal tap-dancing that access to oil still commands.

The overproduction of oil, the Asian crisis and the consequent low price (c. $10 a barrel at the end of 1998) prompted a round of consolidations in the oil industry, e.g. British Petroleum merged with Amoco, Mobil joined with Exxon and France's Total merged with Petrofina of

Belgium. Still one of the most vertically integrated of industries, oil and the oil companies, just as much as telecommunications, computing and the Internet, look set to continue their central role in our lives for the next fifty years or so. As the world's second largest exporter of oil and natural gas Norway has enjoyed budget surpluses that have insulated it against the pressure to cut the social spending facing so many other European countries. This oil-led independence, including the setting up of the Petroleum Fund to serve as a buffer against external economic shocks and to guarantee the solvency of its welfare system, has enabled it to cock a snook at the EU. The 'national savings account' of the Petroleum Fund is a far-sighted investment on behalf of future generations (the UK would have done well to have followed their example). But even the $83 billion that Norway may have built up in its oil bank by 2002 might not be enough to create the new jobs that will be needed in a post-petroleum economy or cover its pension costs which are set to double as a percentage of GDP by 2020.

## Tyrants and nationalism

Whatever we hope for from global connectivity, in terms of the pressure that a group of states might bring on a single state to abstain from violence on its own or another people, we have had to accept that sovereignty within borders is as strong as it ever was. Fifty-three years after the founding of the UN a truly global consensus on almost anything remains an illusion. Late twentieth century tyrants still find it quite easy to manipulate the different vested interests of nations to avoid effective international censure. Saddam Hussein (literally 'he who shakes things up') illuminates the challenges involved. He has outlasted a formidable array of enemies who have long since died or been voted out of office and defied every prediction made about the certainty of his downfall. He represents the classic dilemma for an international community seeking to influence the behaviour of a defeated but not overthrown 'outlaw' government. Despite economic sanctions he has continued to breach international agreements without any sign that an internal revolt against him by his devastated and impoverished population has been made any easier. Worn down by his tenacity and the harm that sanctions are doing to the ordinary citizens of Iraq the world community, via the UN agreement in early

1998, relaxed sanctions on Iraq's exportation of oil and compromised its efforts to stem the production and storage of biological weapons. Saddam Hussein has a long record of breaking agreements and tempting international action before pulling back from the brink simply to start re-negotiating the boundaries with UN weapons inspectors all over again. He has already shown his willingness to use weapons like botulin, anthrax and poisonous gas. In 1988 he used nerve gas against the Kurds in is own country killing 5000 people outright and there can be no doubt that he would use such weapons again to protect himself and his family from facing trial for their war crimes. The US and UK missile strikes on Iraq during December 1998, after UN weapons inspectors left Iraq once again having being denied access to key sites amid a confusing mixture of allegation and counter allegation, left him stronger and the US and UK cause weaker.

The Serb leader Slobodan Milosevic, seeing how Saddam could manipulate the international community, practised the same kind of brinkmanship after murdering Albanian families in Kosovo. His scenario – first do a bit of murder, keep the diplomats talking while you do a bit more; pull the army back just before a NATO air strike; then keep enough paramilitary police on the ground to continue terrorizing the dissident population – is classic copycat Saddam. Such tyrants cannot be defeated by military sophistication alone. NATO's air strikes on Serbia between March and May 1999 demonstrated just how difficult it is to stop genocidal violence without the support of ground forces. The refugee trickle from Kosovo turned into a flood, after the bombings and the retaliatory murders against Albanian Kosovars increased with every bomb that NATO dropped a consequence that the NATO planners (to the amazement of everyone else) seem not to have anticipated.

All the intelligence and all the connecting networks going back to Cain cannot stop crafty tyrants inflicting violence. The UN, set up to promote international peace, security and co-operation, while being able to point to some successes, has also shown just how fragile the desire for multi-national 'peacekeeping' is when weighed against the vested interests of its member states. Born out of a desire to prevent the horrors of another world war the UN has seemed better at intervening in nation-to-nation conflicts than the brutal civil wars (e.g. Bosnia and Rwanda) that have characterized the violence of the latter part of the century. Many of these conflicts have roots in either real or invented constructions of past

conflicts that resurface as vital symbols of ethnic or religious pride. Hobsbawm recognizes how dangerous and self-deluding invented pasts can be:

> History is the raw material for nationalistic or ethnic fundamentalist
> ideologies, as poppies are the raw material for heroin addiction . . .
> If there is no suitable past, it can always be invented. [1]

Two inventions preoccupy modern-day nationalists, both of which
see history as a majestic natural drama or a poem. One is a glorious past
that owes them a fair quota of conquering heroes; the other, and opposite, drama is a history of unremitting oppression. It is common now
for the inheritors of this latter more tragic version, no matter how distant
its origins, to look for opportunities to put right the ancient wrongs
with modern weapons. The iconography of sustained struggles, which
characterize the nationalist version of events and the ownership of the
received historical memory that defines it, is fiercely guarded. Irish histo-
rians raising questions about the accepted 'Republican' version of recent
Irish History often arouse an agonized resentment and are accused of
depopulating Irish history of those great figures who struggled in the cause
of national liberation.

Emigrant communities also have a reputation for keeping very
specific and particular memories of their homeland in aspic. It is almost a
given among emigrants, perhaps as a mark of respect to those left behind,
that the perspective over one's shoulder from a distance should remain
identical to that recorded at the parting glance. No matter that the parting
look may have happened two or more generations back or that the
remembered impression may be spectacularly contradicted by the mother
country itself on return visits. It is a question of relishing being homesick,
the regular tasting of selected memory, rather than a deeply held desire
to return. The hero in Donall Mac Amhlaigh's 'An Irish Navy' eloquently
reflects the tugs and pulls of cultural displacement. Through his eyes
the English market place only achieves meaning in relation to his visits
home to Kilkenny where life assumes its old shapes and colours again.
But gradually the ironies of a life spent between two countries appeals
to him:

> At Hyde Park one Sunday he listens to a Sinn Fein speaker denouncing
> England and holding forth about her evil deeds. This annoyed an
> Englishman who happened to be listening. 'As an Englishman,' he said,

'I should go up and sock you.' Right then a big constable, with a strong Kerry accent, said to the Englishman: 'Move along there now and don't be disrupting a lawful meeting! [2]

The citizens of Ireland, both north and south, have had cause to rue the 'invented' pasts that their respective leaders have encouraged and constructed for them, but they were not alone. Ethnicity, tribalism and nationalism have been used wantonly to justify spattering the last quarter of the twentieth century with blood in Africa and, shocking to 'civilized' Europeans, even within Europe itself. The re-ignition of the old ethnic divisions which lay dormant under the cloak of communism in the Balkans and the regions of the old Soviet Empire during the 1990s suddenly made neighbours aware of differences that had been repressed for over half a century. Once unimportant nuances of religion and behaviour were rapidly elevated to issues that became crucial to self-definition, transforming friends into enemies and neighbourliness into atrocity. Ascherson, although writing primarily about the rise and fall of communities around the shores of the Black Sea, clearly sees lessons for us in their history. Among their comings and goings he recognizes the fragility of perceived identity and cultural harmony and draws our attention to the potential for the rapid decomposition of even those human relations that seem to have lasted the tests of time:

Peoples who live in communion with other peoples, for a hundred or a thousand years, do not always like them – may in fact, have always disliked them. As individuals, 'the others' are not strangers but neighbours, often friends. But my sense of Black Sea life, a sad one, is that latent mistrust between different cultures is immortal. Necessity, and sometimes fear, binds such communities together. But within that binding-strap they remain a bundle of disparate groups – not a helpful model for the 'multi-ethnic society' of our hopes and dreams. It is true that communal savagery – pogroms, 'ethnic cleansing' in the name of some fantasy of national unity, genocide – has usually reached the Black Sea communities from elsewhere, an import from the interior. But when it arrives the apparent solidarity of centuries can dissolve within days or hours. The poison upwelling from the depths, is absorbed by a single breath. [3]

## Shivers of recognition

The more serious shiver of recognition that we feel about 'the apparent solidarity of centuries' dissolving within days or hours is fuelled by all the media apparatus of a connected world and the increasing examples it provides, sometimes sensationally, of the fragile foundations on which many of our connections are based. From personal experience we know that bonds of friendship that have lasted 10 or 20 years can be destroyed by a thoughtless word or a careless action. We know that on the murder of a husband or a wife, the central figures in the ubiquitous 'family' of the politician's rhetoric, that police forces the world over, initially at least, suspect the other partner. We know that neighbours can become strangers or even aggressors if they perceive someone to be 'different' while many cases of proven slaughter in our communities turn out to have been done by individuals who looked and behaved just like us. We have seen how easy it is for brutality to emerge from environments that we once assumed were safe and we often by-pass areas where the poverty that we escaped from still persists 'just to be on the safe side'. Such knowledge about 'the hanging by a thread' connections that we make with others has left us increasingly insecure about who, and when, we trust. During October 1997 when I was beginning this book the BBC screened a six-part series called *The Nazis: a warning from history*. While watching this series the strongest 'shiver' for me came from the interviews with neighbours who extorted money from Jews in the Ghetto and who profited from the release of their property and who spoke as if it was all part and parcel of normal business practice. The testimony, often given without compassion or remorse from those of the same nationality as the persecuted, who had worked with the SS units involved with ethnic cleansing and mass murder, was shocking in its re-called normality: 'this was just the way it was in those days'. One man actually said that there was about it 'a sort of curiosity that you aimed and shot at someone and he fell down, pop'.

Like many such images and impressions we see them, leave them and get on with our lives perhaps vowing to be better friends and neighbours but never quite knowing how we would behave under similar circumstances. However much we play up the homogenization of cultures, the spread of the liberal idea that forms the cornerstone of western ideologies and the dissemination of common standards for computers or the Internet, there is no such thing as a global standard of morality. There is no such thing as a commonly accepted construction of neighbourliness and no such thing as a common definition of the rule of law. Common technical standards for information flow may be the foundation on which all 'e-commerce' will be built but we must avoid transplanting the language of electronic networking to social protocols or to deceive ourselves into believing that technology can iron out the multiplicity of undulations in individual or group behaviour. Global harmony is never going to come pre-packed down a wire. A small ray of humour, among the otherwise frantic re-bordering of the former USSR, was captured by Marsden-Smedley [4] in his wanderings around the Caucasus Mountains in search of the Doukhobors or 'spirit wrestlers'. He met a man in Tiblisis, Georgia who, inspired by the chaotic nationalism that infects the myriad of 'Do-It-Yourself' countries in the region, had declared his flat to be an independent republic. He had written a constitution, created a bill of rights, established a national park in his bathroom and he inspected passports at his front door, all before renting it out to an American businessman to help with the national debt.

## Interdependence, cash-back and racism

Paradoxically, and despite the fears and misgivings noted above, the twentieth century has been a time of growing interdependence. The cult of the individual, so hyped by some politicians and the media during the latter half of the century, has sometimes provided us with a convenient and transient rationale for opting out, but it is a 'cult' rather than a general reality. The reality, including technologies that celebrate the paradox of the lonely screen watcher 'seeking interesting other', is of a growing dependency on often unseen forces as our networks of interdependence multiply and the range of connections that we make becomes more complicated. They range from legislation developed in the EU that has legal writ over a dozen or so sovereign states, to an investment by a company 6000 miles away that creates, saves or loses us our job, to the regular arrival of a day-care worker to check on distant parents.

The last half of the century saw many families in poorer economies relying on regular income from a father, son or daughter working away in another country. Indian expatriates remit around $9 billion back to India every year, while a growing army of Turks, Greeks, Portuguese and Chinese support and sustain families back home to the extent that they often gain separate listings in compilations of their home states' fiscal statistics. Migration from poor countries to rich countries has been a major feature of the century and the proportion of foreigners as a percentage of the population in OECD countries has increased dramatically since 1950. However only four OECD countries – Canada, Switzerland, Australia and Luxembourg – had more than 10 per cent of their total population made up of foreign citizens in 1996 and the UK had less than 5 per cent [5].

The difference in the welcome given to foreign citizens is vast. Luxembourg clearly welcomes the highly skilled, highly mobile knowledge workers that make up nearly 35 per cent of its population while France and Germany remain ambivalent about the bricklayers and plasterers who live in twilight communities around their building sites and vineyards. Immigration to the UK from the countries of the old empire has created, by accident, a multinational society, the strains and tensions of which break out now and then in racist attacks and the exposure of discriminatory practices.

The continuing wide differential in wealth between rich and poor countries remains a powerful magnet to immigrants from the latter prompting all OECD countries to tighten their controls on illegal immigration and to enforce tighter quota systems on the legal kind. Whether it be poorer people just moving around seeking work, the Vietnamese boat people trying to escape a particular regime, Bosnians escaping violence or Albanians fleeing from poverty and chaos, they all share a common belief that they will find a better life in western Europe, Australia or North America. Rich countries once welcomed immigrants from poor countries because they needed greater numbers of economically active people to bolster their traditional industrial base. Today's knowledge industries need to work smarter with fewer people rather than harder with more. Manufacturing industries were the first to invest heavily in technologies that reduced labour costs and the scope for poorly educated immigrant workers has been shrinking steadily. There are still some niches where poor immigrants can operate effectively, usually at the poorest end of the service sector, but many countries, like Australia, now only accept legal immigrants who bring a definite skill or enough cash in the bank to start a business or be self-sufficient.

The darker side of immigration is racism and highly organized groups in the UK, US, Germany and France have been active in using their demo-cratic freedoms to protest about the presence of different races in their countries. The White Supremacist movement in the US extends from the 100-year-old Klu Klux Clan to the neo-Nazi Aryan Nations, The Christian Identity movement, the prison-based Aryan Brotherhood, George Lincoln Rockwell's American Nazi party and the National Alliance. They all seek various flavours of a 'white only' society and many of them condone or even urge violence in order to achieve it. William Pierce's 'The Turner Diaries', a fantasy about a race war where whites kill blacks and Jews at the end of the twentieth century, is the bible of the racist right in America.

It is estimated that there are 474 'hate groups' in the US [6] and like many others seeking a bigger audience to influence and persuade they use the Internet to promote their messages of hate and white supremacy. The 1999 UK report of the judicial enquiry into death of Stephen Lawrence, an 18-year-old black student stabbed to death in 1993 by a gang of white youths as he waited at a south London bus stop, accused the Metropolitan Police of a collective failure to tackle the endemic racism throughout its ranks. The Lawrence family had long campaigned for a full judicial enquiry suspecting that police indifference to racially motivated crimes allowed all the suspects in Stephen's case to escape scot-free.

There are relatively few black police officers in the UK and those that are recruited often complain of uncomfortable racial attitudes among their colleagues. Incidents of 'stopping and searching' black people by police in the UK (black people only account for 2 per cent of the popu-lation over 10 years of age), currently run at around 11 per cent. This 'favouritism' reflects the long held belief in the black community that blacks are under-policed as victims of crime and over-policed when going about their law abiding business. Thanks to the tenacity of his parents in pursuing the way his case was handled via every avenue open to them Stephen Lawrence's murder may lead to some far-reaching reforms of racial policing in the UK.

Like war and violence racism remains virtually untouched by the harmony dividend that we might expect from an increasingly connected world. It continues to ebb and flow, sometimes below and at other times above the surface of things. But it is always there, brazen and quick to seek popular support during the economic downturn and much shyer when capitalism delivers one of its spasmodic booms. It will creep into the new millennium with us showing its teeth now and then and proving that longitudinal harmony between different races living together is one of the connections that the twentieth century only partly got right. Mitigating its worst effects by education, the economic regeneration of our cities and by vigilant moral and legislative pressure remains a big agenda item. This is all the more so as the economics of electronic networking, although providing nourishment for 'live well with your neighbour' ideals and offering new platforms for anti-discrimination groups to disseminate their message, has so far had little impact as an engine of opportunity to escape the ghetto.

## The US: leader and loser

The rise of US hegemony since 1945 has certainly been one of the most significant issues on the global stage. The US has successfully deployed the software, the movies and the influence of its great media corporations to export its 'land of the free' ideas on lifestyle, consumerism, democracy and capitalism to places without anything like the history or experience that underpins its own institutions. The explosion in access to new media that has characterized the second half of the century owes its genesis to the US's predominance in media technology, media creativity and media entrepreneurialism. This is the conduit for the US's peacetime influence and we cannot help but be schizoid about it. In Europe and in the UK particularly, via the kind of old-world condescension that we are still so good at, we find it easy to sneer at American weaknesses, while cherry-picking the bits that we like: 'holding our skirts up in horror while tapping our feet to its tunes'. [7] The twentieth century has taught us that full-blooded democracy the US way often yields outcomes that we despise. Excess is the daughter of freedom and if we sincerely believe in freedom, excess is what you get because the curbs we might want to put on one freedom will inevitably interfere with another seemingly unrelated one, e.g. freedom of speech, freedom of assembly or freedom of choice. That the US produces the worst and the best of so many things is what happens when the human spirit is unshackled from gentility, deference and convention. It is true that the easy rush to litigation makes the US a lawyers' paradise but where people are treated as free and equal and the constitution enshrines their rights in solemn documents it follows that an excess of litigiousness will characterize many of their doings (see Chapter 4). The courts in the US are where many of the great social and political issues of the day – civil rights, abortion, free speech, anti-trust actions – are thrashed out and resolved. Ironically the fathers of US constitutional institutions appropriated the principles that underpin these freedoms from Europeans like Tom Paine, John Locke, Thomas Hobbes, John Stuart Mill and Montesquieu. In the US, however fragile it may sometimes seem, the source and disposition of power is vested in the people at every level of its operation and when they delegate this power to elected officials they do so with the utmost of care. Americans jealously, sometimes obsessively, guard their rights and are suspicious of government authority and are all the freer because of it. All this runs counter to the way things are run in the UK where an unwritten constitution keeps individual rights always secondary to those of the state and where class and education still shadow how and what most individuals can achieve. Without a written constitution or a Bill Of Rights the UK is a poor democracy and the US, however dysfunctional it may sometimes seem in other arenas, is a good one.

## US Burdens and the Asian miracle

It was clearly a century where 'instant democracy the US way' guaranteed US support however totalitarian its local manifestation. This was particularly true in South America where the US seemed happy to support any regime (e.g. Pinochet in Chile) that was not communist. Indeed the last half of the twentieth century can be seen as a time when one power, the US, declared that it and it alone shouldered the burden of global interests and responsibilities. This burden, defined and paid for by the US, increasingly came to be seen by them as a responsibility that justified unilateral action when they thought it necessary. France, China and Russia, although rarely for any altruistic motives, emerged as the three powers most likely to resist such patriarchy while the UK, somewhat poodle-like, always found good reasons to follow in the wake of its old colony whatever the issue. The collapse of the Berlin Wall in 1989 (something that many of us did not expect to see in our lifetime) and the end of the Soviet Empire in 1991 have accelerated the US's 'guardianship' role.

With the failure of so many centrally planned economies, all of them born in the first half of the century, it is not surprising that the second half was dominated by the political acceptance of market forces as a way of regulating the economic affairs of most states. The pendulum had swung over the hundred years back and forth between various shades of intervention and 'hands off' economics but clearly ends the century stuck squarely in the *laissez-faire* corner. What it meant to be a rich country, despite protestations about 'information' replacing manufacturing and natural resources as the key motor of wealth creation, didn't change very much. Those nations that started the century rich also look like ending it rich, albeit joined by a few others who, like Japan, came, saw, emulated and created a new economic dynamo, the 'Pacific Rim' – a concept that would hardly have been imagined before 1950. The inhabitants of the 'Asian miracle' are now going through their own particular form of boom and bust. Triggered by Thailand having to float the Baht in July 1997 the repercussions provided conclusive proof, if proof were needed, of the serious interconnectivity of regional and global financial markets. Within one month Malaysia, South Korea and Indonesia were also in trouble; within four months Wall Street suffered its worst ever points loss, the IMF began putting rescue packages together for Thailand, Indonesia and South Korea and several large finance companies went bust in Japan. Just under a year later, in May 1998, students rioted in Jakarta and their long-time President, Suharto, reluctantly resigned. During the autumn of 1998 Russia teetered on the brink of economic and political collapse and Brazil, the bell-wether economy of South America, needed a $49 billion injection from the IMF to avoid financial meltdown. Having opened their gates to capital inflows from foreign investors these 'emerging' nations ended the century coming to terms with the reverse side of the capitalist coin, i.e. the speed with which that capital can be moved to safer havens or simply called home again down the same wires over which it left. At the time of writing (January 1999) no one is sure if the 'Asian crisis' and its ramifications have bottomed out or whether there is still some depths to plumb, particularly among the debt-ridden Japanese banks.

As the century drew to a close China began to awaken to the potential for blurring the lines between communism and capitalism; sternly keeping communism to govern while exploring the natural proclivity of its citizens for private enterprise in certain designated regions. Containing these 'experiments' within 'designated' spaces without them boiling over into the more general economic sphere will tax all the tenacity of Mao's heirs. Whatever other changes may be taking place in this populous country the official information provided by China about itself to the wider world continues the old Communist mission of half-truth confusion in every area. Western businessmen, keen to tap into this New World of demi-capitalism, have often had their fingers burnt when they meet the truth on the ground.

France found the century somewhat bemusing as its cultural protection of all things French, outside of France itself, became a wistful dream as English consolidated its position as the lingua franca of the EU, the Internet, pop music and the western cinema. All the developed nations began to consider how they were going to pay for the increasing number of their citizens who were living longer and retiring earlier, particularly Japan and Germany who are becoming the oldest of the developed societies. By 2010 more than 20 per cent of their populations will be aged 65 or over and demanding high-cost medical care while living off pensions and state benefits. In 1997 a Japanese government report noted that the number of Japanese children aged 14 and under had dropped to 15.5 per cent of the population, from 35 per cent in 1955. By 2010 Japan could have proportionately the smallest workforce and the largest number of elderly people of any developed country. A birth rate that averages 2.1 children per woman is necessary to achieve long term population stability and only the US, and Sweden among European countries, have reached this kind of replacement rate. The triumvirate of successful medicine, the changing structure of the family and the delights of contraception have lit the fuse for a demographic time-bomb for which too few nations, particularly in Europe, are making any plans [8].

## We cancelled politics in 'the public interest'

As if to vindicate our love affair with inanimate objects and the transforming possibilities of technology that most human of human mysteries, conventional democratic politics, proved to be pretty much of a disappointment. The triumph of presentation over content in democratic politics, begun by J. F. Kennedy in the early 1960s, reached its apotheosis at the end of the twentieth century where the policy claims of 'different' candidates for high office in western democracies became almost indistinguishable from each other. The institutions of democratic government have lost rather than gained respect over the century as the media revealed the lives of our leaders to be as fraught and fallible as our own and their beliefs just as fragile. Thanks to the media that must generate new products for us every day we now know so much more about politicians than our parents or grandparents ever did and this knowledge has made us miserable. The Duke of Wellington, Lloyd George and John F. Kennedy are just three past leaders whose reputations would hardly have stood up to a week of late 1990s media coverage. The concomitant has been that leaders dare not lead in case they are found out.

In the last quarter of the century our days were blighted by an overwhelming sense of mediocrity as the lives of politicians 'became' politics camouflaging the dangers of the corporate–state–military–media complex with its weak national and strong corporate economies and easy acceptance of economic casualties. The allegations of perjury, obstruction of justice, witness tampering and abuse of power made against President Clinton towards the end of 1998 and that formed the basis for his trial for impeachment in early 1999 seemed to capture the spirit of the time. Although the perjury was real the other charges could easily have been made against any number of the Representatives who charged him and the Senate who tried him. As one US citizen said on TV at the height of the Lewinski–Clinton exposé: 'if we impeached every politician in this country who had lied we'd have no government'. President Clinton, the UK Conservatives and some New Labour politicians (continental European politicians suffer less from exposures about their sex lives as their media have a lot more real corruption to talk about) have been paraded before us in a sparkling Anglo-American redefinition of 'the public interest'.

For the first seventy years of the century media intrusion into the private life of a politician was only sanctioned if it could reasonably be argued that such an intrusion was in 'the public interest'. Now there is no argument, reasonable or otherwise, just a profitable pretence. The pretence is that concern for the public interest is what motivates curiosity about politicians' private lives. The media know that the public, some of whom will vote, like to hear about the private lives of public figures just as they do about film and rock stars. The media simply feed this curiosity and under the pretence of being helpful offer personal details to aid us in reaching a judgement on the character of those who seek or who hold public office. No 'public interest' defence is needed for intrusions into the lives of film and rock stars and it is becoming dangerous to invoke what is left of it for politicians. The serious justification it seems to demand to denounce the latter puts editors on the defensive and fuels long editorials and detailed supportive commentary just to emphasize their belief in the public interest value of the story. A bit of infidelity, an act of poor judgement or a long forgotten misdemeanour thus gets the full panoply of the moral high ground.

But we all know now that the public interest defence is dead in the water. A plausible one can be knocked up in a few minutes by anyone who reads the papers. No verbal formula on earth will chart a patrollable boundary between those elements in a person's character which bear upon their fitness for office and those which do not, but we could begin to reclaim some vestige of sanity by dropping the 'public interest' defence of such stories. All parties could admit that the same curiosity that prompts intrusions into the personal lives of say Cher or Leonardo de Caprio also drives the search for a 'public interest' justification for publishing the peccadilloes of politicians rather than the other way round. The new sport of 'warts and all' exposure may put off some good (but flawed) candidates from seeking office but they can be reassured that, while media prying into their private life can be intense and spiteful, forgiveness and redemption now comes round quicker than it did.

Richard Nixon's fall in 1974 – he escaped almost certain impeachment by resigning – for a different set of 'crimes and misdemeanours', did not inhibit his box office pull on the lecture circuit. For many years before he died he was solicited, and paid well, for his views on both US domestic and foreign policy. His crimes were great but his rehabilitation, no doubt in 'the public interest', only took a few years.

Despite the technological possibilities for improved communication with citizens the organs of state do not seem to have become any more accessible to the man in the street. Despite the impact of the Internet in exposing President Clinton's particular moral vacuum (see Chapter 6) power structures among all democracies continue to remain distant. The fibres of US government remain largely untouched by the existence of a White House Email number and vigorous parliamentary involvement in the UK long ago gave way first to cabinet, and then to special committee government. Under New Labour connecting with the centres of power in the UK seems to have got worse. The perception that a small group of ministers and advisers run the country has been reinforced by the number of times that the Speaker of the House of Commons has had to ask the government to stop making important policy announcements before the House knows about them. Her plaintive call just to be *informed* is all the sadder as it tacitly acknowledges that the opportunity to debate them properly is unlikely.

Some of this arrogance and contempt for MPs by the UK government comes with the turf of a large majority. When the Conservatives were hanging on by a few votes individual MPs mattered because success in a critical vote could be on the line. Now, kept 'on message' by their vibrating pagers, Labour MPs, many of them totally surprised to have been elected, toe the line like lambs blissfully unaware of their part in the circumcision of the mother of parliaments. New Labour in the UK has already seen in close-up that power can corrupt in record time and how steering too close to luxury and enterprise politics can melt the wings of even their most polished communicator. In the age of the designer baseball cap those Labour MPs who stay clear of the perks, gifts and trappings of office are mocked for their cloth cap eccentricity and Old-Labour ways.

There was a brief period in democratic politics when serving the people used to be its own reward: orchestrating social change, having a hand in lifting communities up and out of the base line and constructing new levels of social justice. But such service is now expected to provide access to greater wealth, privilege, directorships and future consultancy contracts and the voters stay away from elections in their droves. Elections in the US have become even more a question of not asking or answering questions, while the issue of funding presidential and other campaigns has become so scandalous that even the recent beneficiaries cannot now ignore it. It is not surprising, given the difficulties they face in recognizing the difference between the sound bites of different candidates, that citizen involvement at all levels of elections in the US and most European countries has got worse rather than better over the last half century. A referendum in Portugal in June 1998 concerning the liberalizing of the law on abortion, a topic that can usually be guaranteed to generate considerable emotion in most countries, produced only a 32 per cent turnout, well below the 50 per cent required to give the referendum legal force. The result gave a marginal victory of less than 1 per cent to the 'No' vote against a bill allowing pregnant women to terminate pregnancies during the first

10 weeks. The Portuguese government (at that time planning a further two referenda) though disappointed at the low turnout agreed to respect the verdict and abandon its bill. The Portuguese are not alone; since 1970 voter turnout in mid-term congressional elections in the US has always fluctuated between 37 per cent and 40 per cent with only 38 per cent turning out for the mid-term elections of November 1998.

## Abortion, animal rights and the Taliban

As conventional political institutions fell into disrepair single-issue politics experienced a reformation. In Belgium the intensity of the street demonstrations in 1997 following the discovery of a particular nasty group of paedophiles surprised and shocked the government out of its torpor and led both to an escalation of the police enquiry and the sacking of the relevant minister. Extra-parliamentary groups disillusioned with the way their democracies work have been active throughout the century, but the last two decades have seen an unprecedented rise in 'do-it-yourself' action. In the US the pro-gun, white supremacist, militia, patriot and anti-abortion groups have been vigorous and effective in using all the media available to get their message to a wider audience and, at the extremes of their movements, to advocate and use violence to achieve their ends.

The influence of extra-parliamentary groups has increased as they extend their reach via the Internet. Doctors who perform abortions in the US have been demonized by pro-life groups who have listed them in Internet directories. They identify where they live, their telephone numbers and where their children go to school, and urge their members to keep up the 'pressure' on them to stop performing abortions. Until recently the Aryan Nations W3 site hosted a section called the 'Nuremberg Files' which urged visitors to visualize abortionists on trial and to 'e-mail us with your evidence' of alleged abortionists, and their accomplices. The right to a legal abortion (passively supported by the majority of US citizens) is becoming more difficult to exercise after a spate of vicious attacks have left nurses maimed and at least one doctor assassinated. There are now fewer clinics prepared to conduct abortions and those that do are finding it increasingly difficult to get insurance or landlords willing to take the chance that their premises won't be firebombed [9]. The groups behind the 'Nuremburg Files' were fined $100 million in damages for incitement in early February 1999 by an Oregon court but they have vowed to fight this judgement in higher courts.

In the UK animal rights groups protesting at the transportation of live animals for eventual slaughter in France were equalled in their ardour by those, as in the great countryside demonstrations of 1998, who sought to retain the right to hunt them down as part of a traditional sport.

Islamic groups in particular became forces to be reckoned with during the last third of the century with the high profile Fatwa against Salmon Rushdie, atrocities in Algeria and Egypt as well as organized opposition to the intrusion of western consumerism in many Muslim states. Muslim opposition to what they see as the 'bad bits' of western culture (they are not immune to 'cherry picking' themselves) is uncomfortable for them when they live in western societies and are bedevilled with contradictions within their own. The organizers of the Commonwealth Games in Kuala Lumpur during September 1998 had to hand back around £2 million in repayments to the Danish brewer Carlsberg. They were the original sponsors of the games until the Malaysian cabinet succumbed to Islamic fundamentalist objections to them despite alcohol being readily accessible to most citizens in the country. In July 1998 the Islamic fundamentalist Taliban in Afghanistan banned television programmes in the areas that they controlled and conducted public hangings of the boxes and screens that they said served the cause of Satan. On the other hand they enlisted the no less satanic Internet to proselytize to their cause via a home page that, among other things, alleged that Mecca and Medina were occupied by millions of American commandos, most of them Jewish, who drank wine and feasted on pork. It will probably be a long time before large populations of Afghan citizens gain easy access to the Internet and the world of ideas beyond Afghanistan. When (and if) they do the Taliban's love affair with the Internet is likely to wane and computers and keyboards will join the television sets hanging from the lampposts of Kabul.

## The death of the liberal project

The great, late nineteenth century liberal project, that in the UK grew out of civic pride, the creation of public works and a sense of responsibility for the 'whole' community, encouraged and nurtured in its wake a form of give and take solidarity. The community was a space where people worked to satisfy their own personal needs alongside equal efforts to build civic and communal structures with hopes and purposes that were at least equal to the drive for personal enrichment. This project began to decompose during the late 1970s and has faltered during every decade since. Civic life in public spaces has given way to the pleasant comforts, security and 'edutainment' of wired homes. Here we embrace the paradox of being able to view more of the world from a distance than ever we could from the Town Hall steps, but it is a view that we digest and discuss in private rather than in the active engagement with others that so animated our fathers. In November 1994 I opined that:

> Citizens, once involved as actors in a vibrant and public national polity, have also been seduced. Lodged more and more in private rather than public worlds, they face becoming units of consumption rather than the lifeblood of a democracy. Within such changes hard won community priorities can seem less important and may be easily surrendered in favour of more immediate, if trivial, private convenience. In such private worlds we may also lose that sense of community wherein the information that fuels liberty and oils the limbs of dissent also lies. By envisaging a world of home-wired information we may be feeding new depths of isolation where families have little connection with each other, other than by the common use of similar services. The political association and social kinship that has always been the prerequisite for articulating the common demands required to satisfy common needs, will find little to nurture it in this new privatized social life. Such conditions may lull peoples into a somnambulance where they will discover too late their loss of authoritative citizenship. Their participation will increasingly be limited to that expected from the members of a market, a place where the rights of consumers always have more protection than the rights of citizens. [10]

Five years on our rush to seek 'lodging in private worlds' seems as strong as ever. Before we abandon ourselves completely to the addictions of the private consumerism that twentieth century capitalism has bequeathed to us as its most seductive gift we might stop, step back a little and reflect on the costs. One of the great challenges of the twenty-first century will centre on the way we choose to construct self and community. Indeed it might centre on whether we intend to construct community at all in the sense that it requires something from us, something selfless, something as much to do with the well-being of others as ourselves. The spaces that we occupy and the way that we connect across them are continually refined both by technology and the social environment that spawns it. We are blessed with an ingenuity that knows no bounds but our most recent refinements to the way we connect have tended to feed the selfish rather than the selfless gene.

## How sensate can we get?

Pitirim Sorokin in his mammoth pre-war analysis *Social and Cultural Dynamics* [11] set out to chart the extent to which the material world comes to be regarded as the only reality within a particular culture. He saw this progression toward untrammelled materialism as ultimately determining the moral and aesthetic climate of all societies and suggested that we might inhabit three types of society either in transition or in destination.

- An *ideational* society is one that gives priority to the immaterial and transcendent. Such a society distrusts the experience of the senses as illusory, believing that reality is immaterial, transcendental, eternal and unchanging. Reality is only to be experienced by looking inwards into the soul, not outward at the world around us and truth is attained through revelation by interpreters, the priests and prophets, and frugality and asceticism are admired and emulated.
- An *idealist* society is one that takes the material world seriously but does not regard itself as having much authority in the world of values. This society is less worried by a sense of impotence in the face of occult forces. It is more confident about its ability to control its environment. It dares to relax and enjoy the material world; happiness and human aspiration are legitimate objectives although their achievement should be realized through the moral framework established through the transcendent world. But while the material world is valued and enjoyed for its own sake it is not seen as having any authority in the realm of values, either moral or aesthetic.
- A *sensate* society is one that locates all its values in what can be observed and enjoyed by the senses. This is a society in which materialism is the only reality and the purpose of life is the fulfilment of

'here and now' gratification and happiness in the material realm. The pursuit of such happiness is worthless unless each individual can pursue his own definition of what for him or her constitutes happiness; thus individualism is a marked characteristic of all hedonistic societies.

In moving from the first to the third type societies lose all moral restraint to the point where crime and lawlessness make the pursuit of happiness a hollow goal, the resulting loss of cohesion eventually leaving the community defenceless. In the end the sensate society commits suicide [12]. Sorokin's simple and yet grand classification will always be flawed at the boundaries for no society of any size or complexity is or has been a pure manifestation of these three world views. Variants of them exist in all societies, though unevenly distributed among different social groups and different historical epochs, but the situation of many of our own societies, hovering between the 'ideational' and the 'sensate', cannot fail to resonate with us.

One obvious aspect of our move towards the 'sensate' is our immersion in consumerism. The consumer culture that much of the connecting technologies described in later chapters are designed to serve has not been uplifting. It is too often a 'carrier' of low self-esteem. By encouraging people to identify themselves by their purchases, their car, their house or their clothes, a thing becomes an extension and the chief 'explanation' of a person. This is an age of false consciousness and alienation, the shift towards wanting to have rather than wanting to be, always thinking that we are losing out by the constant comparisons that we make between ourselves and others – 'That car looks a bit boring for you doesn't it?'

Civic institutions represent the halfway house of the 'idealist' society, where transcendent values are preserved within a context which takes material reality and the hopes of human happiness seriously. Our current situation is that the 'idealist' drives that lay behind the development of our civic institutions are running out of steam as, starved of interest and funds, they linger like ghosts representing values alien to the increasingly 'sensate' society they are still trying to serve. One symptom of this is how we are re-defining 'needs' (once funded and supported by the community) as 'wants' (which we believe should be funded by the individual). This is not to maintain that 'needs' always remain the same – they patently don't – but health care, access to information, protection and pension provision are all examples of 'needs' that are currently in the process of being revised as wants by those planning social policy in many industrial countries. Social policies are being reconstructed within a 'sensate' context rather than an 'idealist', framework. This 'context' derives its power source from the centrality of an old idea, the liberal idea of individual freedom, which in its 'old' guise always assumed that effective civic institutions would act as a brake on naked self-interest. Mulgan spends some time exploring our growing impatience with the order that manages both our freedom and our interdependencies.

> Today it is hard to focus honestly on the question of order. Our attitudes have been so shaped by the centuries-long battles to win freedoms from kings and the church, and to liberate the powerless from oppressive orders, that it is hard to acknowledge that what was once the solution may now have become the problem. We have grown so used to struggling against authority that it is not easy to acknowledge that any institutions – whether they are firms or families, sports teams or nations – need some basis of authority if they are not always to take the line of least resistance, but rather to act for the long term. [13]

Consumption as a god and conspicuous consumption by elites, the velocity with which community needs are being defined as wants, and the willing away of any constraints that we see as limiting our capacity to live out our desires, are not movements unique to our own time. Other societies – the Greek, the Roman, the Ottoman – went through a similar stage. But coinciding as they do in our time with the deployment of technologies that facilitate and encourage individual detachment, while at the same time celebrating connectivity, these sensate tendencies are enlarged and magnified, and

> ... thin our sense of obligation to others, enabling us to hide behind pseudonyms, or surround ourselves with more fleeting transactions that demand less in terms of understanding and intimacy. [13]

Liberalism as it operated in real space may be a construct that, as a theoretical issue, has no more value than the construct of disconnected individuality. However we have the evidence to show that, as well as furnishing themselves with a good life, many individuals were happy to divert part of their personal energy, intelligence (politics) and resources (via taxation or philanthropy) to support the common good, however capable they were of just looking after themselves. They did this because they inhabited and moved around the same spaces, shared the same problems and saw for themselves the variety of circumstances and conditions that their neighbours experienced at first hand. We cannot, even with access to the most sophisticated virtual worlds, see and feel moved in the same way. Remote means remote, and while occasional remoteness may corrupt only slightly, a culture bent on celebrating absolute remoteness stands a good chance of corrupting absolutely.

## Educating to separate

President George Bush was once reported as registering astonishment at seeing a supermarket check-out scanning device for the first time. According to the late American historian and iconoclast, Christopher Lasch [14] this kind of 'astonishment' is emblematic of the kind of profound isolation that elites in the US (the same could be said for many European countries) have come to have from ordinary life. The notion of social mobility, i.e. a proud detachment from the masses, has gradually crept into the lexicon and psyche of what passes for a 'normal' and 'healthy' ambition all over the western world. Equally the overriding purpose of education, and the comprehension of connecting technologies to which it gives access, has now become to separate oneself as far as possible from the masses. The original democratic ambition of education to raise the level of a 'whole' society so as to make all of its citizens more capable of intelligent self-government, and to be richly fulfilled via self-actualization, has given way to the much-vaunted cult of selective meritocracy. Indeed it is a notion that has been elevated to symbolize the healthiest of societies, when in fact, as it is now practised, it is totally antithetical to the durability of a truly democratic culture. Social mobility in the west is an idea that now serves to maintain an elitist pool of individuals far too bound up with personal wealth creation, international corporate affiliation and naked self-interest to extend helping hands or spare any time for their neighbours or their country. In communities dominated by the word 'global' and all that it is supposed to mean by way of 'competition' and 'trade', the values of middle America and Little England have long been disdained as too parochial and provincial to be of any use as illuminating beacons or compass points. Where once the US took seriously the ambition to establish at least some semblance of equality for all, now it all too easily countenances the 'climb as high as possible and then kick the ladder away' school of personal advancement.

The youth of Europe are living within the post-modernist context of no context, a world where there are often precious few ladders leading anywhere past the next year or so. The fragmented politics of gender, race, employment, religion and sexual preference, which characterize the waning of the twentieth century, have served only to splinter youth further. Of the 360 million people in the EU 25 per cent are between 15 and 29 years old and the average unemployment rate for under 25s in the EU is 21.5 per cent; in France, where the young have been called 'the waiting room generation', it is nearer 25 per cent. Although they do not live in a world war or in the shadow of a cold war young Europeans still live in an age of economic anxiety, blaming and disowning most institutions, be they religious or political, for the lack of worthwhile work. According to a 1997 survey by the European Commission of 9400 people between 15 and 24 more than half belong to no group or organization whatsoever [15]. Struggling to replace those certainties that once came from work, many of them can only secure work in 'McJobs' – underpaid, part-time, temporary and menial. They also face reforms of the social security systems that their parents always took for granted as part of the 'harmonization' EU package. Theirs is a 'do it yourself, for yourself' time in a place that lacks the 'seize the day' imperatives that US parents and institutions pass on to younger generations. Older Europeans still look at social justice as essential to the deeper values that give true meaning to the value created by the market but the young of Europe are caught in the cultural crossfire. On the one side are all the support systems that make Europe a good place to live in, and on the other American-style social fairness – low taxes and lower provision for welfare – are trumpeted as the way forward for a rich and prosperous future. The age of freedom meets the age of anxiety.

## Post-modernism and the no rule rule

Anxious people, expecting to choose for themselves how they wish to behave in the face of the collapse of moral restraints, are very much a part of the post-modern condition. The 'modern' world up until c. 1950, was a place of certainties where everyone knew their place in society's hierarchies. Modernity was first and foremost about being restless, travelling rather than arriving, a process of continuous modernization. To be modern in the first half of the twentieth century, for a community as much as for an individual, meant to be preoccupied with 'bringing things into a better order', while accepting that no existing state of affairs was fully satisfactory – in other words being constantly on the move. At the same time there was usually a point to aim for. This was a point just down the road or round the corner which, when achieved, would see all our problems solved once and for all and where no further improvement will be possible or needed. It would, of course, take a lot of thought and effort; it would need a few more discoveries, a few more clever gadgets, another big push and then we would all be there.

Today the rules that regulated those hierarchies no longer apply and we live in a 'deregulated', 'flexible' world where the only foundation is a vague notion that everyone has a right to individual liberty. The post-modern world is characterized by unprecedented velocities of change accompanied by radical uncertainty and anxiety. It is a constellation of ambiguity and rates of change amid which the old certainties of the 'modern' age can never be reclaimed. As in the 'sensate' society freedom is the overriding priority and there is deep resistance to any attempt to impose any order that inhibits individual desires.

Zygmunt Bauman describes post-modernism as 'modernism without illusion' – that is without the comforting, but in his view, misleading belief in that satisfying 'point' just down the road. For him the post-modern condition comes with the realization that there is no clear direction, let alone an end to the road, and that in attempting to solve problems we must accept that all the choices will involve risks and these in turn will make new choices inevitable. How we live in such a society can no longer be answered by religion, politics, or art [16]. Bauman celebrates the pluralism that has replaced the old certainties of modernity and the spirit that questions the vision of a continually progressing world because he cherishes its openness and scope for alternative interpretations. He see society at a crossroads: one road points to capitalism and socialism together, married in their attachment to modernity; the other destination (possibly the new post-modern mix) is, as yet, unknown. Human beings in the post-modern world have succeeded in achieving instantaneousness and abolishing space, an idea perfectly mirrored by W3 where distance no longer exists. 'Jobs and relationships are temporary, the future is unforeseeable and unforcastable, we can no longer take the long-term view – even the medium-term view is becoming rare – and globalization, which just happens and there is nothing that we can do about it', has become the current fad. But Bauman is concerned about the impact of the culture of consumerism. Worse than industrial capitalism, he sees consumerism as duplicitous whereas capitalism was a straightforward mix of 'bosses' and 'workers', winners and losers. Consumerism promises something it cannot deliver – universality of happiness:

> Everybody is free to chose and if everyone is let into the shop then everyone is equally happy.' (an equality of entrance to the fairground but not the rides and 'fun of the fair'). That is one duplicity. Another is the limitation of its pretence that you resolve the issue of freedom completely once you offer a consumer freedom. So it is a reduction of freedom to consumerism. [16]

As a consequence of such freedoms people forget that there could be better ways of forming an identity than buying a new outfit – a mistake their forefathers would never have made. The de-regulated or 'flexible' post-modern world is one full of uncoordinated, often contradictory chances and voices but devoid of clear-cut standards by which the superiority of any of them can be measured. It is a world overflowing with a multitude of tempting and seductive possibilities and haunted by the excess of values worth pursuing. Freud said 70 years ago that our psychological and social troubles emerge from surrendering a lot of freedom for the sake of more *Sicherheit* (certainty, security and safety); now he might point out that they result from surrendering Sicherheit in exchange for fewer constraints on freedom of choice and self-expression. Formulating new rules and values that retain some of the Sicherheit of the 'idealist' world while we contemplate how total our surrender to the 'sensate' world should be is probably one of the most pressing tasks facing developed societies today.

## Hijacking Darwin

The twentieth century has been a struggle between the one ideology (Marx's) and one theory (Darwin's). Both have been hijacked and put to the service of political and economic dogma. The free-market capitalists, and some other strange bedfellows, hijacked Darwin while tyrants and self-seeking bureaucrats hijacked Marx. Unlike Marxism Darwinism is not a manifesto but an insightful description of biological evolution that has gained a remarkable level of acceptance. At its heart is the observation that at any moment in time, given a particular set of environmental conditions, some variations on a particular organic theme will flourish, biologically speaking, more than others: i.e. via natural selection. Certain characteristics and types thus become favoured over others as long as these particular conditions prevail (survival of the fittest) but they only lead to significant biological change over a very long time. Change is thus driven by changing conditions, including social ones, but only very slowly. Human beings and all our biological attributes, including behaviour, are embraced by Darwin's description but, try as we may to find it, there is nothing there that tells us how we ought to behave, how companies should behave or how we should arrange our societies. Unless it becomes normal over the next millennium to control social environments deliberately to favour certain human variations, given its incredible time-line, Darwinism is not a very useful basis for considering our more immediate social and political concerns.

Although Darwinism has increasingly been embraced as a basis for exploring social options, as Bond [17] forcefully notes, it is all about where we came from and not about where we are going or why we should go in any particular direction. Sir Carl Popper pointed out that Darwin's idea was 'feeble' as a scientific theory, being neither predictive nor testable (and therefore not refutable). It was, and is, not strictly possible to define the fittest as anything other than 'those who survive'.

Because it is irrefutable and non-predictive it is an inherently flexible idea that can be used to 'describe' but not explain a range of sometimes contradictory observations. That Darwinism has become so influential across a range of disciplines, from psychology and economics to computing and medicine, is indicative not of its strength but of its weakness. As we end the twentieth century, with our bag of post-modern uncertainties intact, perhaps Darwinism is seen as a welcome vestige of nineteenth century certainty, the last gasp of modernity in the face of what science sees as the terrible post-modern tide of epistemological mayhem. But Darwinism is both 'certain' and infinitely 'flexible'. Its certainty is reflected in its 'almost' universal acceptance as explaining the origin of man. Obviously the caveat 'almost' is important as many religious groups would not 'come out' and admit that Darwin was a credible alternative to the creation as set out in their religious texts. In the gubernatorial election in Alabama during November 1998 the incumbent governor's campaign still included (after all these years) ridiculing his opponent for believing that he was descended from an ape. This Governor, ever concerned for academic precision, had insisted that an insert be placed in the biology textbooks in all state schools just to remind children and their teachers that evolution is only a theory. Given the number of theories knocking around that may be commented on in school textbooks the Governor of Alabama may have to order many more such inserts in the future [18].

Darwinism's flexibility is signalled by its attraction to so many different causes with mostly opposite ideas. Darwin was a hero to Karl Marx, the social Darwinists, Fascists, anarchists (to support ideas of natural order) and an inspiration to followers of the Thatcherite creed of free markets and reduced state intervention. Biological description is neither a full understanding nor an agenda for action yet the centrality of Darwin's idea has been celebrated and uncritically absorbed into political prescriptions as if it had meaning over a range of public and policy arenas. However misused it greets the twenty-first century in better shape than the ideas of Carl Marx, though the greater intensification of technology that he envisaged may be more central to our day-to-day lives, affirming as it does those features humans exhibit which distinguish us from the rest of nature.

## Marx on the back burner, for now!

The Marxist, materialist theory of history implies that there is no fixed (biologically or otherwise) human nature; rather it changes with every change in the mode of production. This belief in the malleability of human nature has been important for the left because it provided them with grounds for hoping that a very different kind of human society is possible, i.e. the perfectibility of man living co-operatively and in harmony with one another. For Darwin the struggle for existence, or at least of one's offspring, is unending, competitive and brutal, but:

> If the materialist theory of history is correct, and social existence determines consciousness, then greed, egoism, personal ambition and envy that a Darwinian might see as inevitable aspects of our nature can instead be seen as the consequence of living in a society with private property and private ownership of the means of production. If there were no private property and the means of production were communally owned, people would no longer be concerned about their private interests. Their nature would change they would find their happiness in working co-operatively with others for the communal good. [19]

Sadly in the twentieth century the dream of the 'perfectibility' of humankind turned into the nightmare of Stalinist Russia, China under the Cultural Revolution, starvation in North Korea and the killing fields of Cambodia under Pol Pot. The debate about whether genes or social existence are triumphant in determining consciousness will travel with us well into the millennium. But we have enough evidence now to declare that some aspects of human nature are universal, e.g. systems of marriage, the creation of some form of government, ethnic identification, suspicion of outsiders, etc. We also know that most cultures are social: very few humans choose to live alone and finding time to help immediate family and relatives, forming co-operative relationships and recognizing reciprocal obligations are universal features of most societies. The existence of hierarchy or a system of ranking people is also a nearly universal human tendency and few human societies operate without any difference in social status. When we get rid of one system of ranking another one always emerges to take its place and we do not abolish the 'idea' of hierarchy in a society just because we eliminate a particular variant. Another one based on wealth, military power, birth or education will be waiting in the wings to take its place. Failing to understand the 'grain' of human nature is a major reason for the failure of political and revolutionary philosophers who, living in a more intensely cerebral world than most of us, often plan their reforms without taking the trouble to learn about the people who will have to carry out or live with their grand schemes. Typically failure is then always attributed to traitors or sinister agents rather than to the fallible tendencies that humans have accumulated as part of being human.

Interestingly the non-hierarchical, team-conscious, co-operative ideals of the left have been plagiarized by management theorists over the last ten years or so. They talk of flatter hierarchies, empowering people, de-centralization, devolution and delegation all in the cause of getting closer to the customer, doing better business and making more profit. But organizations, like governments, have found that what they give away, for a good reason at one time, they want to claw back for a different good reason at another time. The hierarchy, and its privileges, is a force that doesn't know where else to go and we, having become so used to one form of hierarchy or another, find it difficult to believe that there can ever be an effective, if flawed, governance of a community without one. Some commentators expect there to be a new mutation of capitalism, between the owners of capital and the owners of intelligence and knowledge, a new form of natural selection and mutual dependence where neither party dominates or controls the other. Such 'high-end' contracts already exist between that happy minority who can sell their intelligence to others who need it. Electronic networking will enable more of it to be done, faster and over great distances but the demand for such 'high-end' knowledge is not going to transform the nature of capital or most of the labour that still turns it into products and services.

## End of tour

During the first half of the century the world was torn asunder by two great wars which started in Europe; by contrast the last two decades of the twentieth century for most developed countries has been prosperous and triumphant. A child born in Europe in 1950, outside the Balkans and parts of Eastern Europe, has reached middle age after half a century of peace and material progress; this is no mean achievement when we consider the turbulence that characterized the first half. Travel and other communication systems have blossomed all over the world and the ICTs are astounding us on an almost daily basis with new ways to connect, share knowledge and conquer distance. Ten years ago who would have considered that we would be accessing a space called cyberspace or having the features showing at our local cinema Emailed to us on a weekly basis.

But dropping out to log on also poses a threat to some hard-won liberties and once cherished ideals of community and civic life. For Sorokin it is the changing convictions about what constitutes ultimate reality that fashion the choices we make and that explain the rise and fall of civilizations. In true post-modernist mien summing up the convictions that would constitute ultimate reality for most people in the west, let alone the rest of the world, would be a search for unicorns. The universal nature of human rights and individual liberty would figure highly but the different perspectives on what constitute human rights and how 'universal' they should be would pose as many questions as answers. The same challenge would face attempts to define 'individual liberty'.

Of course a huge portion of the world's population would love the luxury of debating the constitution of ultimate reality rather than struggling for survival in the harsh reality of their lives. Wrestling with the seductions of consumerism and materialism would be the least of their worries. Although this discussion of connectivity will concentrate on the issues nd concerns facing western/developed nations, who do most of the long-distance connecting, it is chastening to remember that although many millions of people enjoy the fruits of our connecting ingenuity many more millions do not. Many of them will have to wait decades before their lives are secure enough to enjoy anything like the same degree of social and technical convergence that we in the west take for granted every day.

# References

1.   Hobsbawm, E. (1977) *On History*. London: Weidenfield and Nicholson

2.   As quoted in Foster, R.F. (1993) *Paddy and Mr. Punch: connections in Irish and English History*, London: Allen Lane, pp. xii–xiii

3.   Ascherson, N. (1996) *Black Sea: The Birthplace of Civilisation and Barbarism*. London: Vintage

4.   Smedley-Marsden, P. (1998) *The Spirit Wrestlers*. London: Harper Collins

5.   Economic Indicators, 'Immigration'. *The Economist*, 26 September 1998

6.   *Heart of Darkness*. BBC One, Sunday 25 October 1998

7.   Walden, G. (1998) *Daily Telegraph*, Sat 4 July

8. McRae, H. (1994) *The World in 2020: power, culture and prosperity: a vision of the future.* London: Harper Collins. Chapter 4, although written before the present crisis, still provides an excellent analysis of the strengths and weaknesses of the Asian economic miracle and his Chapter 5 on demography clearly sets out the challenges facing developed countries as the age distribution of their population changes

9. Carlson, M. (1998) 'The Passive Majority'. *Time*, 9 November, p.42

10. Haywood, T. (1995) *Info-Rich – Info-Poor: access and exchange in the global information society.* London: Bowker-Saur

11. Sorokin, P. *Social and Cultural Dynamics.* London: Allen and Unwin. Four volumes published between 1937–1941

12. I owe a great debt to Anne Glyn-Jones's (1996) *Holding up a mirror: how civilizations decline.* London: Century, for much of this material on Sorokin's theories

13. Mullgan, G. (1997) *Connexity, how to live in a connected world.* London: Chatto and Windus, p.6/7 and p.5

14. Lasch, C. (1996) *The revolt of the elite's: and the betrayal of democracy.* New York: W.W. Norton and Co

15. Gleick, E. (1998) Visions of Europe; the new youth'. Special *Time*, Supplement, Autumn, pp.173–175

16. Bauman, Z. (1998) discussing the post-modernist age's rejection of the illusion of total solutions in *THES*, 15 May, p.16

17. Bond, R. (1998) 'Darwin's distracting description'. Letter to *THES*, 29 May

18. I am grateful to Professor Michael Malinconico for this intelligence

19. Singer, P. (1998) 'Evolutionary Workers' Party'. *THES*, 15 May, pp.15, 17

# CHAPTER TWO

# A seminal moment?

'The mess on the floor is always the organised mess.'
                                    Paul Krugman, Economist, MIT

## The 'Big' debate

Every generation believes that it stands at a seminal point on the time-line of social and technological progress. To help us comprehend the past we have constructed shorthand 'ages': of iron, of enlightenment, of steam, of flight, etc. Since the middle of the nineteenth century the pace of technological change has quickened and we have become accustomed, with the 100 per cent certainty that comes with retrospect, to present these ages as a continuum rather than sudden bursts or blips. Despite the best objections of post-modernists to the idea of linear purposeful time, in which the historical achievements of one generation are passed on to the next, schoolchildren still grow up believing that we hopped from one key date to another in the neat and harmonious linearity that has come to express the western ideal of continuing progress. We have also grown accustomed to assessing and measuring, in the light of past compartments, just how 'transforming' the latest 'transforming' tech-nologies will be. In the 1970s and 1980s we considered ourselves to be living in a transforming 'information age'. Since every past civilization processed information into knowledge which they then passed on to us, appropriating 'information age' for ourselves suggests an arrogance and supremacy akin to that found adorning some of the monuments built by the Victorians towards the end of the nineteenth century. The ancient Romans and Egyptians may not have filled their worlds with modems and photocopiers but there is no doubt that information, processed into knowledge, made them champions in ways that we still celebrate today.

Access to information and knowledge has always been important. Our particular 'spin' on it is the increasing emphasis that we have been giving in our discourse to the instruments that handle the delivery, and in particular to the speed of delivery, rather than the quality or value of the content. In the next millennium, having got over the excitement of being able to access once closed information quickly, quality and value will perhaps loom larger. We will demand that the promised intelligent agents filter out the dross for us and deliver, with much more precision, the kind of value and quality that we each construct as necessary for ourselves – although I suspect that creating precise information boundaries for ourselves may not be as easy as some might expect.

As we grapple with the frustrations and false starts generated by the browsers and search engines that have transformed the Internet since the early 1990s we might reflect on the frustrations that those pioneers of just 20 years ago faced as they explored the vague promise of the electronic networking. Jack Meadows has noted how the team leader of an experimental electronic journal in the 1970s declared at the conclusion of the trials that 'I have seen the future and it doesn't work'. He also noted that one colleague heralded the experimental electronic communications of the 1980s by remarking that 'I have seen the future and it goes beep, beep, beep'. As the amount of information in circulation increases and we face up to the anxieties of information 'overload' Meadows wonders if our cries will be more like 'I have seen the future, but I can't seem to find it again' [1]. My own exclamation would be more like 'I can't see the future for the trees' as knowledge stored on paper still continues to cover the space around me in ever increasing piles.

As the century ends we are still embroiled in the 'big' debate. Does information and communication technology (ICT) represent a massive turning point in social development (creating completely new kinds of societies) or is just a natural evolution of all the 'labour-saving' technology that has gone before, i.e. is it just one turning point among many? This debate has fostered questions like: What is a turning point? What is the defining feature of a society? What is continuity? How does our information society differ from the information societies of the past? What exactly do we mean by 'revolution'? Commentators like Manuel Castells clearly believe that IT is at the heart of the transformation that has globalized the economic system, reduced communism to ashes, intensified a retreat into religious fundamentalism, ignited the fires of raging internationalism, marginalized trade unionism and created a new militant environmentalism. In his mammoth three-volume work Castells seeks to show how this technology has captured all the processes that constitute human societies and altered the terms within which they function [2]. He sees the depth and suddenness of the impact of ICT as a natural concomitant of its pervasiveness throughout the social structure and the reason why everyone is now immediately affected by it. The industrial system that is now being transformed was, like a father, preparing the way for the vastness of the influence of electronic text with its incomparable memory, storage capacity, processing speeds, ubiquity and mastery of space and time. For Castells the last years of the twentieth century were characterized by the hurried arrival of a new technological paradigm, with information machines at its core.

> Networks constitute the new social morphology of our societies, and the diffusion of network logic substantially modifies the operation and the outcomes in processes of production, experience, power and culture. [2]

Negroponte [3] would share many of Castells' views, although the latter is more cautious in his optimism than Negroponte about the universality and depth of the ICT revolution; Neil Postman [4] and others would not. Essentially the debate boils down to whether ICT is a 'revolution' that is changing what we call society and the condition of being human, and will ultimately change it beyond recognition, or whether it is just another step in the evolution of our relationship and mastery of our environment which, although always impacting on our social structures, rarely revolutionizes what it means to be social. The revolutionary school also tends to be the most optimistic about the impact of ICT while the evolutionists tend to be pessimistic and wary about the 'go with the flow', 'it's unstoppable anyway' schools of thought. The evolutionists would also argue, I think, that not only should the evolving technology be a tool of humans in social settings controlled by humans, but that it should always be that way, i.e. technology kept on tap, not on top. Neo-luddite or techno-liberator, we seem to like our debates about new technologies served up rare and on clearly segregated plates. There has to be two sides and we feel happier buying into one of them − it feeds naturally off either the dominant optimistic or pessimistic sides of our characters. The media, in search of the simplicity and polarization that they think is necessary to explain modern technologies to a mass audience, are perhaps also to blame for the black and white nature of some of the popular debate.

## Genes: slow, slow, quick, quick . . .!

In the world of evolutionary biology a similar debate is set to run and run. There the 'ultradarwinians', led by George C. Williams [5] and Richard Dawkins [6], who maintain that evolutionary history is the outcome of 'oh so slow' natural selection working on available genetic variation. They emphasize the supremacy of the gene rather than the organism in the struggle for reproductive success. Genes need organisms to house them, nurture them and to provide the energy and physical apparatus for them to function but the genetic information (the instructions for constructing an organism) is more important than the system (the organism) it builds. For them evolution is strictly a competition among genes for representation in the next generation; theirs is the ultimate reductionism scenario. On the other side the 'naturalists', represented by Stephen J Gould [7] and Niles Eldredge [8], argue that gradualism is not intrinsic to the process of evolutionary change but a cultural bias, the response of nineteenth century liberalism to a world in a state of revolution. For them the history of the world reads as a series of stable states interspersed by sudden convulsions, major events, that make possible a later period of stability. In attempting to establish a better fit between evolutionary theory and the fossil record these two palaeontologists announced their theory of punctuated equilibria in 1972. Both groups support a theory of evolution − they just differ on how the evolutionary process works. Eldredge likens this debate to painters of different schools, who necessarily produce different pictures of the same landscape. Neither can claim exclusively to paint the 'correct' picture of nature but they must both acknowledge that they are engaged in a joint enterprise to paint a better one. Here also then are 'revolutionaries' who favour a sudden convulsion scenario that threw up completely new forms of life and the 'evolutionaries' who see individual organisms plodding through adaptation and accident without explosion. Like these protagonists around the detail of the theory of evolution both sides of the 'how transforming is IT debate' agree that IT does transform our lives. They differ on the depth and degree to which that transformation will, or should, change what it means to be human and this debate will hot up even more as we start linking machines to our bodies.

## Defining moments

I cannot be alone in confessing to feelings of both optimism and pessimism about all the ICTs, sometimes at the same time and over the same issue. Like many others I feel very comfortable with much of the new technology; I experience how it saves my time and how it helps with some of my daily challenges and I eagerly anticipate improvements that will further increase both its ease of use and my convenience. Yet I am also aware of how, say, using the Internet/Email/computers, etc., changes my behaviour in some ways and takes me away from other, just as valuable, activities and I guess that this is just the way it's going to be. As an adult making adult choices the onus is on me to get the balance that suits me right (if I don't know what it is I can't expect any one else to) and it has ever been so. If I get too engrossed and diverted by the tools and instruments of ICT, if I spend a lot of time waiting for slow modems to download information that I am not quite sure that I want, if I give up the hills and valleys or family life to sit all day with plastic and silicon then that's my choice. I can change, refine and modify this behaviour, as I did when I used to mess with cars, as and when I want. Perhaps it is time to develop a new language when exploring the impact of electronic networking on our future: one that avoids the simple verities of hope and dread, hyper-optimism or dark pessimism; one that assumes winners and losers, great benefits and some serious downsides; and one that recognizes that there will be liberating transformations alongside the continuing longevity and importance of many non-tech habits and behaviours. If we can start from this point to sharpen our faculties in critique of the bigger issues at the centre of our lives then we can build on these assumptions and they need not be constantly repeated.

One important part of such a perspective is to take stock of the things that we value and then consider how the ICTs have helped, or could help, to facilitate these what I would call 'defining moments' of our lives. The pleasures of child-rearing, talking with friends, travelling, falling in love, developing ideas, reflecting on our relationships, handling illness and old age etc. – none of these 'big' behaviours, though sometimes affected, is much influenced by computers or electronic networking. Testing out technologies with regard to their impact on these 'defining moments' is a valuable test of their place in our world. Late into marriage I have no doubt that Bill Gates would regard the birth of his daughter as a 'moment' quite a few notches up from the take-off of Microsoft! We have been told that the world of electronic networks is transforming the way that we connect with each other and there can be no doubt that in certain domains this is true. Looking around we can see people whose lives have been transformed by ICTs but equally we also see many others, probably the majority, whom it has touched, but hardly re-defined their world. Radically new ways of working are still work, Email is still person-to-person communication, surfing the Net is still 'browsing' among words and pictures and word-processing is still about creating documents. The world's universities are still built on towers of paper and few computer users opt for life without a printer, while in the wider world many of today's big issues have been with us since the beginning. Racial differences still inflame peoples, gender differences remain complicated, different languages still hinder human understanding, unemployment is still unemployment and wars are still wars! Charles I on reading a declaration of his treasons, squirted down a fibre optic cable from Oliver Cromwell's headquarters somewhere in England during 1649, still gets to hear that he is going to lose his head! The 'defining moment' has nothing to do with the technology that brings him the message.

This is not to denigrate or disparage the impact that ICTs are having or will have: rather it is just to recognize that who we are and much of what we do has nothing to do with any kind of technology. The future may be different. Many technologists (e.g. at the MIT Media Lab and Reading University in the UK) are working on portable communication devices that they envisage will become part of us, a bit like an external-ized nervous system. They believe that in the not too distant future such devices will blur the lines between our biological functions and our (attached) machine functions and we will intuitively manage both as if they were one (see Chapter 9).

## Been here before

Standage's history of the telegraph [9] in which he points out its many parallels with the Internet is a reassuring tale for those of us who belong to the 'one thing follows on from another' school. After its invention in 1835 and Morse's practical patent in 1837 Morse had to struggle on with scanty resources until, six years later, the US Congress grudgingly granted $30 000 for a telegraph line to be built between Washington and Baltimore. In 1844 Morse sent his famous 'What hath God wrought?' message across this line and we have been sending messages down lines ever since. Standage notes the self-hype that accompanied the development of the telegraph, its utopian overlay, the fears of information overload, its encouragement of new industries, its hospitality to new forms of crime and the opportunities that it generated for new forms of wealth creation. Although many governments were sceptical about using it at first the pursuit of profit and military advantage ensured that telegraph wires were soon laid all over the world. Many commentators at the time pronounced that the telegraph would so transform the world that universal and eternal peace between nations was now a possibility. How could there be the kind of misunderstandings that lead to war when communication was instantaneous? As we know neither understanding nor misunderstanding has anything to do with the speed at which communication takes place as the ice warnings, then using Marconi's wireless technology and Morse's code, sent to the Titanic in 1912 clearly demonstrate.

Like the Internet the telegraph spawned some new crimes and new ways of solving crimes. Industries soon came to depend on the instant communication of prices and, like the Internet, the telegraph generated a whole new circus of economic activity. The more direct of these included the manufacture of the cables, cable-laying ships, gutta-percha farms to supply the special insulating material, the organization of large and small telegraph offices and the employment of regiments of messenger boys to fetch and carry the data (telegrams). Like the Internet its utility grew as its user base grew and soon no business could be without it. No general could command without it either, but neither was he free from the once impossible interference of politicians. News media were some of the obvious beneficiaries but it also instigated some less obvious changes. It helped usher in the era of the distant expert who could be quickly and easily 'tapped' for opinions and advice, its pricing system mirrored and reinforced the class order and it exposed people to new concepts of time, space and racial differences. The Internet is causing similar changes; like those instigated by the telegraph some of them, such as gutta-percha farming, will be temporary while others will form the foundations for radical new ways of communicating and doing business. Morse code has been resilient in surviving many changes in communications technology. It only ceased being used as the distress 'language' of the sea on 1st February 1999 (155 years after its first use) when GMDSS (Global Maritime Distress and Safety System), using satellite global positioning technology, became mandatory for all large sea-going vessels. However a large band of amateur enthusiasts scattered around the world will still keep its tap, tap, tapping alive as they shun the Internet for the tactility of a hand on a key rather than fingers on a keyboard.

## Global voyeurism

Television, by bringing so many images of entertainment, joy and suffering directly into our homes, justifiably lays a claim, after the telephone, to be one of the twentieth century's most ubiquitous connecting technologies. Although the communication has been mainly one way from broadcasting networks to a passive audience it has exposed us to some powerful moments and has become the principal medium by which ordinary people connect with the wider world. There cannot be many who have forgotten the image of the skinny man holding two plastic shopping bags blocking the path of a line of tanks as they came down Chong On Street during the Chinese crackdown on the pro-democracy students' demonstration in Tiananmen Square in early June 1989. He was eventually pulled away by Chinese solders to disappear forever. He was a worker named Wong Wai-lam and although the images of a man standing against those great war machines will forever symbolize the lone citizen's stand against military repression, he is lost to us.

Although through the window of television we see, pity and weep for the victims of famine, war and flood, we are not sure about our obligations to these distant peoples, just because we know in ever more vivid detail what is happening to them. Although a great fan of the part that television plays in our connecting saga I fear that it has also led us into some bad habits of global voyeurism where, cozy and warm in our multi-media hut, we ooh! and ah! over the troubles of the world in between making the coffee and taking Lucinda to ballet, and hardly differentiate between them. We salve by seeing and having seen we are salved. This is not to suggest that as 'watchers' we could have any instant influence on distant events but rather to remind ourselves of the numbing effect that the regularization of tragic news, brought temporarily closer to us by modern communications, can have on us. Phillip Larkin's famous acid test 'Did I care about it, and if so what was the quality of the caring?' seems an appropriate question to ask ourselves as we ooh! and ah!

Television has certainly mobilized citizens in rich countries to contribute money to suffering communities at home: e.g. Children in Need and Red Nose Day in the UK which help to support overseas projects in the third world. However some of the larger issues, e.g. the suspending of crippling third world debts, arms sales, child labour and pollution, still remain largely untouched by viewer opinion. Although the linking of support to developing countries, as in the 'aid for trade' practices of the 1980s, has largely been eradicated by western governments, the dotted lines of commerce and trade that connect the tragedy of many poor countries to our own government polices rarely gets much airtime.

Will Wyatt, giving the Huw Weldon Memorial Lecture in 1996 [10] dedicated it to 'television presenters and their audience'. In a timely comparison with 'voice-over' and 'speak-for-yourselves' documentaries he explored the value and challenges of television presenters who talked directly to their audiences. He underlined the great bond that he believed many presenters build up with viewers as a result of this directness, representing to them the sole ownership and essence of the programme. He opined that the multi-channel/digital television of the future would make it more difficult to grow the kind of magisterial presenters who had done so much to bring both popular and non-popular culture to big audiences in the past. He appealed to producers not to be afraid of pedagogy; he urged them to seek out those who have profound knowledge and to find ways to let them share it with a wider audience. His concerns will resonate with many who believe in magisterial television. I have to say that I don't share his worries. I don't believe that audiences make deep connections with television presenters, they just recognize them and possibly become fans of particular individuals. The public response to the murder of the BBC's Jill Dando in April 1999 highlighted the affection that the public build up for some TV presenters. However I am sure that she would have been horrified to see how her own tragedy pushed the stories of the accelerating genocide in Kosovo to second place in the news bulletins of the time. Since mass broadcasting started in the UK during 1936 the personality of presenters has always been important to the viewer, but, at its base, it is a trivial connection and one that I don't see multi-channel TV giving up altogether. I also see no dearth of profound knowledge on TV – it is there if people want to seek it out, and I also remember being quite moved by voice-over commentaries and 'fly on the wall' documentaries. But in the end a TV story is just a TV story; only small numbers of people ever get worked up or shaken out of their armchairs to do anything about what they see on TV. Television is a great informer but only an occasional motivator.

## The future is already here

The greatest proponents of the 'information age' saw access to more information as a surrogate for the unqualified and unproblematic access to more knowledge – they saw 'width' so they assumed quality. The multiplicity of man-made disasters that we have experienced since the 1970s, from oil spills and the mistaken destruction of passenger planes to nuclear melt-downs, clearly shows that the human component of converting information into effective knowledge can be as capricious as it ever was. As we enter the twenty-first century we envisage ourselves living in an electronic networked age where information and knowledge are increasingly transferred by an invisible global nervous system of connections linking individuals and organizations. We have been in this 'information-come-electronic network age' compartment for some time now and so theoretically there shouldn't be too many surprises. Many commentators have emphasized that the technologies that the more fortunate of us will be using in 10 or 20 years' time are already in existence, albeit in an early form in research laboratories or in regular use by select bands of assessors. Also much of what we still term as 'new' has been in play for some time now. The Internet has been around since the early 1970s. The W3 has been in the public domain since 1993 and many citizens of the developed world already enjoy the distribution of information and knowledge by electronic networks for business, education and pleasure, and their numbers are growing exponentially every year. The US consultancy Dataquest estimates that 15 million US households in 1998 owned at least two computers and expects inexpensive high-speed Internet services to become available to millions of US homes through modified cable systems and new fast telephone links during the next two years.

Many other forms of 'connecting' have also been refined to high levels. Delegates to seminars and symposia meet in hi-tech conference centres having travelled thousands of miles to meet each other in aircraft that regularly transport 350 or more people safely. Postal and delivery services use the technology with which they also compete to move our bulky, more tactile communications faster and more efficiently. Telephony is much cheaper than a decade ago and will get cheaper still over the next few years as a more competitive spirit pervades a business once controlled by state monopolies. The mobile phone is becoming as commonplace as the incomprehensible contracts that once hindered its penetration give way to simple pay-as-you-call charging systems, and the fax machine now seems so familiar as to belie its two decades of commercial use. All of these connecting tools will continue to be refined and improved over the next ten years. They will become cheaper, smaller and more powerful and will integrate more functions. They will improve our lives but they will also make new demands on us. Some of them may also turn out to have a sting in their tail.

## Testing, approval, marketing, crucifixion

Most people would accept that all technology is something of a Faustian bargain, in that it giveth and it taketh away. However, the value of the giving and the adverse impact of the taking cannot be discovered quickly. It often takes the jury, i.e. society, many years of observation and participation before it can deliver its verdict with any accuracy and it usually requires further advances in other sciences or in scientific inquiry before a comprehensive assessment of all the factors can be made. Rachel Carson's critique of DDT in the US during the early 1960s was one of the first great exposures of the damage that a seemingly helpful and benign chemical can inflict on humans as it enters the food chain. Many other cases have followed. Atomic power was to give us cheap power, but we learn, many years later, that the radioactive waste it creates is almost impossible to clean up. In the 1930s we found CFC's to be a handy and convenient way to keep food cool and help spray all kinds of things only to find out later that they eat ozone. Motor cars give us tremendous freedom and personal mobility but at the cost of filling our atmosphere with a host of dangerous pollutants that may be turning our world into a greenhouse. In 1950 each of us emitted 2.4 tons of carbon dioxide; in 1992 is was nearer 4.1 tons each and the people of China have hardly started driving yet!

With the introduction of any new technology we enter an initial period when the missionaries enthusiastically declare the new scripture. They are often the researchers involved in its early development or the enthusiasts who, as well as using it, also tend to predict the even bigger and better things that it will do. Then comes a period when the corporations test it for commercial viability, then a time of early market testing on the public and then, sometimes surprisingly quickly, it takes off and we all have it or want it. The crucifixion comes many years later when another set of researchers reveal how damaging all or bits of it are to humans, plants or animals. Networking computers to communicate rapidly and to disseminate information couldn't look more benign. There's no radiation (although the radiation that emanates from computer screens is currently being researched); there's no obvious pollution (though computers do consume energy that may have been generated from fossil fuels) – indeed it could help to cut down on some vehicle pollution by reducing the need to 'go' somewhere. No bits or bytes are likely to enter the food chain and it creates lots of possibilities for housebound people to make contact in a way that they never could before. We may hear of a few cases of screen-blindness, some repetitive strain injury and the odd electric shock here and there but clearly, taken as a whole, it looks like we're on to a winner!

For those who can gain access to it there can be no doubt that the 'network option' is one that can enrich and empower, helping them with big projects as well facilitating the myriad of day-to-day conveniences that communicating rapidly over long distances enables. We have only just moved out of the missionary phase as far as the Internet and global networking is concerned and so the jury is a long way from assembling in the courtroom. Fortunately the very technology it is judging can also help the members to discuss the case quite effectively, however scattered they might be. It may seem bold, particularly at a time of such euphoria in anticipation of the wonders of bandwidth and content to come, even to suggest any contemplation of potential downsides. Nevertheless scientists and technologists should always be grateful to early sceptics and cheerily embrace any and all criticism, and even resistance, to new technologies. Firstly they can regard it as the understandable distress signals of the animals who will eventually be 'tagged' by them, including themselves, and secondly, as Microsoft, Netscape, Sun, Linux and many others have found, they can take it on board as a cheap contribution to future product refinement. Such an open-minded approach is unlikely to get in the way of the fiercest of the determinists who, as noted above, see their 'version' of the electronic networking idea as nothing less than a revolution and the distinctive feature of all future societies.

But obsessions need antidotes and perspective. Having access to more information doesn't translate unproblematically into having more knowledge or always being able to use it effectively. The potential disadvantages of electronic networking, unlike ozone depletion or radiation sickness, are likely to be more messily associated with the much wider social, political and economic imperatives currently occupying the communities from which networking will be orchestrated rather than as a direct result of networking per se. Some disadvantages may arise directly from the way we behave with networking technology and how this behaviour compounds and coincides with the wider economic and political behaviours of both communities and individuals. In contemplating the value or likely impact of new technologies citizens want to be able to trust the institutions that approve, test and market them. Despite the proliferation of information sources now available to us just asking, let alone answering, questions about the intricacies of technical or chemical innovations generally require some specialist knowledge. We expect to get this information from the 'official' agencies that act on our behalf, but in reality we have increasingly come to rely on individuals, who may have to risk their careers, to let us in on the real story (see Chapter 7). In anticipating the impact of new technologies our motives are always mixed, but socially negotiated factors such as accumulated knowledge about how science has been applied before and whether our institutions have knowingly or unknowingly done us harm are starting points. Many governments insist on secrecy to exclude us from knowledge of potential harms or side effects during the development and testing phases of medical and technical research and as long as these harms are corrected well before exposure to the public this would seem reasonable to avoid unnecessary panic. Nonetheless our experience with the workings of such systems, with the past role of market forces and our faith in the capacity of our political systems to distribute the benefits of technology; all represent reasonable axes of concern. The cycle of utopian discovery and doom-laden revelation in the sciences now follows an almost predictable pattern, and even if the precise nature of the particular downside takes us by surprise we are not surprised that there is one. Science has never waited on society – if it had we might still believe that the sun moved around the earth; however we do expect scientists, as members of our community, to share our values. We expect them to respect human rights and human dignity and, given the opportunities that they have to push forward the frontiers of knowledge, we expect them to do it within the moral and ethical frameworks of the time, whomever they work for. The evidence so far is mixed. Some of it, in its exposure of unexplained secret testing and experimentation on babies and adults, is extremely disturbing.

## Apologies and paranoia

In 1977 the US government made a $20 million payment to the survivors, and to the families of those who had not survived, in compensation for the infamous Tuskagee experiments carried out between 1932 and 1972 in Macon County, Alabama. Twenty years later in May 1997 President Clinton apologized on behalf of the US government for the damage that these experiments had caused to the men and their families. In these 40-year long experiments around 700 men, infected with syphilis, were used as a 'control' group to see how the disease developed and how it eventually caused death. They were denied the penicillin that was available from the same clinics that they attended for 'close' monitoring for 30 of those 40 years. In a chastening reminder of how callous scientific testing in a civilized country can be a group of very poor black people, who were unlikely to raise any effective objections, were sentenced to a slow death. This was the second presidential apology made for unethical scientific research in two years. In October 1995 the US President had also apologized for some radiation experiments that had been carried out in the

1940s and 1950s. These experiments had included injecting people with plutonium without their knowledge, feeding radioactive oatmeal to retarded children and releasing radiation near inhabited towns and cities just to see what it did! Although the apologies were welcome as an overdue recognition of the misuse of power by previous governments, such an exposure of the disregard for human life by a government during scientific and medical testing does not by itself re-establish our confidence in it. Indeed it begs the question of what kind of research on humans is going on today for which a US, or some other President, will be apologizing in 2020? The Swedish government's recent offer of compensation (the equivalent of about £13 500 per person) to those people who were sterilized without their consent between 1935 and 1975 under the sterilization laws of 1935 and 1941 is another example of how inhuman practices can be carried out in this case in the name of preventing 'undesirable' births, even by governments whose social policies normally inspire admiration.

During mid-1997 the UK government admitted for the first time that radioactive waste had been dumped 40 years ago close to the shipping lanes in the North Channel between Scotland and Northern Ireland. The low- to medium-level radioactive material, contained in metal drums encased in concrete, had been disposed of during the 1950s in Beaufort's Dyke. This deep-sea trench had previously been used for dumping upwards of one million tons of 'conventional' armaments including bombs, rockets and chemical weapons and other unwanted munitions since the 1920s. Since 1984 ministers of the crown in the UK had repeatedly denied that any dumping of radioactive material had taken place in this area. A 'spokesman' for the Scottish Office at the time of the exposure explained that successive 'governments had been unaware of the dumping'. If this was true it poses as many questions as it answers, including the effectiveness of monitoring, the secretive nature of this and other disposal activities and the issue of what else may have been dumped in that sea trench or indeed in other places around the UK coast.

Such revelations cannot help but flavour our confidence in governments, our faith in the testing and disposal phases of science and technology and our concerns about the real motives of those who seek us to adopt science and technology. Science transforms human identity but we also want it to be subject to the scrutiny of independent moral principles. But these principles themselves are shifting as science, as in bioengineering, genetic crop modification etc., declares new possibilities that in themselves transform the cartography of what we chose to regard as acceptable. Electronic networking operates on many levels and it couldn't look more benign. It is heavily diffused throughout the pantheon of many other technologies from missile systems and financial networks to real-time medicine over distance and the monitoring of dangerous chemical processes. Its valuable contribution as a 'carrier' within these domains will no doubt go from strength to strength but who out there can be trusted to tell us if there is a downside? We have come to accept that the 'cover up' is now as much a part of political life in democracies as in the continuing and one-time communist regimes – perhaps the revelations seem all the more shocking for being so unexpected. Wars always produce mistakes to which governments are always slow to admit and, when found out, are slow to answer for. The many soldiers killed by 'friendly' fire in the Second World War, in Vietnam and in the Falklands whose relatives had to fight for years to discover the truth form just one example. The various exposures to chemical weapons involving servicemen in the Gulf War and the mystery surrounding the 1500 men left to drown in the North Sea after the sinking of *H.M.S. Glorious* in 1941 are two others.

With so much of this kind of history behind us we may be forgiven for wondering why a citizen's contract with its government cannot now be more transparent. While governments and corporations always hang on to be 'found out' we will always be slightly suspicious about what exactly they are doing in regard to the testing of scientific and technological knowledge. The last part of the twentieth century has seen something of a plague of paranoia in western societies. Although some individuals may thrive on paranoia it is not a state that most of us seek or desire. But part of the blame for the spread of what we might call popular paranoia is the almost constant trickle of revelations about past or current wrongdoing by the agents we trusted most to protect us. It may also be part of the reason that so many Americans are joining the kinds of sects and groups whose obsessions so often bear the 'trust no one – least of all the authorities' kite mark. These often outlandish groups offer people a way to register, however unfocused it may seem to those of us on the outside, a protest at the collusion of the military–industrial–scientific complex. This is very much a 'Catch 22' situation. The widespread anti-authoritarian attitude of suspicion among such groups has often gone too deep to be brought back by common rationalities which just end up looking like arguments from the tongue of the oppressor seeking to justify its role. Such people will not be cured of their attraction to conspiracy theories simply by the inoculating force of common sense, so bringing them back into the world of active, 'normal' citizenship is going to be a long haul. It will only start to happen when the trickle of state and corporate wrongdoings dries up and people begin to have more faith in their traditional institutions. The Internet has been a great boon to conspiracy theorists and to the whistle-blower who can't find any other outlet for their exposés. It may be less reliable as a source of information about its own failings or misuse.

## The malice of inanimate objects

All of us at different times get caught up in the 'tension-ground' of 'wondering' if we know enough. This is the modern no man's land of information shell-holes and barbed wire. It used to be the malice of inanimate objects, those piles of newspapers and cuttings in the corners of rooms, that intimidated us. We kept them there because we were convinced that there was definitely something among them that we wanted to refer to again. We sometimes even took scissors to bits of them to improve our hit rate. But we soon forgot what it was that we wanted and as the pile increased the time needed for retrieval seemed less and less worthwhile. Their silent screams sometimes became unbearable enough for us to blow away the dust and throw them away amid curious emotions of angst and liberation. Once connected to the Internet and linked to a notionally infinite pile of cuttings via a fixed or mobile device that, like a whispering Iago, never ceases to hint at what we're missing, the screams could get even louder.

Academics, as most publishers know, do not respond well to having their urgency constructed – often resisting even the generous time-scales associated with a contract, made between consenting adults, to deliver a text or a review at a particular time – but they are not by any means immune to information anxiety. The sheer weight of information available in a large library can cause them delirium if not sickness. Walking down the steps, after many hours of browsing in a large library, they feel the walls behind them murmuring mischievously about all the stuff that they've missed. Academics are particularly bedevilled by the fear of incompleteness and the constant worry that the key ingredient of their argument is lying somewhere they haven't been. So they worry, go back again and put off actually writing something useful or creative, based on their researches so far, for another year or so. 'So far' never seems to be 'far enough' and they are not alone.

As more and more information is brought to the attention of other groups – businessmen, doctors, lawyers, etc. – via the Internet and other sources, learning to handle containment rather than just facilitating access may be our biggest challenge in the future. As seekers after information we often desire a mix of specificity and serendipity. When we know precisely what we want, we want to go straight to it, retrieve it, use it, discard it. When we are unsure about our precise needs we want to browse among likely sources hoping for interesting discoveries and connections to emerge. But to be able to browse we need big collections organized in some way that facilitates 'stumbling' across happy discoveries, and yet, given our addiction to speed, we are also anxious to expedite retrieval. Now there is no doubt that the Internet is big on serendipity. To help us with our twin desires of specificity and surprise nineteenth century libraries developed rational classification schemes based on subject relationships which, as well as helping us find specific titles and subjects, also realized a modicum of serendipity. The specific item would be shelved alongside related items which we could 'stumble' across and make 'happy discoveries' which we might not have anticipated. We found the specifics we were looking for and we also found some related stuff and most of this was 'manageable'.

The Internet is the exact reverse of this experience – an infinity of information, poor specificity and overwhelming serendipity. In 1996, visiting Bolton for the first time, to speak at a conference, I checked out 'Bolton' out on the Internet. I found very little about Bolton the town but a great deal about Melissa Noack in Minnesota. She had a boyfriend called Darin Bolton and her home page came complete with a nice black and white picture of them sat together on her sofa. Now I appreciate that this kind of mismatch will be less common in the future. We will describe our needs more precisely and intelligent agents will trawl the Internet, vastly improving the precision of retrieval. However my guess is that in instructing our personal electronic 'ferret' we will still 'oversubscribe' because we will also want those 'happy discoveries' that come from not being too precise! Our desire to hit more and more bases, because they are there, will lead to the regular chore of having to re-specifying the parameters within which our electronic retriever operates. Like many others I have a collection of 'bookmarks' in my Internet browser (over 40 of them), Internet sites that I have been to at least once and might want to go to again and which give me some degree of specificity. The only difference between these 'bookmarks' and the malignancy of my pile of newspaper cuttings is the lack of dust. There is no difference in the guilt they instigate by my being continually reminded of their riches and yet never finding the time to use them effectively.

## The Shire: unspoiled by progress!

We are now bombarded with predictions about the way that our world will grow even smaller, grow more democratic, grow more empowering and enabling and offer us more opportunities, as broadband networking becomes commonplace. We believe that there will be changes, but we don't believe that things will necessarily work out quite as the prophets say. The predictable unpredictability of the human condition will ensure that there will be some surprises in the way that all new technologies are explored, taken up or dumped by large populations. Many commentators now see our futures inexorably driven by ICTs like wooden houses driven before a hurricane. I would resist such a vision.

The history of our relationship with technology has always been mixed. We are always enmeshed in a crisis of progress that tugs us back and forth between memories of less anxious, more leisurely and satisfying days gone by, and the excitement and convenience offered by new technology. A UK brewery (Banks's of Wolverhampton) has, for a number of years now, been using an advertising slogan 'Unspoiled by Progress' to sum up the advantages of traditional beers over those made by more modern methods. The idea of progress always having a serious downside is quite well established in the view of a certain 'Frodo' generation who, like J.R. Tolkein's Hobbits of 'The Shire', love their cottages, dingles and neatly ploughed fields and, though good at handling small tools, resist the onset of bigger machines. Such a conservative view believes that quality, reliability and utility, in nearly all things, is always sacrificed as we organize ourselves to satisfy mass markets, plump for more speed and facilitate the sating of immediate desires. Pride in one's work, craftsmanship, those days when we had more time for deep introspection and a greater sense of community – all these memories are recalled through the rose-tinted spectacles of a nostalgia sustained by real or imagined images of the past and they can be very strong. This looking backwards generation is always with us, always re-inventing itself. The baby born today amid a multiplicity of devices for accessing and exchanging information and entertainment will be scratching its head as a 60-year-old reflecting on a time when things were better and had more meaning than the trivial gadgets and gizmos that occupy the time of his or her grandchildren. As we enter the last gasp of the twentieth century, we find ourselves immersed in a melting pot of ideas about the properties, limits and opportunities that the convergence of so many technologies might bring about. We will triumph. The future will mix and match our past and present as it has always done but, as always, we will need to revise and hone our skills of selection and discernment. The new storytellers will tell us of the coming inevitability of certain technologies and behaviours. But there will be many stories and it is up to us to choose those that we want to come true.

## Intel giveth, Microsoft taketh away?

There are of course the usual powerful corporate forces at work that would guide us down this path or that and there can be no doubt that we are increasingly being sucked into new forms of dependency in relation to technological obsolescence, up-grading and speed hype. The rhetoric of the major hi-tech corporations often displays a seamless merging of ideals and enterprise. But we know that there are seams, we know that trade and competitiveness demand one set of standards and the public good demands another and we can usually tell the difference, however cleverly the rhetoric may be mingled. In the area of IT we know that many of the 'revolutionaries' are also in the business of selling us the hardware and software that will keep the revolution going. We need to stimulate our critical faculties in ways that retain the healthy scepticism that warns us that such a confluence of ideas and trade are rarely motivated by the general good.

We know that Andy Grove of Intel must declare the fast-chip, rapid obsolescence, Pentium faith in order to feed our hunger for the interminable 'next generation' processor that will keep both the revolution, and his business, hot. We know that Bill Gates must then add more whistles and bells to his software in order to eat up the new processing power. 'Intel giveth and Microsoft taketh away' and oftentimes we are not really sure why. One serious symptom of our new dependency is that as consumers we buy the message that we must discard one-year-old technology in order to have the fastest, irrespective of what we use it for. This is a captivity based on messages about obsolescence that we accept without much critical analysis of our needs, a kind of hi-tech keeping up with the neighbours but without the visibility of polishing the new car on Sunday mornings. We also see the alliances being forged, almost on a daily basis, between media content providers and those who provide the drivers and connections to the new networks. We can guess that these alliances have more to do with extending markets and profits than with high ideals or unsullied altruism. The history of recent information technologies suggests that the general good has to wait a long time for big critical masses to be reached, before we get any serious 'trickle down' of wider, and often unintended, benefits. In the world of commerce evidence of need is measured and confirmed by 'take-up', and in a world where market forces now dominate the posture of nearly all our institutions 'take-up' is emerging as the only measure and confirmation worth having, irrespective of the value or richness created.

All stories told about the future of technology are told from a particular point of view. These stories can't be wishy-washy affairs – they have to have the ring of inevitability about them if they are to sound convincing and hence the reason why they always come on so strong with them. The view of the corporations selling hardware and software is that we want faster processing, more memory, more features and more flexibility and so this forms the basis for all the stories they tell us. The view of the corporations selling communications devices is that as more bandwidth becomes available we will approach something verging on 'perfect' communications, e.g. with portable video phones, and that we will all want this. However the evidence for the latter is not as clear as has been the take up of more 'whistles and bells' on PCs. Email is probably the most impoverished form of communications that we use – no voice intonation, no body signals, none of the non-verbal stuff that we know makes up for a rich transaction – and yet it has been a phenomenal success compared with the slow take-up rate of video phones. Talk to anyone about using a fixed or mobile video-phone and they are very cautious. They are not sure that they want all that rich non-verbal stuff communicated during every phone call – some yes, but all – they are not so sure.

## Reducing space/cutting time

The twentieth was a century where technology became boundary-less. Apart from television, medicine was the fastest mover with antibiotics and other drugs being mobilized to save millions of lives across all continents, allowing us to live longer and to control population growth. Some diseases like AIDS emerged, in the west at least, as an export from poorer countries that coincided with new lifestyles in rich ones, or like dementia and Alzheimer's disease out of the success of other life-extending health-care. We saw just enough of biotechnology and genetic engineering to know that they will feature strongly in both the pantheon of 'achievements' and as the source of many ethical controversies during the first half of the twenty-first century.

After television and medicine we will remember most the new technologies of transport and communication. Advances like the jet engine, the mobile phone, satellite and cable TV, the fax and the Internet helped people in developed countries to connect with themselves and with others more than ever before. Indeed a large number of the technological advances over the twentieth century continued our ancient struggle to overcome the limitations of distance and time in order to connect, trade and communicate. Reducing the speed that it takes to connect, whether over real space or in cyberspace, became the icon of our century to such an extent that progress in all decades is inevitably measured against improvements in it. Any decade that passes without accelerating the speed of travel and communication would now be regarded as a serious blip on our progress curve. We expect technologies to continue to speed things up and it looks like we will not be disappointed. While passenger aircraft may not go much faster in the twenty-first century they will certainly carry more of us further on a single 'fill-up', while in digital space the limitations of bandwidth will be overcome by turning our current electronic 'footpaths' into real, rather than imagined, superhighways. The 'new' computer industry was born schizoid in that it cannot tell us what it is doing today without adding a caveat about just how different it will be tomorrow. Always quick to tell us that today's technology is already obsolete, so that we can never really complain when it is, our cheque-books have come to live their prophecies. No other industry has done so well out of its own obsolescence or lived so much in the future as computing has done. We expect computer chips to process information faster and modems to send and receive it quicker across cables and beams with greater capacities because we have been told that it will happen, and so the only emotion left to us is surprise if the industry fails to deliver. The incessant re-definition of urgency that is the natural bedfellow of speedier access to anything has spawned some unhealthy side effects including new kinds of anxiety and frustration. This emphasis on getting some kind of a result, almost any kind of result, quickly always reminds me of those old cartoons where the farmer shoots off a blunderbuss full of nails and rusty bits in the hope of hitting something and a host of unexpected animals drop from the sky. As we speed things up, keeping one ear open for how much faster they will be tomorrow, we have created a new range of pleasures and disappointments for ourselves.

## Addicts and pushers

The increasing speed that characterizes the way in which we measure the success of all communication technologies has become something of a universal yardstick by which we now measure success in many other arenas. We have become addicts to urgency, much of which we construct ourselves or have constructed for us by other addicts turned pushers. From casual discussions about the efficacy of one Roman charioteer over another we have spent the last 2000 years constructing a speed curve which has continually re-defined urgency to the point where hardly any activity, apart from the laying down of fine wines, is satisfactory unless it is accomplished quickly. Accordingly we increasingly give status and privilege to those who can secure the fast track in everything. Indeed the constant re-definition and privileging of urgency has provided us with a long-standing basis on which to hang social and economic distinctions. Those who have to wait for anything – a bus, share prices, a table at a restaurant, graphics to download via a slow modem or a standby ticket on a charter flight – are regarded, and regard themselves, as less privileged than those who never have to wait. We all have our personal 'waiting' stories, the resolution of which inevitably required more cash or occasionally more status. No other metaphor for the impoverished societies of communist eastern Europe and the USSR has stuck in western minds quite like the pejorative images of the long queues that turned up now and then on our TV screens before the fall of the Berlin Wall. In contrast the long queues that we saw in Russia, as its citizens clamoured to retrieve their money from banks before it became worthless, will be regarded as just a minor blip in the onward progress of capitalism.

During our early evolution urgency, and the valuable adrenaline that it called up, used to be reserved for life-threatening situations where a slow response would prove fatal. Now our minds too often have to respond to trivial definitions of urgency. This results in the harmful over-use of adrenaline, poor recall, poor pattern recognition and, ironically given the abundance of information available to us, greater recourse to guesswork, poor outcomes and stress-related illness – a spiral that inevitably generates more urgency, more pressure and more stress. The concomitant fear of having to process more and more information, because it is available, in shorter and shorter time scales compounds the problem. Constructed urgency plus information anxiety equals heart disease is an equation that may come to dominate our personal frustrations during the twenty-first century.

As we have seen revolutionaries always emphasize the 'transforming moment', and on the Internet that moment is very much associated with the 'speed' at which something happens. Nowadays waiting 75 seconds for our computer to warm up seems tardy, waiting four minutes rather than two for graphics to download via a domestic modem, notwithstanding that they are coming from the other side of the world, feels like an eternity. We now expect instant connectivity with every call that we make and every button we press. Even more worrying is that the privileging of such concepts as response time, Internet time, real time, nano seconds, etc. is trickling its way into our discourse about more general social and economic matters. Personal access to speed in private is now an iconic status symbol that clearly sets those who have it apart from the rest. Paradoxically the very source of these 'speed' metaphors, the Internet, can also be the most frustratingly tedious when measured against the hours – the 'World Wide Wait' that we clock-up in scoring false hits or meandering down hierarchies of interminably irrelevant 'hot' links. I note these trends as a confirmed addict who would like not to be and who is trying to step back and reflect a bit more on the 'why' behind my own and all other urgent requests (see Chapter 7).

The only challenger to 'speed' in the icon stakes has been our desire to avoid sharing space with others. We are willing to sacrifice speed, as in wasting long hours in urban traffic jams, as long as it is traded for privacy as in sitting in our car, listening to our own music in our own space while talking to ourselves. The 'minimum two persons in a car' lanes on some US highways is an explicit recognition of the extreme steps that have to be taken before we will give up the joys of solitude, in this case sacrificing some privacy to help us move a little bit faster. Speed in unison with privacy, as in private jet, private yacht or a private railway carriage, has increasingly come to be regarded as a pinnacle of personal achievement while any activity in 'public' spaces, as in public transport, libraries, parks, swimming baths, etc., has been starkly designated as clearly a second best.

## Tracks and trees

Consider for a moment how communities in Europe during the Bronze Age might have looked from 3000 feet up. In this pre-urban world we would have seen various sizes of clearings surrounded by heavily wooded countryside cut through with an embryonic network of rough roads and footpaths linking some of them together. Go higher to take in a wider view and the clearings would begin to look more and more like the server nodes on a late twentieth century computer network plan linked by lines that represented signal carrying entities. Many of these nodes, the early settlements of metalworking man, would grow to become the towns and villages of the early Middle Ages. Before then only a few people moved back and forth along the narrow network lines linking the 'servers' to do business, carry news and have some fun, much as we use motorways, airlines and modern computer networks today. Local 'area' networks of tracks and pathways were the main carriers of information; the wider 'area' networks were still not very well developed and the doings of the various Chiefs and their followers would carry on hardly known about or noticed by other groups just a hundred miles away.

By contrast, in June 1953, over 20 million people watched the coronation of Queen Elizabeth II in Britain. Many of them crowded into the houses of friends and neighbours to watch small television screens very much as villagers in developing countries sit around a communal

television now. In a tribute to the limpet-like tenacity with which old technologies hang around a more cosmopolitan, global audience now watch,
with even greater fascination, the ups and downs of her middle-aged
children on screens that haven't changed very much, just bigger and with
colour, 46 years on.

Constructing ways to connect with each other for co-operation,
profit, news or play quickly became a defining feature of early man's move
into societies and the history of humankind has been a history of ever
more sophisticated and speedier connection making. The drama of
evolving communication technology has stimulated and enriched us on so
many levels that we now take for granted the sheer volume of information that we have at our disposal. But, less evident to the techno-optimists,
it has also generated some great dysfunctions including the paradox of
so much human isolation in the midst of so many tools to make contact. New strains of alienation, the potential disenfranchisement of many
whose economic, social and intellectual circumstances keep them out of
the new networks and serious doubts about self-value in the face of
so much advertised opportunity have left many individuals and groups
unsure of their place in their communities. Similarly the inhabitants of the
smaller clearings in the landscape of Bronze Age Europe who were not
connected to the bigger ones, often did not know what was going on,
felt more vulnerable and stayed poorer because they were not yet big or
important enough to get connected. They were the isolated ones, their
databases were small and so their value to others was low and 'value'
to others, to a system, to a government or to an organization has
continued to be an important pre-requisite in gaining access to all
'connecting' infrastructures. Those early clearings and the many dots on
maps like them in poorer countries today, were caught in a common trap.
They knew less because they weren't connected and they weren't
connected because they knew less. The trouble involved in setting up
the infrastructure to connect the smallest groups (cutting down the trees
to make a better track), didn't look like it would have much of pay back.
As the clearings (database) grew bigger or more important, e.g. the
discovery of useful minerals, their proximity to a handy river crossing
or their natural evolution as a market centre, their claims to be connected became more persuasive and so more so trees were cut down.
Today we speed along eight lane motorways and we worry that we
haven't got enough trees! Now your dot gets bigger and more important,

metaphorically at least, the closer you are to knowledge rather than a mineral store or a river crossing.

The Silicon Valleys and Golden Triangles of the world, where concentrations of scientists and researchers reside, despite being connected to each other via broad band electronic networks, still gain comfort, prestige and kudos from being close to each other physically. Communities inhabited by like-minded people, such as Wall Street in New York, 'The City' in London or 'Motor Sport Valley' in the UK (see Chapter 8), still thrive alongside the fast electronic networks which theoretically render spatial proximity irrelevant to the effective transfer of ideas and knowledge. The desire to have a presence on the ground among talented people brought Bill Gates to Cambridge, England in October 1997 to talk about building the first Microsoft research centre to be located outside the US. No one better than he would know how easy it is to squirt sophisticated information effectively down lines and cables over vast distances. But he wanted a centre where his people would rub shoulders with other 'like-minds', where unanticipated spin-offs would arise, where insights gained in unlikely places and between unlikely people would generate new ideas and where the scope for serendipity would be greater than that facilitated via remote contact across wires. Clever people operating in real space change the world. This is not to say that the lone genius working at his or her computer and pulling information down to their screen cannot achieve insights that change things. But it is to say that the quality of the exchange in real space is different. It is richer, serendipity is easier to facilitate and the messy amalgam of ideas that produce new knowledge seems to grow more abundantly. But collecting humans together in real space, especially clever ones who command a premium in the market place, is expensive and electronic networks can compensate for enforced distance by providing a start, a catalyst or a foundation for the building blocks of inspiration and innovation.

## The comfort of parallel running

One valuable characteristic of human technological enterprise, highlighted in the example of television noted above, is how it mixes the comfort of continuity with seemingly radical change allowing us time to 'change over'. Running in parallel, although the obvious reality, is not an exciting theme when pitched against the exuberance of the technological re-volutionaries. Indeed the producers of new technologies must persuade a critical mass of users, the installed base, to abandon the old for their 'new', or at least get them to run them in partnership, if they are going to make any money and thus have any incentive to keep on innovating. Their impatience to gain quick market share is often manifested in over-exaggerated claims (in the early stages at least) for a technology, media-sponsored hype and the concomitant disappointment with early versions of communications technology. The mobile phones that only covered 60 per cent of a country or that would not work outside one's home country are typical examples.

However, no matter how exciting it looks, or is said to be, most human response to new communications technology is to wait and see how comfortable it is before embarking on risky or expensive trials. A lack of common standards is the most common cause of failure closely followed by 'why?' for gizmos and gadgets that demand attention without filling much of a need. Sony's Data Discman, a portable CD player with a 200 Mb capacity, a liquid crystal display and small Qwerty keyboard that played 8 cm electronic books and billed as 'tomorrow's portable library', was a good example of the former and the latter combined. Incompatible with conventional CD-ROM drives, deliberately designed not to plug into a PC for fear of downloading and having a monochrome LCD screen that made you blind, this particular mobile library flopped. Postal services, tele-phony, civil aviation, fax machines, Email, the motor car and railways – all these forms of communication continue to live together. Indeed some, like postal services, now depend on computerized processing and effec-tive road and rail networks to make their own service work. It is true that sometimes the impact of one severely affects the value, convenience and efficacy of another. Canals suffered as the UK became covered with railway lines by the 1870s and the economics of the world's railways suffered dramatically as the convenient and private, if less environmen-tally sound, motor car took over their short-haul passenger schedules and civil airlines much of their long-distance passenger list.

Travel for business and pleasure has accelerated in all developed countries. While postal services all over Europe face privatization to enable them to raise private capital and to deal better with competition from the fax machine, telephony and Email there is no doubt that they are still major players in the world of communication and connection making.

Deutsche Post, the German postal service, due to be privatized by the year 2000, recorded an increase in pre-tax profit of 54 per cent during 1996. In the face of new competition older forms of communication tend to ratchet up their efficiency and sophistication by using the very technologies which in another guise may be or become a competitor, with labour costs usually being high on the agenda for scrutiny. Deutsche Post shed over 37 000 jobs during 1996 and 1997. In March 1997 the UK's Royal Mail unveiled a new road and rail distribution centre in North London, ironically containing the largest railway station to be built in the UK during the twentieth century. Already handling 100 million letters a week in 1996 the seven-platform railway station and 40 loading bays for road vehicles form the nerve centre of a £150 million Royal Mail project to cope with an expected 20 per cent growth in mail volumes over the next five years. Letters of all kinds, and the literacy required to produce them, seems alive and well in the 'Internet Age'. Those who hold shares in paper-making companies would be unwise to sell them just because of the rise of electronic messaging. Paper production is booming in the western world as computers connected to the Internet look naked without a printer and the comfort of a paper copy remains a high priority for just about everyone. If you have any doubt about this try disconnecting your own printer from your PC for a month or so. There are organizations that will help you with the withdrawal symptoms but be warned – it will be bad!

## Distant events

Recognizing the possible connections between seemingly different and distinct events is a skill for which many organizations now pay a premium. One of the qualities now expected from all highly paid 'knowledge workers' is that they should be able to see profitable connections between separate bits of data and suggest possible outcomes from unlikely assemblies of information. This is why financial institutions invest so much in electronic information systems that mix news, market and economic information on their screens. The slick screen-watchers of the city are on the look-out for trends (in their case these trends may last only minutes) and the likely connections between seemingly disparate pieces of information.

Natural disasters, which can have ramifications far beyond their epicentre, are often unpredictable, although increasingly sophisticated computer software is helping us to anticipate weather systems, as in predicting the likely force of hurricanes approaching the Caribbean and the Gulf of Mexico. We now understand the origin of many of the natural upheavals which our ancestors believed originated from the anger or malicious playfulness of the gods, even if we can't predict all the links in the chain. An example of an unlikely connection between a natural disaster and a business based many thousands of miles away from it was the Kobe earthquake in Japan in January 1995. As well as causing deaths, injuries and homelessness in Kobe itself it was also the final trigger for the downfall of an ancient merchant bank in London. Nick Leeson's special 5/8 account held in Singapore in which he had hidden the massive losses he had made while betting on the Japanese Stock Market would have come good, and he would have avoided detection, if the Nikkei Index had remained more or less stable. Had it stabilized and then stayed that way for a few more weeks the 5/8 account would probably have started to break even. The Kobe earthquake however sent the Nikkei into a rapid downward slide, and Barings, a merchant bank that had been founded in London in 1763, tumbled into insolvency.

The unilateral activities of sovereign governments or collections of governments will always continue to surprise and we should not assume that the growing economic interdependence of nations, via global financial markets, means that nations no longer can, or want, to influence their own destinies. The oft-trumpeted decline of the nation state doesn't add up against its continuing ability to take important policy decisions independently of the global network. The UK government's ambivalence towards a 'fully integrated' European Union prompted some nervousness among potential Far Eastern investors who saw the UK as an otherwise stable bridge into the EU, but the UK has remained ambivalent. In 1994 Malaysia imposed a temporary embargo on giving big contracts to UK companies after *The Sunday Times'* exposure of the 'Pergau Dam/Arms For Aid' scandal and Malaysia has continued to adopt a maverick-like stance in its response to the Asian financial crises. The search for inward and outward investment by states, although a clear sign of interdependence, is such a moveable feast that all countries now recognize how temporary it can be. They know that the damage from sudden closure or cutbacks due to a downturn in the economic cycle is really no different from that incurred when indigenous industries collapse. They also know that the key knowledge at the heart of the enterprise never gets left behind, if indeed if ever travelled far from the corporate head-quarters in the first place. We are at a tension point in the development of the global economy. Nation states recognize their interdependence and the way in which distant events can impact on them but they also wish to retain their independence across a range of domestic and foreign policies. This desire will surface now and then as they react against particular, but not always predictable, kinds of interference. Distant events will continue to have a fickle impact on people and places that at first seem unrelated to them; e.g. the prominence of the Green party in the new German parliament and changes in policy with regard to nuclear fuel re-processing that might make it more difficult for a British government to sell off British Nuclear Fuels.

## The machine made flesh

In 1926 Fritz Lang confronted the promise of industrialization and tech-nology in his great silent film classic 'Metropolis'. This was a future where people were made slaves to the machinery of the city and the film clearly saw the boundaries between humans and machines merging, with humans treated as parts of machines with a single controller switching them both on and off. Its worst expectations have not been met, although the more brutal aspects of industrialization, in some places and in some ways, may have come close. Today the objective of many researchers is to tame the machine by exploring how we can link people and machines together for the benefit rather than the enslavement of humans. The keyboard and the mouse are slow and inefficient ways to communicate with a computer and so more intuitive and natural ways of communicating with machines are high on the agenda of a number of ICT researchers. Talking to machines in 'natural' language to get them to do what we want is heralded as being only a few years away, while linking us to them so that they can react to our thought instructions is probably a little further over the hill. In 1998 Professor Kevin Warwick of Reading University in the UK had a silicon chip transponder inserted into his flesh for nine days. This allowed his body to send out a unique signal that could be picked up by sensors attached to a computer that controlled part of his physical environment.

Locked doors knew who he was and opened for him and he had no need of keys; he could easily be tracked around the environment and contacted if need be. It is easy to see how the 'embedded chip' idea taken further, and encoding much more information, could transform us into a mobile electronic record. We could be a credit card (not so easy to misplace or get stolen), a passport (couldn't lose it) or driving licence (we would always know where we put it) or various other things (a library ticket) that took our fancy. Professor Warwick attracted a lot of attention from media around the world but it was the 'violation of the flesh' that seemed to disturb most people who heard about and commented on his experience.

The UK government, in modifying its 100-year-old quarantine laws, plans to introduce a microchip passport to facilitate the movement of animals between the UK and some other countries in early 2000. Each animal would have a microchip embedded in its flesh and a special scanner at airports and docks would detect all the information, about injections, history, place of origin, etc., needed to satisfy the authorities that it was 'safe' to move in and out of the UK. A re-chargeable microchip, one that can have its information changed or amended, suitable for embedding within humans can't be too far away. The MIT Media Lab is working on the 'nomadic radio', a close-fitting, hands free device that could be the precursor to a wearable 'pipe' for all the information that we might want to access and accessible to all those who might want to contact us. Such a device would integrate the kinds of things that we carry around separately now, e.g. pagers, mobile phones, electronic organizers, etc.

Steve Mann at Toronto University has spent the last twenty years exploring the 'fit' between humans and communicating machines, including video transmission to and from a head-based apparatus. He has now honed down his personal equipment to a small device that is able to route the information and image display to a pair of eyeglasses. Mann believes that personal communications technology of this kind can be refined until it becomes intuitive and as much a part of a person as their bloodstream. Implants to compliment the human nervous system may seem an alien idea but 'digital flesh' is really no more alien than artificial limbs, heart pacemakers or embedded microchips to resolve deafness. As always this 'violation of the flesh' will depend for its acceptance on whether it is us or another power that is suggesting (or insisting) that we receive implants of this kind. Those found guilty of heinous crimes may have no choice in the future but to receive an implant describing who they are and what they've done; others, e.g. epileptics, may need one for their own safety. The rest of us may decide that being hijacked for the credit limit that we represent or being kidnapped so that someone can rip our passport out of us is a risk that, even if we have to forego the magic opening of some doors, we would rather not take. The sheer wonder of the human ability to work on ways of connecting is not the stuff of dry objectivity and the canon of unpredictability is too voluminous to confine it within the rationality of a precise academic taxonomy. Almost every day sees a new technology that is heralded as helping us to do it better and the rate of change, at least among the techno-elites, seems breathtakingly fast. Cataloguing the seminal moments of the twenty years to 2020 will inevitably include some of this technological wizardry but the defining moments are unlikely to be dominated by it.

# References

1. Meadows, J. (1996) 'I've seen the future and it goes beep, beep, beep'. *THES*, 18 October

2. Castells, M. (1998) *The Information Age: economy, society and culture* (3 vols.). London: Blackwells. [Vol. 1. *The rise of the network society*, Vol. 2. *The power of identity*, Vol. 3. *End of Millennium*]

3. Negroponte, N. (1995) *Being Digital*. London: Hodder and Stoughton

4. Postman, N. (1994) *Technology: the surrender of culture to technology*. New York: Blackstoneau

5. Williams, G.C. (1966) *Adaptation and natural selection: a critique of some current evolutionary thought*. Princeton, N.J.: Princeton University Press

6. Dawkins, R. (1976) *The selfish gene*. New York: OUP, and Dawkins, R. (1986) *The blind watchmaker*. New York: W.W. Norton

7. Gould, S.J. (1996) *Dinosaur in a haystack: reflections in natural history*. London: Jonathan Cape

8. Eldredge, N. (1995) *Re-inventing Darwin: the great evolutionary debate*. London: Weidenfeld and Nicolson

9.  Standage, T. (1998) *The Victorian Internet: The Remarkable Story of the Telegraph and the 19<sup>th</sup> Century's Online Pioneers*. London: Weidenfield and Nicholson

10. Will W. (1996) The Huw Weldon Memorial Lecture, BBC 2, Saturday 16 November

# CHAPTER THREE

# Changing spaces

A Biologic: the name for a natural parent and a washing powder.
'Would you like to be buried with my people' (Old style Irish marriage proposal)

## Fleas and soft grunts

Each of the spaces we have constructed as part of our mastery of nature
– families, homes, villages, towns, cities and nations – offers different
kinds of opportunities for connecting; each demands different responses
from us and none of them operates effectively without some involvement
by us. All of these spaces are regulated or ruled in some way either by
adherence to agreed codes of behaviour (the family and villages) or legislation (towns, cities and nations). Although most of the spaces we inhabit
have boundaries they rarely exist, outside the Balkans or the 38th Parallel,
as other than lines on maps or signs of the 'city limits' variety. Nonetheless
they often occupy our mental space as part of the way we define ourselves
at a particular time, e.g. at work, in church, at the bank, etc.

Concerns in the UK about giving up individual parliamentary
constituencies in favour of a party-nominated list of candidates for
European Union elections was not only a debate about loss of influence
to far distant political regimes. It was also about the loss of notional boundaries that, relatively speaking, had a human dimension and that were
comprehensible to those who imagined them. Despite the death of
distance and the conquering of geography via the Internet or mobile
telephony an important comfort factor for humans is still the ability to

'imagine' the boundaries in which they are operating. For thousands of years we have 'stopped' to talk. Where we talk and who we talk to defines the various communities to which we belong, at work, home and play, and who we are within them.

Biologically we're built to talk; indeed some anthropologists believe that our brains are as big as they are because sorting out the truth from the lies in language takes a lot of processing power. Language enabled us to cheat, as in saying one thing and meaning another, so our brains had to get bigger to help us spot the cheating. Communication between humans was originally concerned with social grooming, bonding, developing relationships, caring and building cohesive groups, it is only very recently that we've begun using communication to transfer data. I guess that for most people on most days their acts of communication are still principally taking place through talking rather than in transferring data. Talking for humans is very much like those soft little grunts that apes make, as they tidy each other up and pick the fleas of each other, useful and a comfort. I'm not sure where the phrase 'talk the hind leg off a donkey', as applied to Olympic talkers, came from but perhaps 'talk the fleas off a monkey' would have been a more appropriate description. All the spaces we construct to live, work, or play in are also places to talk. Each one thus becomes a location for myths and behaviours that we process into stories, as in stories from the village or the city, or stories from the gym or the aerobics class. Places are central to many of the stories we tell about ourselves, and the family, in its habitat, produces some of our most important stories.

## Family life: the nuclear fallout

It is within spaces occupied by families that we first learn to connect. They hold within them some of the most important information and knowledge that we will ever use. A baby looking out on the family and its environs from its high chair is in the midst of a revolving knowledge base that will carry its mark on it, for better or worse, for the rest of its life. The intimacy of family living, of partnering, parenting and kinship, despite all the changes going on in its formula, is still the single most important feature of most human societies. The warm Irish greeting of 'and who do you belong to?' is typical of the desire to place another in an understandable context. Although this context may seem less important in northern Europe than it once was it would still feature as important in most southern European countries.

Over the last fifty years the family in industrialized countries has been engaged in re-defining itself in terms of what it is, what it means and what we might expect from it. These changes include smaller nuclear families, extended families that are often separated by great distance, single parent families, gay parenting and women marrying and bearing children much later in life. They also include more childless families, the separation of practical from genetic parenting, families that are mixtures of the adopted, the genetic and the fostered and families with mixed ethnic origins. The old-style biologically determined, fixed-core family has given way to more diverse and fluid groupings. Such a liberal–pluralist view of the family has often been characterized as a disintegration of family life 'as we know it'. It is currently the subject of much political (see below) and popular concern, particularly among those who would like a stricter definition of what a family should be in relation to its receipt of state benefits. Nonetheless, whatever its form, numbers or level of attachment, it is within the family that we first learn to connect and view the world. From this base, however fluid, we build up information which we use to compare others with our kin and us and we construct internal pictures of ourselves which we carry around with us all of our life.

An important part of our experience within families is the places with which they are or have been associated. Having lived in the same small town where I was born all my life I often envied those who were born in different countries, whose parents' work took them to different places or who, later in life, simply moved around the country for a variety of reasons. My own experience has left me with some very clear pictures of my family and the various spaces in a growing town that they occupied. These links now seem rich and satisfying, but when I was younger the experience of those who moved about always seemed so much richer to me. This trade-off between the pleasures of staying close and the joys of pulling away is a common one in relation to families. Its fallout is embedded in the way that we relate to others, how sociable we are and how easily we develop non-family networks.

One's home locale exerts many influences on our perception of things. For instance it is well known that when people are asked to draw lines on a map from memory to show the distances between places the results depend on where they live. They tend to exaggerate distances in their home regions, while reducing distances across the rest of the country. The space occupied by one's family, where they lived, their occupations and their recreations, also emerges later in the way we interpret behaviour in other families in other places. However much we try or want to escape from it, home is where the old code is. Like the millions of lines of code included in a new computer operating system to handle older applications, home is a legacy system whose old code is always with us. The amount of old family code that we carry around with us obviously varies greatly between individuals, particularly in their degree of emotional attachment to it. In operating systems millions of lines of old code (bloatware) can slow a computer down forcing the new applications to run slower. Old family code can do this as well; it can take up space, interfere and hold us back but it can also give us confidence and furnish us with patterns and examples that help us cope effectively with new circumstances.

## Governments and families

Throughout history governments of every hue have sought to influence the scope, conduct and role of families and family life. Augustus the first Roman Emperor attempted new laws to reduce adultery and divorce, to encourage marriage and the production of more legitimate children:

> His marriage law being more rigorously framed than the others, he found himself unable to make it effective because of open revolt against several of its clauses. He was therefore obliged to withdraw or amend certain penalties exacted for a failure to marry; to increase the rewards he offered for large families; and to allow a widow or widower three years grace before having to marry again. . . . When he discovered that bachelors were getting betrothed to little girls, which meant postponing the responsibilities of fatherhood, and that married men were frequently changing their wives, he dealt with these evasions of the law by shortening the permissible period between betrothal and marriage, and by limiting the number of lawful divorces. [1]

Augustus himself was no stranger to adultery – a habit, which his friends maintained he only followed 'for reasons of state'. He became intimate with the wives and daughters of his enemies in order to discover the intentions of their husbands and fathers, thus forestalling potential disruption to the (his) legitimate government. Many US Presidents from Jefferson to Clinton have maintained 'extra-family' relations of the carnal sort which have beleaguered them in one way or another.

Fewer hypocrisies have dominated the history of both rulers and ruled more than those relating to sexual conduct and the boundaries of family life. In the past, as with J. F. Kennedy, a more servile media turned a blind eye in return for other favours. Today few political issues are more booby-trapped than pronouncements on 'the family', particularly as they often confuse sexual relations for family relations and vice versa. Not withstanding the pitfalls all political parties still seem to want to be 'the party' of 'the family'. Their problem is agreeing on what kind of family they want to support as many of their voters now live in what traditional political activists might regard as unusual, and possibly even unacceptable, family groupings. A decomposing Conservative government in the UK during the mid 1990s called for a re-think about the centrality of the traditional family in national life and urged a return to 'old fashioned' family values at the same time as many of its own MPs were succumbing to rather different 'urges'. The almost weekly exposure of these 'non-family' values among its MPs and ministers undoubtedly contributed to the scale of the Conservative losses during the May 1997 General Election. Unlike Augustus they could not control the media and no justification by pressing 'reasons of state' looked probable.

The growing conservatism and market orientation of all western political parties, i.e. that personal choices should not concern the state, has now begun to create a number of dilemmas for them. Family breakdowns patently do concern the state in the way that they impact on housing, pensions, tax policies, divorce law and, most of all, welfare policy. Around 80 per cent of lone parents in the UK rely on welfare, so they are plainly a policy matter in the sense that their private choices can have a serious impact on public funds. Thus the 'official' designation of what constitutes a family is very important to those who rely on welfare, particularly mothers who have never married. This is the fastest growing group of lone parents, whom also tend to be the youngest and the poorest of all lone parent groups.

The UK is experiencing something of a leadership role in the lone-parent family stakes and its divorce rate is among the top end of Europe's league table. Around 45 per cent of UK marriages currently end in divorce compared with an average of 30 per cent in the EU and 55 per cent in the US, and it also has the highest rate of births to teenage mothers. The current UK political consensus that welfare benefits make it easier for young mothers to decide to leave their partners and that cutting these will cause them to stay together ignores the violence and abuse that is often the precipitating factor in break-downs within poor families. Government intervention in the family in Europe seems paradigm-locked. It has yet to catch up with the complex web of relationships that now pass for 'family life' in many communities.

In the UK as many as 40 per cent of absent fathers fail to stay in touch with their children after the first two years of separation. This prompted the government to set up the Child Support Agency (CSA) in 1995. Despite its admirable intention to ensure that absent fathers paid proper maintenance for their children the CSA found few friends. Due to changes in the disposition of families strange alliances grew up against it which seemed to take everyone by surprise. In 90 per cent of cases fathers are the absent parents; many of these have second wives, a lot of whom worked, who were offended at having part of their earnings find their way to support the children, and often the wife, of a previous relationship. The CSA, to its great surprise, thus found itself pitting women against women rather than just an ex-husband against an ex-wife. Beset by problems of accuracy and lacking allies the CSA was restructured in 1998.

As well as creating lone parents, the huge growth in divorce rates often creates composite serial families. This serial monogamy, second and third marriages, is now so common that it has left governments floundering about what to do. In one (new) family the father is present and in residence, possibly helping to manage a mix of natural and step-children, while in the other, more often than not, the natural father is an occasional visitor and a lone mother does most of the managing. Ironically the weight of convention and social approval now seems to have shifted towards the new family with less and less official sympathy being shown towards lone parents. Governments want to be involved with families for many reasons including trying a bit of social engineering here and there to reduce future welfare costs. In the UK the daughters of single mothers tend to do progressively worse at school and have a 60 per cent chance of becoming single mothers themselves. Children whose parents split up can suffer lasting consequences, both economic and emotional, and they seem to do worse as adults in terms of educational attainment, earning power and the ability to form stable relationships. They tend to co-habit, marry and have their own children earlier than their peers, offering the risk of another generation of broken homes. Single-parent families in poverty spend most of their energy just getting by and so thinking ahead to the future for the children is much harder for them even if they are educationally equipped to do it. Their connectivity is weak and tends to be limited to small circles of friends and the official agencies that handle welfare. The range of knowledge sources available in the home to help children with their schoolwork is poor and the richness of their own connections outside school is limited, often taking place on the street rather than in a library or clustered around a friend's TV or computer. The clear danger, which neither government policy nor moral imperative seems strong enough to prevent, is one of serial deprivation, with lone parents passing on poor economic prospects to their children who in turn become lone parents, and the cycle continues.

One of the most common areas of government interference in the 'natural' flow of family life is in the area of birth control, i.e. setting up incentives for families either to have more, or less, children. China's unique one-child policy, still widely observed in many Chinese cities, means that a generation of only children, including a new 'red army' of much coddled boys, is now reaching sexual maturity. Not having experienced the ups and downs of sibling rivalry, and without any of the 'touch-and-go' play which characterizes the behaviour of young boys and girls together, these youngsters are open to greater influence from their friends and the newly spiced-up media than from their parents. Chinese teachers believe that this emotional isolationism, often linked with both parents working, now warrants a new approach to sex education – one that in addition to explaining the pure mechanics also emphasizes the emotional and social aspects of sexual relations.

Other Far Eastern governments are finding that the extended family that they took for granted as part of the 'eastern way', and the systems of support that came with it, is changing, particularly as the number of women working outside the home is growing. If the rising age of some populations in developed countries is the most important force deter-mining future social policy it is closely followed in second place by the year-on-year growth of women in the workforce. The close relationship between this trend and other social variables like a fall in the birth rate, a retreat from the marriage contract, the rise of the divorce rate and the rise in the proportion of children born to single-parent families is now well established. The countries of 'the Eastern way' will have to struggle with the social and economic costs of a woman's right to choose just as the those in the west have, and Confucius is unlikely to have all the answers.

## Turning the tables

The family meal with all members present is still preserved in a few households as a moment in the day when 'incident reports', a bit of bonding and some catching up can take place without everyone being on the move or too busy to communicate. Such 'islands' of family connectivity are becoming rarer as the agendas that concern one family member or another increasingly occupy the time once reserved for gathering around a table. Families now to have to work hard to retain any sort of occasion when everyone can be together to do the sharing which was once so effortless. Like so much of our behaviour this change is complicated by the coincidence of a range of social, economic and technological factors. The economic factors often depend on, or can be traced back to, a technology that has enabled the new behaviour. The social factors range from various members of the family eating out with other groups, more competition from recreations that occupy the time that was once set aside for meals and the elimination of a discipline that insisted that children join and emulate their parents in the social protocols of eating. The economic factors include less time available for working members of the household to do the shopping and the ubiquity of the pre-packed convenience foods that have come about to save that time, the latter deriving much of their utility from being easily transferrable from supermarket to home freezers. Women in paid work, still by far the greatest shoppers and cookers of family meals, have been particularly liberated by this coincidence. The purely technological factors include improved kitchen technology (refrigerators, freezers, self-timing ovens, microwaves etc.) which frees all the players to pursue different timetables and tastes.

Gaining a new connecting technology always attracts attention and celebration, but losing a social medium that facilitated rich and robust connections passes almost unnoticed. Those tables that once provided a gathering place for families to connect with each other now often serve as an information point and clearing house for our connections with the outside world. In a clear salute to the continuing importance of postal services in all our lives these tables mostly, but not always, accumulate paper that came through a letterbox. We have a table which, in lieu of ever being used for any serious eating, gradually gets cluttered with papers from work, half-opened letters, bills, receipts, magazines, credit card statements, junk mail, etc. Over a month or so we dump all this stuff on it in the clear belief that the visibility of all these items will remind us that we have to send a cheque somewhere or respond to something in the not too distant future. To a large extent this works and, trawling the table now and then, we pick up something that catches our eye and we deal with it. The need to decide what to do with an invitation or to reply to a utility or some such often catalyses a discussion of the 'what are we going to do about this?' variety. At such times, usually dressed and ready to leave for work, we snatch a few begrudged minutes to stand about re-reading things and demanding answers of each other in order to make a decision whose time has come, or more probably, past. Although never really regarded as such the table has become an important information centre on and around which we conduct much of our business with the outside world. After four or five weeks the table begins to look a mess, and more importantly it begins to break down as a flag of reminders, as things get interleaved and mixed up with each other, or covered up entirely. It is getting out of control and the 'loss' rate is much higher. When this happens one of us gets frustrated with the mess and starts to tidy it up, re-arrange things, throwing away stuff that is no longer relevant and re-distributing stuff to other household locations – a mantelpiece is a common secondary location. This table-clearing can be quite a tedious job but after it there is a sense of relief that some things thought to have been lost were found and some things forgotten about, but which needed action, were happily retrieved. There is also a fresh satisfaction that the table surface is now clear enough for us to start the process all over again, usually in association with a firm resolve to keep it under better control and not to let the paper mountain build up to such an extent again.

Such a table, or something like it, exists in most homes and in all busy places. Desks and offices all over the world replicate examples of the steady growth of printed information on flat surfaces which move from a state of the visually useful, to surprise, to action, to overwhelming and, finally, to dumping. Academics, writers and journalists feature among the groups who suffer badly from spatial 'paper on flat surfaces' information anxiety. This can be a mild or quite serious illness depending on the imminence of lecturing, marking or publishing deadlines, but they are not alone. The world is full of brief-cases that have been filled in offices, carted home on subways, left unopened by their exhausted carriers and brought back again the next day for the whole process to start all over again. Only osteopaths and physiotherapists profit from this nightly transportation of heavy loads, which although carried around with the best of intentions, often yield little by way of satisfactory processing. The cluttered table is a handy metaphor for the way humans seek visual signals to remind them of things. The old newspapers and magazines we accumulate signify our desire to know but our difficulty in finding the time to know, and the heavy brief-cases, they just signal the triumph of backache over optimism.

## Talk in the day time

Families may be finding less and less time to talk through the problems and challenges facing them in their own space but there is a place where they can join in observing and settling other people's problems. Day-time talk shows in the UK like *Kilroy*, *Trisha* and *Vanessa* and in the US like *Jerry Springer*, *Ricki Lake* and *Oprah* offer platforms for the public display of family issues and emotions complete with a studio audience guaranteed to have opinions about anything that crops up. Relying as they do on a mixture of confession and comment from people in situations made to look extreme they allow viewers to identify vicariously with family controversy, exorcize skeletons in their own cupboards and provide surrogate family situations and crises for those who no longer have families around them.

Confessional, some might say 'victim', TV is hungry. There are up to 20 such programmes going out every day in the UK alone on cable, satellite and terrestrial TV, all competing with each other head-to-head for the small numbers of viewers that characterize day time or late-night TV. All of them, in varying degrees, are designed deliberately to provoke confrontations/conflict as the main source of entertainment. Jerry Springer, who pulls in viewing figures of 70 million world-wide every day, is in quite a different league from most of the others whose viewing figures are only nationally based at around the 1.5 to 2 million level.

These shows have little to differentiate between them other than the skills of their presenter, the controversy of the topic and the hoped-for high Richter scale of turbulence achieved by their audiences who are fast becoming the stars of the show. Jerry Springer's US show is con-sciously designed to cause as much emotional mayhem as is legally permissible and fist fights among his guests and audience have become commonplace. In the spring of 1998 Springer cut out the studio violence after a number of US protest groups complained of its gratuity, and its ratings slipped causing it to fall from its coveted number one slot. He brought back the studio scrapping in the summer and the ratings came back up soon after.

These programmes are often accused of playing fast and loose with the emotions of people who are less articulate, confident or fortunate than the norm and of allowing audience participation to turn into bullying. Vanessa was censured after she caused shock and distress by infringing the privacy of a murder victim's children during an item on the relatives of victims of crime. On another show she was found to have acted unac-ceptably, by the Broadcasting Standards Commission, for humiliating a woman who had given up her son for adoption. The woman was keen to pursue reconciliation with her son, whom she gave up for adoption, following an earlier meeting that had gone wrong. Instead she found herself in the middle of a hostile studio audience who had no tolerance or sympathy for her. She was howled down and harangued as she tried to explain the circumstances that lay behind her situation before her plainly resentful son, who had been listening out of sight backstage to her words, confronted her.

Hungry programmes like these are easily hoaxed. A man who claimed to be a paedophile on *Kilroy* generated a large number of complaints but the show itself was later humiliated when the same man explained later that he was a hoaxer who had appeared on the programme a number of times in different guises. He said he was never detected because the researchers were always too desperate for sensation to check up on his unlikely stories. The 'faker' syndrome has also affected *Vanessa*. The BBC had to apologize in early 1999 because it was discovered that some of the issues that had been paraded on her show were fabricated and had used actors rather than 'real' people in 'real' relationships.

There is currently some concern in the UK that audience rage Jerry Springer-style may just be around the corner. Springer admits that his shows are a 'circus', that all his guests have to sign a legal waver agreeing that they will take no action if they get struck on the set and that his aim is to get as much heated emotion/rage out of the audience as possible. However much television producers claim to abhor violence they know that the expectation that there may be a good fight over an issue pulls in the viewers and that those lethargic daytime audiences won't stay long unless things get spiced up a bit.

An overriding desire for spectacle, particularly violent spectacle, is one of the characteristics of a move from the 'ideational' to the 'sensate' society. After their 'ideational' phase in Medieval times the Mystery plays in Britain marked a similar transition to that which had seen the Greek theatre move from tragedy to pornography. On stage Heaven and Hell became places rather than states of the soul, the torture of the crucifixion was lingered over and indecencies such as turds dropping from the rear of the hobby-donkey bearing Christ into Jerusalem were included to delight rather than to 'improve' the audience. Agreeing to go on national TV to sort out a family problem seems a bit like volunteering to be put in a modern version of the medieval stocks. Like the groundlings at a Mystery play all the signs are that audiences sitting at home will only watch if the audience in the studio is prepared to pelt the victim hard on their behalf.

What is clear is that such 'confessional' programmes, alongside the well-established soap operas that all western nations support on their TV channels, are successful because in addition to entertaining they also fill in some of the gaps left by the changes in family structure noted above. Families have never connected on just one level, e.g. by being loving and emotionally supportive, but have also bonded by disagreement, arguments and rows. While many households still enjoy both sides of this family coin many now patently do not, and so connecting vicariously with the more robust side of family life obviously fills that gap. The exaggerated and glad-iatorial form that is becoming the norm for this portion of day-time TV may seem a somewhat dramatic way to connect with the universality of family life. Nonetheless the issues covered in these shows – sibling rivalry, single parents, co-habitation, inter-racial marriages, age-differences between partners and so on – are central to many lives as they are lived in the Western world.

## Village life

The village, as a memory, an idealized image or a reality, has achieved a desirable status in the developed world ever since large numbers of people moved out of its understandable, if often poverty-stricken, dimensions to find work in the expanding towns and cities of the industrial revolution. A bit like the memories of homeland that immigrants might preserve in aspic the family in the village has, in the west at least, always loitered in the imagination as an idyll of safety, comprehensible community and happy interdependence. The village likes to present itself to the 'others' as unique and desirable although the latter quality is often flaunted in a coquettish 'see but don't touch' behaviour that can be misunderstood by those who take it at face value. Villagers often boast of their 'special quality of life' and harmony to townies who in turn (if they are below retirement age) shrug off rural life as a place for has-beens and bumpkins who couldn't cope with life in the fast lane. City dwellers moving to villages often meet with the suspicion that small communities reserve for interlopers and, however willing the newcomers might be to adapt, twenty years might pass before they lose the name of 'newcomer'. In the early 1970s when I was a District Councillor representing a ward in a (very small) town I was often chastised by rural councillors for wanting to fund warden support schemes for old people across a district that encompassed three towns and many villages. The rural councillors maintained that such expense was not necessary in their areas as, so they maintained, such support arose naturally out of the good neighbourliness of village life, a quality of course that the selfish and unfeeling towns had lost.

The towns and the industrial environment which they built around them once sucked in their factory workers from the poorer countryside and now country folk see the tables being turned with rich townies wanting to return to the country to gentrify and plagiarize their lives. The late Richard Critchfield [2] spent 25 years observing villages all over the world, learning and writing about what makes people belong together –

about what the word 'community' means. The village life that took shape after the passing of the primal hunter-gatherer era was, at its best, a way of fitting individual and personal self-interest into a recognition of other people's self-interest. The village, and later the town, created a defined, material and recognizable space where groups shared information and developed ideas together, and where they developed a wide range of relationships and obligations towards each other which we often summed up as a sense of belonging. We cherished life in these spaces because we made fruitful, enriching and rewarding connections with each other. We engaged in something we called 'community' and we all received something in return for our engagement. It is a paradox, given the popular desire of city folk to 'escape from it all', that one of the characteristics of village life has always been a lack of privacy. In villages everyone knows each other's secrets and the fascination of knowing 'theirs' has to be balanced by our knowing that they know ours. This reciprocity is the information bargain of small communities − support in exchange for voyeurism. The 'postmistress knows everybody' culture of village life (although post offices are now increasingly in short supply in UK villages) which at a distance seems so comforting can also become claustrophobic as the every-day stories of village life inevitably includes us.

As industrialization rolled over the landscape absorbing a village or two, we strove to retain the idea of a 'village' in the city, e.g. Parsons Green in London and Greenwich Village in New York. Who could now imagine the villages of Twickenham, Battersea or Bow still separated from each other and the urban sprawl by farmland or market gardens in the London of today? The garden suburb movement in the UK, which straddled the end of the nineteenth and beginning of the twentieth centuries, was an attempt to bring rural aesthetics to the masses. Speaking in praise of garden suburbs like Bedford Park and Hampstead Garden Suburb which grew up around London, the Liberal politician C.F.G. Masterman wrote in 1909 that 'something of the larger sanities of rural existence could be mingled with the quickness and agility of the town'. Even during the first part of this century 'mingling' the pleasures of the country within striking distance of the city seemed a happy compromise for the growing middle classes. They needed access to their offices and the ever-improving transport systems snaked out into the countryside to them to help them get there.

The 'larger sanities' of the countryside can now be enjoyed while staying in touch with the 'quickness and agility' of the world via telephone, fax, Email, the Internet and more effective postal and delivery services that also use IT to deliver bulky items quicker. There have been moves by some people to seek modern forms of re-assembling themselves into groups whose members choose to define what is good for themselves in the context of what is good for others – a kind of 'elective village'. This has become manifest in the rise of 'alternative' life-style groups, alternative religious affiliations and in the language and rhetoric of the 'global village' used by the Eco-branch of the proponents of teleworking and electronic networking. The latter see the technology of interconnectivity such as that of the Internet as an instrument for the virtual reconstruction of village life with modems and telephone lines helping to rescue individuals who have become isolated by the post-urban world.

## Homework

Teleworking, working from home via a computer, a modem and a telephone connection to another computer is growing slowly all over the world particularly in Scandinavia. To some it represents the answer to a range of contemporary problems, conjuring up the possibility of pleasant living in the isolated thatched cottage of yester-year but with all the benefits of high-speed ICT connections to the business and commercial world of the distant and busy city. Teleworking facilitates the merging of home-space (residence) and work-space (also residence), eliminating the distinctions between home and work that have long been the tradition of the first Industrial Revolution. The Internet has fostered the growth of some real village-based teleworkers located far from any urban sprawl but the evidence suggests that the boundaries of the city are where most teleworking is located.

During the late nineteenth century, in the West Midlands of the UK, an area called the Black Country (the skies were always dark with industrial smoke), nail and chain makers often worked from home in small family groups. They mixed the joys of domestic life with the routine production of big and small nails and chains. Their reported comments on this seamless relationship cannot be repeated here but had something to do with exploitation linked to the parentage of the exploiters. Many of the new 'outworkers' operating from home and connected by lines and beams to a distant employer, far from always feeling released or liberated from the shackles of routine, often feel something similar. Today the computer network allows for both reasonable and unreasonable supervision from a distance. Some teleworkers find themselves being checked up on by the automatic counting of the number of key strokes they make; they generally find it impossible to represent themselves via collective bargaining and they have poor, if any, contractual protection. For them a two-tier system of home working is as evident now as it was when the 'outworkers' of Yorkshire delivered their woollen cloth to the middlemen who collected it from the weavers of northern England in the eighteenth century.

Higher levels of knowledge work – consultancy, computer programming, translation services, design and editorial work, systems analysis, etc., delivered by sophisticated and educated people often working for themselves clearly flourish in a 'teleworking' environment. Such workers can take control of the mix between work and leisure in providing a richer quality and quantity of life for themselves. They avoid time-wasting and irritating commuting, they can organize their workload as they see fit and they can stop to do a bit of fishing when they want.

However taking the more mundane/ordinary work out of the office and putting it at home does not change the underlying *leitmotiv* of work that dominates a particular culture. Sweden's 400 000 teleworkers benefit from a social system that has a long history of team-working in consensus-oriented corporate structures. When transferred to a teleworking situation these translate well into the kind of respect and mutual trust needed to support people, at both ends of the wire, who do not now engage with each other in real space every day. In the UK and the US, where a more competitive office environment often reigns, the tensions will be different. Many UK managers still find it difficult handling individuals who work on their own or away from the main centre. They have come up through a work culture where seeing people at work has been an important part of the control system deemed necessary to ensure that the work gets done. The thought of all those people watching day-time TV when they should be working is just too angst-ridden a possibility for them to contemplate. Thus outside of the freelance arena the growth of teleworking in the UK is going to have to wait for these old ideas of control to fade before it becomes a more significant way of organizing work.

Some of the disadvantages of teleworking, e.g. detachment from colleagues, worries about promotion prospects, isolation from the soft information flows that occur naturally in the office and the possibility of suspicions arising between those at the centre and those on the periphery, are now well known. The prospect of teleworking for a growing proportion of the workforce has been around for a long time now and its take-up is increasing throughout the western world. Shorn of its utopianism, via our early experience of its appropriateness in different cultures, it is now understood better and approached more selectively. In 1998 BT, obviously keen to sell the idea of teleworking to keep its telephone lines busy, commissioned some research to discover the extent of teleworking in the UK. They discovered that 6 per cent of those organizations with more than 50 staff had a formal definition of what teleworking means while some 34 per cent of them had a loose definition. They also discovered that 20 per cent of those firms without any formal definition at all were hoping to introduce some form of teleworking scheme over the next five years [3]. In places where urban growth is outstripping the resources necessary to support it, such as traffic management resources, and where the Telecommunications infrastructure is good companies will certainly put 'telecommuting' on their list of future options. In 1997 a group of economists in Japan estimated that in 2017 15–28 per cent of the Japanese workforce will be telecommuting [4].

In the early days of teleworking the growing cost of office space, office support and car parking were frequently cited as reasons to get people out of the office and working from their own space. Helping the environment by reducing the number of cars on the road, and thus the amount of exhaust emissions pumped into the atmosphere, was also added to the list of 'good' reasons along with that of allowing mothers to spend more time with their children. Sometimes a planned change of location by a firm prompts an exploration of alternative scenarios to help retain staff that might otherwise be lost by the move. For the Swedish branch of Siemens Nixdorf teleworking was initially introduced as a stop-gap measure in 1995. The company had relocated to the outskirts of Stockholm and was worried about losing a large number of valuable employees unhappy with the prospect of a long daily commute. The 'stop-gap' experience proved valuable for both the employees involved and the company and Siemens Nixdorf now hosts the largest teleworking project in Sweden. Again the local culture including the Swedes' hospitality to innovation and a readiness to embrace new technology, their geography (the telephone has long been a firm part of daily life) and some of the lowest telephone charges in the world contributed to the success of the project.

The reasons to explore teleworking are multi- rather than uni-faceted and not all of them function as 'good' reasons in every place. A common formula, emerging across Europe and the US, is the 'handy mix' solution. This is where people work from home for, say, three days a week and spend the other two days at the office where they can use (share) a desk and any of the other facilities that they miss when they are at home. They can also use this time back at the office to re-connect with the apparatus of working life including catching up on news and gossip during social interchange with colleagues. Secure in the knowledge that 'someone knows that they are out there' they can go back home again where they can pace their work to suit their domestic and private lives.

## Cities: becoming other things

To paraphrase Mark Twain when responding to an Associated Press story about his having passed on: 'reports of the death of the city have been greatly exaggerated'. The death of the city, as predicted by 'digital deter-minists' who see a short-lived future for expensive city locations as cheap and reliable communications networks render cities obsolete, is an idea that has been around since the 1960s. Since that time cities have continued to grow rather than shrink and half of the world's population now chooses to live in them, not to mention the hours spent sitting in cars in them. But a city has always been a number of places: a place of business and government, a place of recreation, a place to live, a place of culture and a place simply to be located in order to tap into its energy and its hospi-tality to plural lifestyles. Within each of these places there operates a wide range of economic and social activity, largely reflecting their dispositions in the wider society, and the priorities of each can be quite different. Cities attract a communications infrastructure and because of this attrac-tion communications technologies always have their most powerful concentration around cities. Technological investment does not exist in a vacuum. We always see more investment by companies and governments in the places from which they operate and, for better or worse, those places tend to be in urban areas. Many cities now have buildings that promote themselves as 'wired workplace' locations that offer high speed, broadband Internet access alongside traditional utilities such as heating, electricity and air conditioning.

We are also seeing the development of what might be called the 'Edge City'. The core activity of any business may still be located in places like Wall Street or the City of London, while back-office activities like marketing and data processing are located in less expensive places around the city in, say, a business park or a new industrial estate. Demand for office space in cities from professionals and government remains strong. These organizations realize that they have to pay a premium for the kind of social interaction that they cannot achieve down a wire. Solicitors who moved to cheaper locations on the edge of cities thinking that 'connecting' technology would compensate for the lack of a city address have soon moved back as their business suffered and they realized that the key component of their business, the personal interaction with clients, was missing.

Since Medieval times the idea of clustering trades in cities has worked well. Wood Street, Bank Street, Baker Street – all names that you might find in any modern city – bear testament to the success of the like-minded congregating together to glean and assimilate information and knowledge off one another. We are learning that physical proximity has an important commercial function however much communication technology improves, and cities have proved to be adept at changing their roles as the ebb and flow of economic and social life changes. In the nineteenth century they were just places to work. In the twentieth century they have become places of social interchange, culture, art galleries and museums and government, all activities that require people to congregate and meet up with a consequent increase in the services needed to support them. In the twenty-first century the city will be a mix of all these but it will also host a dense concentration of the wires and antennae that will connect it to all the other cities. The one-time attractions of being near a river crossing will be replicated by being where the electronic 'hub' is. So the future of the city is not as one thing but as many things and its potential to change and become other things is as rosy as ever.

## Cities: fixed and moving

Cities are giant engines of communication – physical, social and electronic – and yet the impact of communications patterns in cities with regard to information flows has suffered from the myopia of urban planners. Locked in a paradigm of traffic management and physical movement on the one hand and the electronic utopians on the other the future of the city is perceived as lying in the hands of just one of two ideas rather than in a rich mix of many. Yet we know that all relationships are social and economic as well as technical and that it is this glue that holds groups and organizations together; it is also the glue that shapes the urban and electronic space of cities. The movement of traffic and the physical flows of gas, water, electricity, commodities and manufactured goods are all supported by a parallel netherworld of wires, hubs and repeaters that monitor, control and direct them around real space as well as tracking all of us via the various electronic footprints that we leave behind. We are witnessing a growth in the movement of both humans across urban space and information and data flows across networks. They are interdependent, feeding and building off one another rather than competing for dominance. The mixture is the thing and rather than preparing to cope with an 'inevitable' dematerializing of commerce into invisible electronic spaces we need to be honing our skills to navigate around both the tower blocks and the Web pages.

As noted above the future is not going to be much of a rural idyll as far as executing most knowledge work is concerned. The main focus of innovations in teleworking is around major cities and not in widely dispersed electronic cottages. Being able to draw on the information 'mud' of a city is something that will remain of critical importance for those who wish to share in the intelligence of other cities. Cottage-to-cottage may share all the resources of the Internet library but complex negotiation across the wires requires a broader spectrum of social experience much of which can only be gleaned from rubbing up against the collective intelligence located in towns and cities. Urban places remain unique fora that bring together the webs of relations and 'externalities' that sustain global capitalism. Much of what goes on in cities cannot be telemediated; we are moving into a new type of urban world rather than a post-urban world and there will be a complex terrain of winners and losers. While the growth of electronic spaces is not leading to the dissolution of cities, they are clearly melting pots where the social and economic extremes of Internet working will reside. Multinational corporations, amid their clusters of fibre optic cables and satellite dishes, will coexist beside vandalized communities that are lucky if they find a pay-phone working, physical proximity to the infrastructure having little to do with easy access to it. We know that the same technologies that disenfranchise, control and exploit disadvantaged groups can just as easily be used to empower and release them and this ambivalence and contradiction will be seen most poignantly in cities. Urban spaces are becoming more complex. They are not only fixed sites, which 'hold down' social, economic and cultural life, but also movable feasts of knowledge, using electronic networks to lift themselves out of their immediate geographical context to become important nodes on the global business system. The collective intelligence within urban spaces thus becomes available for smarter and easier distribution but not necessarily for replacement [5].

## The new monasticism

Whatever their advantages or disadvantages over one another in their particulars villages, towns and cities all provide social spaces that allow us to engage in rich exchanges of information and knowledge and to resist the temptation to default into remoteness. Electronic networking, on the other hand, is about maximizing returns by being remote; therefore we should not be surprised if one of its consequences is to tempt us into getting along by being more remote from each other. This is a big paradox: that the same ICT which can connect us with others in far-off places and overcome distances which we cannot travel easily can also reduce and inhibit the richest and most satisfying of human intercourse when we use it, over short distances, to replace meeting each other in real space. By succumbing to the 'remote' temptation we are disregarding the benefits that accrue to societies from people being socially connected in their physical environment. Most community-based activities that involve getting together in real space, e.g. attending specialist clubs, voting, attending political, trade-union or voluntary club meetings, have already become a minority interest largely occupied by children and old people. Children are still ferried by tired (and anxious) parents to 'do things together' and older people often travel to dances, bingo, clubs and social outings, while the rest of us shut ourselves away to watch TV, to log on, or to shout down telephones. The 'Pub' is probably now the most ubiquitous place of human engagement in a small space in the UK and, important and delightful a place of recreation as it may be, it would be a dangerous pillar on which to maintain the discourse of a democracy.

Accomplishing things together looks like becoming a forgotten art as associations of humans striving to achieve common goals look like becoming extinct. Even the voluntary work that contributes so much to the hidden GDP of the UK economy is in severe decline in many towns and villages due to the 'disconnect and stay inside' tendency. The vital connectedness between hearts and minds that once so animated social and informational exchange in the US and Europe is in danger of losing the important sparkle that it always gained from humans engaging with each other in small spaces. Many factors are encouraging these tendencies – fear of violence, cheap entertainment at home, long-distance commuting, dormitory neighbourhoods, etc. – but overlay a popular culture of electronic communication from remote terminals on top of these trends and we are looking at a world without legs.

As citizens we operate in a number of spaces. Our communities have, up until comparatively recently, been largely built up and developed around activities and transactions carried out in real space. Networking, by privileging the ever more efficient production, analysis and consumption of information in digital form, is turning each of us into an audience and a market of one. As part of a spectrum of communication this is OK but as an addiction, which drives out the serendipity and richness that we derive from conducting our affairs in real spaces, it is not OK. Murdoch, an academic active in the area of the unevenness of access to technologies, summed up well some of the tensions in 1993:

> The history of communications is not a history of machines but a history of the way the new media help reconfigure systems of power and networks of social relations. Communications technologies are certainly produced within centres of power and deployed with particular purposes in mind but, once in play, they often have unintended and contradictory consequences. They are, therefore, most usefully viewed not as technologies of control or freedom, but as the site of continual struggles over interpretation and use. At the heart of these struggles, lies the shifting boundary between the public and private spheres. [6]

In the UK it is now almost a weekly occurrence for one of the big banks to announce the closure of a branch (often the only bank available) in a small town or village. They sometimes promise a cash machine to replace it and in some areas, where the infrastructure is poor, they even promise cash machines that will also transfer data by satellite so that people can still ask questions about their account, as well as withdrawing cash. It is a common story. Other physical institutions, both public and private, like local post offices, branch libraries, newsagents and small shops, long accepted as key structures in binding communities together, are also disappearing fast. Of course commercial enterprises must compete and if they cannot compete via small units then they have to move on. But we cannot avoid the expectation that, unless we create alternative, useful and convivial real spaces for people to meet in, we will drive more and more of them indoors. Many of them will not have the resources to plug into cyberspace alternatives, even if they found them attractive enough to want to try.

The importance of connecting with each other in real space is of course not easy to measure. Some populous groups, e.g. those older people left in sparsely populated rural areas, those left alone as a result of changes to family structures and those whose economic circumstances still require 'places' to pay bills and talk over problems, represent a fund of experience which should not be ignored. They live the deficit and confirm the value that many people still put on access to familiar connections in real space. The accumulation of these values represents a spectrum of experience and richness that is not altogether replaced by TV and telephone. Information technology rarely makes lonely people less lonely or busy people less busy. Mulgan emphasizes the importance of space and time in producing rich connections:

> Yet even in the most technologically advanced societies there is still a role for connections based on place. Proximity matters because humans are unavoidably physical. . . . It matters because so much communication is non-verbal, and face-to-face communications have an intensity that no technology can match. . . . All attachments and memberships take time, and time is scarce . . . attachments require not just 'quality time' but also quantities of time, to learn about the people involved, their motivations and idiosyncrasies. Most people retain connections with their family and school friends for this reason.' [7]

Of course we don't want the pleasures, or the burdens, of being intimate with everybody, but neither can we expect rich and intense understanding or the transparent and comprehensible reciprocity that we value so much in our exchanges from people we don't know or never see. The issue of time, the time we are prepared to make available for deep connection-making, is an important one. At certain times of our lives, such as when we are at school or university, we put more effort into making these kinds of connections, some of which we will retain on and off for the rest of our lives. But later we enter the 'time is scarce' trap and we invoke it profligately to justify the skimming, *thin knowledge* culture noted above. The by-word of electronic communications is speed and engaging with global networks to pursue faster communications makes a lot of sense in many circumstances. But the 'speed' metaphor has trickled into our everyday transactions to the extent that if we cannot now connect quickly and briefly with people (like a child flicking through the channels of a TV set), we get bored. Many situations where we once found 'time' to engage with others in real space have been traded because we have convinced ourselves that they now take too much time, although we rarely audit our time as precisely as this oft repeated claim would suggest. Technology has liberated us from the limitations of experience and imagination that came from being prisoners of inhospitable geography. Yet out of the enforcement of spatial limitations came some deep and intimate understandings that we have come to treasure as illuminations of self and as the satisfying glue of community life. The question, as so often in these debates, comes down to one of balance. Those ancestral voices that urge us to engage with all the components, verbal and non-verbal, of human communication are strong and won't lie down, yet they demand a premium in time and attention from us. On the other hand so much can be achieved quickly and conveniently without leaving home via ICT that we often cannot see the point in using our time in any other way. We want richness and we want reach and although ICT will deliver more richness and reach via broadband networks in the future we must resist the temptation to sacrifice all the richness we get from our attachments to real people in real space. ICT offers us tremendous convenience and is always seductive because of that but there are times when the inconvenience of moving around to meet people will result in better transactions, better decisions and better understanding.

# References

1.    Seutonius, *The Twelve Caesars*, trans. Robert Graves, revd. edn. London: Penguin Books

2.    Critchfield, R. (1995) *The villagers: changed values, altered lives, the closing of the urban-rural gap*. New York: Anchor/Doubleday

3.    Oldfield, C. (1998) 'Telework generation branches out'. *Sunday Times*, 24 May 1998

4.    'California dreamin'. *The Economist*: A survey of commuting, 5 September 1998, p.26

5.    I owe much of this 'brief word' on cities to Graham S. and Marvin, S. (1996) *Telecommunications and the City: electronic spaces, urban places*. London: Routledge, particularly the conclusions they set out between pp. 376–384

6.    Murdoch, G. (1983) 'Communications and the constitution of modernity'. *Media, Culture and Society*, **15**, pp. 521–539

7.    Mulgan, G. (1997) *Connexity: how to live in a connected world*. London: Chatto and Windus

# CHAPTER FOUR

# The changing face of telecommunications

Question: What's the difference between Jurassic Park and telecommunications companies?
Answer: One is a theme park full of dinosaurs, and the other is a hit movie.
Sir Ian Vallence, Chairman of BT at Telecom 95

## Bell and the State

In March 1876 the United States Patent Office granted Alexander Graham Bell patent number US174 465 covering 'The method of, and apparatus for, transmitting vocal or other sounds telegraphically . . . by causing electrical undulations, similar in form to the vibrations of the air accompanying the said vocal or other sounds' and the telephone was born. Bell made the first long-distance telephone call in 1876 and commercial application of Bell's invention followed within a year, as did the first of hundreds of lawsuits to protect his oft-abused patent. One hundred and twenty three years later all rich countries celebrate their high levels of telephone penetration as an indication of their economic maturity (although the number of Internet servers they host might soon replace this yardstick), and all poor countries see it as a fundamental prerequisite for getting rich. Telephonic messages now travel via various mixtures of wires and radio waves, they are bounced off satellite dishes and zoom through fibre-optic cables. They are joined by the huge volumes of data, millions of Emails, fax messages and digital images that now complement voice communication every day. So important was the telephone to the developing infrastructure of nation states that in Europe, and in many other places, the right to operate a telephone system tended to be a right exercised by government departments as a state monopoly, for better or worse. Only during the last 15 years has a spirit of de-regulation and privatization combined together to generate real competition between providers both within and across nation states.

So important has the telephone been that the vague concept of 'globalization' would have hardly any meaning without it. The telephone has proved to be the greatest 'connector' of people over distance in the history of communications and its part in enabling so many transactions, particularly financial and banking transactions, to be carried out over any distance, irrespective of time zones, lies at the heart of the 'global idea. At the end of the twentieth century it would not be too extreme to say that a nation's success in harnessing the information and knowledge-based enterprises that are expected to dominate future economic growth will be directly proportional to both the density of penetration and the variety of bandwidths available within its telecommunications infrastructure. Statistics concerning the number of lines linking homes, the miles of fibre-optic cable laid in the ground and the number of servers linked to the Internet etc., are the new measures of a nation's industrial muscle announcing the virility, sophistication and dynamism of its business culture.

In the protective but unexciting hands of state or other monopolists the telephone took time to come of age and the cost of telephone calls to Joe public, in Europe at least, stayed much higher and for much longer than they needed to be. The principal justification for high telephone charges, in the age of state control, was the requirement to provide an 'equal' level of public service in the sparsely populated areas where no private operator would venture and the need to cross-subsidize this service from more lucrative areas. While both the technology and the user base was in its infancy and poles and wires were the only way to connect telephones across long distances there was some justification for this position. Today with the help of wireless technology the once 'uneconomic' portion of telecommunications companies' responsibilities, while still expensive, is not the great burden it used to be. Changes in the technology of distributing telephone messages to the remoter parts of the industrial world have made the public service part of the telecommunications companies' mission easier to accomplish while holding out the promise, as yet largely unfulfilled, of greater telephone access for the scattered communities of poorer countries.

## Land of the almost free

In the US the mighty AT&T ruled as a virtual telecommunications monopoly until its break-up in 1984. After 1984 the US market was segregated into three broad groupings: four big long-distance companies – MCI, Sprint, AT&T and WorldCom; five to six regional telephone groups (the 'Baby Bells'); and a myriad of mobile phone companies. Twelve years later the US Congress passed the 1996 Telecommunications Act designed to offer a formula whereby local and long-distance US Telecommunications operators could begin to compete in each other's markets. That, at least, is the theory. So far the results have been a boon to lawyers rather than to competition and consumer choice. The spirit of the new Act has been bedevilled by tensions between the Federal Communications Commission (FCC) charged with overseeing the liberalization of both long-distance and local telephony and the courts. The US courts, obviously unmoved by the 'spirit' of the legislation have been particularly active in upholding the rights of local operators to shut out the aspirations of a long-distance provider and vice versa. In January 1998 a judge in Texas challenged the fairness of the 1996 Act which he said prevented Baby Bell firms from entering the long-distance business until they opened up their local markets. The judge declared the key provisions in the Act to be unconstitutional in unfairly punishing the regional (Baby Bell) operating companies by preventing them from operating in long-distance markets. Before leaving office as chairman of the FCC at the end of 1997 Reed Hundt, having seen how quick local telecommunications companies had been to go to State courts to resist competition, warned of the pernicious effects the American legal system could have on the government's attempt to liberalize the market. He believed that the 1996 Act set out a promise of open markets which, without further government intervention, would flounder in the harsh desert of the law with its long delays and tortured questioning of every phrase, word and punctuation mark.

The speed with which parties go to law in the US is something that non-Americans often find puzzling. But in a country founded on a legal document and populated by many different cultures, the law plays both a prominent and a unifying role (see Chapter 1). However when associated with the temptation to grind away over minute pieces of detail telecommunications companies, regulators and even Presidents have come to find that an over-documented legal culture can frustrate as well as execute the will of the people. Ironically that 'harsh desert' may eventually accelerate the customer-hoarding that the 1996 Act sought to prevent by stimulating competition.

Greater consolidation and 'buying into' new markets via agreed mergers is coming about in the US precisely because individual telecommunications companies have found it so difficult to get into each other's markets any other way. Rather than a thousand telecommunications flowers blooming the US is witnessing an orgy of consolidation that could take it back to the pre-1984 days of big company power. As well as seeing regulatory approval of the massive WorldCom-MCI deal and AT&T's acquisition of TCI (see below) 1998 also saw the $135 billion merger between SBC Communications and Ameritech and the $120 billion merger between Bell Atlantic and GTE. After its link with GTE (a one-time suitor for MCI) Bell Atlantic, who following its acquisition of Nynex is already the biggest local telephone company in the US serving 40 million customers in 13 states, gained 21 million more widely scattered customers. This merger gives their combined operation one third of the US local market with around 63 million access lines and makes Bell Atlantic easily the US's largest domestic carrier. It is also one of the largest cellular providers in the US with over 10.6 million customers and a major provider of Internet services. Such a merger provides the opportunity for the new company to achieve a common goal in the industry, i.e. the bundling together of long-distance, local and Internet services. This is possible because GTE, which was never a part of the Bell system, already offers long-distance services which Bell Atlantic, after proving to the regulators satisfaction that it has opened up its own local region to competition, will be able to plug into without further ado. Interestingly the faster growing GTE agreed to be bought by Bell Atlantic at below its market price while both Ameritech and TCI held out for premiums of around 30 per cent. It suggests that some of this old-fashioned consolidation is going on for the wrong reasons and that fear and desperation rather than a grand vision is pushing some of the partners together.

## Europe and Asia

BT was the first European telecommunications giant to be privatized (1984) and immediately fell foul of both its regulator and Mercury Communications, its one competitor, for dragging its feet in reducing connection charges and 'unbarring' its exchanges so that Mercury could offer an alternative service across its lines to customers. Mercury (now part of the UK's Cable and Wireless Communications) eventually gave up on serving domestic and public telephone-box customers to concentrate on business and commercial services and more latterly cable television.

These early 'spoiling' techniques employed by an old state provider when forced to let competitors travel over their wires were still alive and kicking fifteen years later. It took the intervention by the EU commission in October 1997 before the now partially privatized Deutsche Telekom (DT) would reduce its rates for local area connections to 'closed user groups' in Germany. Companies attempting to bring some competition to the German telecommunications market had complained to the EU about high costs and as a result the rates for local connections were eventually cut by 39 per cent and those for long-distance calls by 78 per cent. The German government had already had to intervene to reduce DT's interconnection charges to 2.7 pfennigs per line from the 6 pfennigs that DT wanted to charge.

Monoliths like DT will not go quietly. The tide is against them but they will continue to resist opening up their privileged infrastructures for as long as possible, despite its having been paid for by past customers and taxpayers. As the US experience proves just having liberalizing legislation in place is no guarantee that the incumbent operators will fall in with the spirit and tenor of the times. Competition for domestic telephony in the UK only really began to bite after 1990 as the largely US-owned and struggling cable companies got more of their cable into the ground, offered some serious discounts to BT's pricing structure and gradually combined to form larger and more cost-effective companies. Originally there were 24 cable companies in the UK; by 2000 it looks like there will be only three: Cable and Wireless Communications and the US-based NTL and Telewest Communications. NTL has set the pace by improving cable penetration rates, one of the industry's greatest weaknesses, by offering cable TV as a lost leader in order to gain telephone customers.

The EU has had to struggle to liberalize telecommunications, just as it had to liberalize commercial air traffic. The deadline for telecommunications liberalization for most of its member states was 1 January 1998. Greece, Spain, Portugal, Luxembourg and Ireland were allowed more time and have to comply by 2000 but no one expects either timetable to be followed closely. Greece has been the slowest to set the necessary structures in place for liberalization to end the monopoly of fixed wired telephony by OTE, the state telecommunications operator. In May 1997 the EU started legal procedures against Greece for failing to implement EU directives on setting up an independent telecommunications regulatory authority, allowing competition in satellite communications and cable television networks and making leased lines available at fair prices. In response Greece eventually agreed to open satellite communications and cable television services to competition by the end of 1998 and to liberalize all telecommunications services by 1 January 2001, a year after Portugal and Ireland.

This slow motion response to deregulation is not confined to Europe. In other countries the break-up of state-controlled monopolies, including those among the far-eastern 'Tiger' economies, has been painfully slow and often acrimonious. However the Asian financial crisis has stimulated some governments to sell off bits of their telecom monopoly to help fund various survival strategies. South Korea listed the state-run Korea Telecom, which has a monopoly on local telephone services and the lion's share of the long-distance market, on the Seoul stock market in December 1998. At that time only 5 per cent of the equity was open to foreign investors but this will increase to a total of 33 per cent by 1999. In December 1998 the Australian Competition and Consumer Commission called for industry submissions on its draft ruling that Telstra, the country's largest telecommunications carrier, should allow competitors direct access to its local telephone network. Previously competitors had been restricted in where they could connect to the Telstra network. If carried, the new ruling would allow them to provide both local calls and high-speed data services at all points in the network, considerably reducing their access costs. Even after selling off four tranches of shares to the private sector to raise funds to finance economic stimulus measures, Japan's Finance Ministry still owns 59 per cent of the world's third largest Telecommunications company, NTT. Prior to the Japanese financial crisis NTT had been tenacious, and very successful, in lobbying to keep its monopoly.

Privatizing a near monopoly national provider is of course only the first step in opening up markets as the new 'private monopoly' will use every trick in the book to block or make uneconomic access to their infrastructure for as long as they can. These tactics may be time-limited but they still boil down to preserving the right to charge higher prices for as long as they can.

## Early 1990's media mergers/late 1990's telecommunication mergers

The early 1990s saw a spate of media mergers and acquisitions that were primarily about bringing 'content' together under one umbrella:

> Like the great dash to forge mergers and alliances that de-regulation is prompting among the world's airlines, the key players in the media business want marriage, particularly that part of the marriage vow that emphasizes 'to the exclusion of all others'. [1]

News Corporation had started the process of 'big' media integration by buying Twentieth Century Fox in 1985 and forming the Fox Broadcasting Company in 1986. Sony acquired Columbia Studios in 1989, Time Inc. acquired Warner Communications in 1990 to form Time Warner, Matsushita purchased MCA/Universal in late 1990, News Corporation bought Hong Kong-based Star TV in 1993 and Viacom bought Paramount Communications in 1994. After Walt Disney bought Capital Cities–ABC in early 1995 Time Warner went on to buy Turner Broadcasting System (including CNN) in the same year to create the world's largest (and most debt-ridden) media company. Many of these mergers were accomplished only by buyers paying over the odds for their prey. Many commentators at the time saw the frenzied bidding games between the key players as being more about ego enrichment than sensible business planning. In late 1997, seven years after its merger, Time Warner was still posting a net loss of $35 million and holding debt of $17 billion proving that media 'synergy' through acquisition is rarely a quick fix as far as profits are concerned.

The late 1990s seem to be heralding something of a re-run of this merger-mania, this time among telecommunications companies. If controlling content was king at the start of the decade controlling distribution, including access to the rapidly developing Internet, looks like being king at the end of it. The 1996/1997 chronicle of BT, MCI and WorldCom's merger/non-merger was a telecommunications soap opera that illuminates in microcosm the turbulence in telecommunications that is still to come. This one drama, encompassing as it does:

- That being big and profitable is no longer enough on its own to dominate a telecommunications market;
- The fierce opposition to competition in the land of competition;
- Poor knowledge by one player of the market into which it is buying;
- The emergence of a young upstart to upset the comfortable world of the established players;
- The incomprehensible (to the layman at least) structures and alliances of the business demonstrates just how complex the business of telecommunication has become, how it stands at a crossroads in the relationship between voice and data transmission and how the certainties of a century-old 'nice line of business' are quickly decomposing.

## Working in concert

During July 1997 BT and MCI both learned that telecommunications were not necessarily the licence to print money that it had once been. Both companies had agreed in November 1996 to merge to form 'Concert', a new multi-billion pound telecommunications company big enough to create a global network with the reach and service depth necessary to satisfy the national and multi-national clients of the future. At that time this was the largest take over of a US company by a foreign one. Then came the bombshell. In July 1997 MCI issued a profits warning outlining that it would cost double the amount (around $800 million during 1997/98 and a greater sum during 1998/99) than it previously thought to break into local US telephone markets using its own infrastructure. Despite having three directors on the board of MCI, including its Chairman and Chief Executive, BT seemed to be caught off guard and unaware of the scale of the potential losses that it would be sharing with its new partner. Not unexpectedly this gave rise to suggestions that BT had entered into the original agreement without a real understanding of the dynamics of the US market. Poor information exchange (these are both communication companies and BT's advertising slogan at the time was 'It's good to talk') between the two boards and even worse between the boards and their shareholders caused a period of great uncertainty which brought both companies into disrepute. After some belated cross-Atlantic negotiations the MCI board agreed, at the end of August 1997, to a price cut of 15 per cent, re-valuing the US's second-largest long-distance operator at $23.7 billion. MCI, a notoriously litigious company – it was once described as 'a law firm with an antenna on its head' – is believed to have agreed to re-negotiate the terms with BT because there did not seem to be a sufficiently credible alternative partner. Also, and despite MCI's reputation for going to law, an agreement would avoid the nuclear winter of litigation that would inevitably follow a 'walk-away' and which could have lasted three years or more. Coincident with the re-negotiation of the terms the FCC approved the merger with some caveats concerning the opening up of local markets in the UK. Since the end of 1996 MCI had been caught in the cross-fire between the FCC 'open markets' policies and the web of state-based legal obstructions being created by the Baby Bells to hinder all attempts to break into their markets.

Despite all the talk of 'globalization' it is the US market, home to over 40 per cent of the world's multinational companies, that BT saw as the key to its wider ambitions – hence the strong desire to link up with MCI and hence the relief among BT's management when the merger was salvaged by the re-negotiations of August 1997. Worldwide telephone minutes, i.e. the volume of calls made, is expected to increase by over 50 per cent to 95 billion minutes each year by 2000. This translates into a one trillion-dollar market, and Concert was to be BT's passage into this brave new world. BT wanted to capture the multinational corporations which are fuelling demand for data transmission, fast Internet connections and multi-media capacity by offering them a seamless global telephone system. To this end BT has also signed up alliances, under the name of Concert Classic, with strategically placed telephone companies in different markets to help facilitate its global ambitions. These included Telefonica of Spain and Latin America, Portugal Telecom, Viag in Germany and Generale des Eaux in France.

## Enter WorldCom: bidding up the future

The relief felt by BT executives was to be short-lived. On 2 October 1997, almost a year after BT and MCI announced their merger plans and little more than a month after they had settled on the new terms, BT's global strategy was thrown into disarray when WorldCom, the US's fourth largest long-distance operator, trumped BT's bid for MCI. WorldCom's $30 billion (£18.6 billion) offer took both BT and MCI by surprise. It was $6 billion greater than the value BT placed on MCI and, if successful, would be the largest take-over bid in history. Interestingly, given that its long-term strategy was in tatters, BT's share price in London jumped by more than 12 per cent over two days on the news of the counter-bid and rose even further later. This reflected the relief among its institutional shareholders that the MCI deal, which had been controversial since it was announced, might not go ahead and that BT might sell its 20 per cent stake in MCI and return some serious money back to its shareholders. For at least two years BT would be sending cash on a one-way trip across the Atlantic to feed MCI's investment in local telephony infrastructure and this short-term dilution of earnings was not attractive to many of BT's equally short-term large UK shareholders. They would have preferred BT to seek a different partner, perhaps one already established in the US local market who could have secured quicker returns to shareholders.

Mississippi-based WorldCom, which had already expanded into local services and the Internet in the US through more than 40 acquisitions in six years, believed that its bid was more credible than BT's. Its bid was worth more (albeit all on paper), WorldCom was already established in all US telecommunications sectors and there was considerable overlap between both companies long-distance and local networks in the US. These advantages would, according to WorldCom, save $2.5 billion in the first year of the merger and an extraordinary $15 billion-worth of cost cuts over five years from better use of the combined network and other cost savings. Like MCI WorldCom had concentrated on providing sophisticated broadband connections to business customers. In 1996 it had acquired MFS Communications, another company operating local telephone networks mainly for business customers in US and European capitals. MFS just happened to own UUNet, one of the largest US Internet service providers which, like MCI, ran one of the national 'backbone' carriers for Internet traffic. This acquisition of UUNet complemented that of September 1997 when WorldCom, in a three-way deal that saw the end of CompuServe as an independent entity and gave American Online its big break, agreed to buy the telecommunications infrastructure of both these online services.

## Enter and exit GTE, exit BT

On the face of it this episode looked very much like a David and Goliath affair. BT, a £48 billion company, has more than triple the revenue of WorldCom ($32 billion) and makes profits of around £4 billion while WorldCom barely breaks even. However the 'Davids' were still coming. Mid-October 1997 saw yet another entrant to the saga when GTE, a local US telecommunications operator put in an all-cash $28 billion (£17 billion) bid for MCI. This was the largest 'cash' offer ever made for another company and, had it been successful, it would have created an enterprise with more than $40 billion of revenues, more than 21 million local lines and more than 24 million long-distance lines. However in November 1997 MCI settled for a marriage with WorldCom at a price of $37 billion, a world record for an all-paper offer, and one that suggested that there was little wrong with BT's judgement that MCI was a prize worth having. BT, though richer to the tune of £7 billion for its 20 per cent stake of MCI (a clear £3 billion profit), was left very bruised by this affair. At home in the UK it faced growing competition, losing more than 50 000 customers a month, as more than 50 well-heeled rivals began raiding the most lucrative, i.e. corporate, parts of its business. The UK regulator predicted in December 1997 that BT's share of the UK market would fall to about half by 2000 compared with its present two thirds. It continues to face tough domestic regulation, 25 per cent of its prices are capped until 2001, and unlike many of its European rivals it has already cut thousands of jobs from its payroll. There would seem little that BT can do with regard to further cost cutting while its profits are so carefully regulated. To avoid being left on the shelf as a UK utility with small 3 to 4 per cent per annum growth prospects it must become a global player and that means finding a partner with complementary strengths to advance its global ambitions. BT continues to look for partners but it was not allowed to seal any new deal with a company in the US until WorldCom had concluded its negotiations with MCI towards the end of 1998. The higher valuations for the

US telecommunications sector, driven up in part by the price which WorldCom paid for MCI, will mean that BT will again have to cross the bridge of diluting its own earnings if it takes the merger plunge again. Its first big step after the MCI debacle was to join in an 'equal' partnership, rather than a full-blown take-over, with AT&T but, if it stays cash-rich, it will still be looking.

## AT&T reply

In June 1998 AT&T (under 'new management' since November 1997) responded to the MCI/WorldCom merger by acquiring Telecommunications Incorporated (TCI), the second largest cable TV operator in the US, for $48 billion. The new company hopes to be able to offer a one-stop-shop over a broad range of electronic services including long distance and cellular telephone calls, cable television and dial-up and high-speed Internet access, all under the powerful AT&T brand. In December 1998 AT&T bought up IBM's data network which stretches across 59 countries and in early 1999 it formed a joint venture with Time Warner (TW) to deliver local telephone services over TW's cables and it hopes to do business with more cable operators in order to extend its domestic reach. AT&T's proposed acquisition of MediaOne the US' fourth biggest cable operator (if approved by regulators) will extend its reach over that crucial last mile to 60 per cent of US homes and if approved, make it the biggest cable operator in the US.

Since the Baby Bells have successfully kept it out of their markets AT&T is busy buying into local calling through the (back) cable door. In July 1998, just one month after its acquisition of TCI, AT&T also agreed to a major joint venture with its old enemy BT, which involves them both in pooling their international operations. This formal association between the largest US long-distance operator and the UK telecommunications group is expected to generate an initial turnover of $10 billion, handle 25 billion minutes of telecommunications traffic annually and generate an operating profit of $1 billion in its first year. The two operators will have an equal stake in a new enterprise that will combine the cross-border assets of each company, including their international networks, all their international traffic and all their international products for business customers. Their aim is to capture a substantial share of the lucrative international traffic generated by multinational companies, by the Internet and by other telecommunications operators. This business is currently worth $40 billion and is expected to grow to $201 billion by 2007. Most importantly the new company will control the design of a new global network, based on the most advanced technology, to provide a seamless service. BT will put Concert into the new pot and AT&T will unravel a number of existing and complex relationships. These include World Partners, a loose alliance of international operators including KDD of Japan and Singapore Telecom, and AT&T-Unisource, a partnership with a European telecommunications alliance which includes the national telecommunications operators of The Netherlands, Switzerland and Sweden.

Because of the loose nature of these partnerships, AT&T's concentration on its home market and, most importantly, AT&T's inability to control service quality across the partner network World Partners has not been a great success. At the end of 1997 AT&T looked like a utility industry laggard with a broad range of strategic problems. 1998 was the year it decided to change. Its acquisition of Teleport gave it a strong base in the local market for big business customers while its acquisition of TCI gave it access to the kind of infrastructure which is crucial for satisfying the needs of its vast domestic residential customer base. Its alliance with BT gives it the international dimension that it needed with a reliable partner. If the confidence of the partnership can be maintained then both AT&T and BT should be able to deliver a full range of high quality international services to large multinational corporate clients and to exploit the Internet technology that is the ultimate competitive threat to the industry's cosy traditions.

The international arena is important to both parties because it is both lucrative and where the cutting edge of technological innovation is often focused. Just as important is the fact that AT&T and BT have taken each other out as enemies and competitors. Without looking over their shoulders at each other they are now free to divide up the world into spheres of influence. AT&T can retain its hegemony in the US, primacy in Europe can be assigned to BT and they can hunt as a pack in third markets. If it works out – one always has to be cautious about big international alliances – this new venture would handle the lion's share of the world's international telecommunications traffic giving it huge economies of scale that should eventually trickle down to customers in higher convenience and lower prices.

## The world moves on

Of course the world will not stand still while these companies join together. Cable and Wireless in the UK, already strong in southeast Asia, is developing a relationship with telecommunication Italia, while Deutsche Telekom and France telecommunication already have a (somewhat problematic) three-way alliance called Global One with the US's current third biggest long-distance provider Sprint. WorldCom has built its own network from scratch in Europe which should, in the long-term, enable it to earn higher margins than some of its competitors because it will not have to pay fees to other telecommunications operators. The international telecommunications business, once founded on cosy collaborations between national monopolies, is now in the throes of getting used to competition and the alliances that need to be forged in order to compete effectively. After the announcement of the Bell Atlantic–GTE deal a spokesman for SBC Communications said:

> American carriers that want to be successful national and global competitors need size, scale, skilled employees and a large customer base. The race is on, and consumers are in for a great ride. [2]

But global aspirations are not just the prerogative of US telecommunications companies. Despite a 20 per cent fall in its net profits from Latin America during the first nine months of 1998 Spain's privatized Telefonica has recently declared Peru, Chile, Brazil and the rest of Latin America to be part of its 'domestic market'. Its aim is simply to redefine Telefonica's market from the 40 million people who live in Spain to the 400 million who speak either Spanish or Portuguese and it hopes to have an established presence in 17 Latin American countries by the end of 1999. Mr Villalonga, the Chairman of Telefonica (it was he who dropped the suffix 'de Espana' from the company's name to show its determination to be more than just a home-based utility), is keen to show that cultural connections can be an advantage in even the most globalized of businesses. Although I doubt if the Portuguese speakers of Brazil see their culture as quite as Spanish as he does:

> Latin America is to Telefonica what the United States is to AT&T. It is our home, our culture, our language . . . we send our best people to Latin America they [the Americans] send them to California. [3]

In order to satisfy local regulatory rules governing ownership Telefonica operates in these countries mostly through consortia and it already has 23.5 million customers in Latin America against its 21.6 million customers in Spain. With competition in Peru already established and due in Argentina after 2000 and the huge privatization of Brazil's Telebras now settling down the next ten years of telecommunications growth in Latin America looks, on the surface, to be a Klondike. Some 4 million people in Sao Paulo are still waiting for a fixed telephone line and the growth in data traffic could be explosive with only 1 per cent of Internet content currently readable in Spanish or Portuguese. However the economies of Latin America are expected to be quite volatile over the next two or three years so Telefonica's alliance with the US's WorldCom–MCI is probably a handy insurance policy.

Elsewhere in Europe the story will be one of continued expansion and consolidation. Deutsche Telekom (DT), partially privatized in 1996 and continental Europe's largest telecommunications company, will be selling more of its equity (around $12 billion-worth) to raise cash for future investment in the international arena. Like BT in the UK DT has been under increasing pressure in its home market, losing an estimated 30 per cent of the peak time long-distance calls to competitors during 1998, and also like BT, it has been shedding staff to cut costs. Although it has shed 30 000 workers DT still needs to take more costs out of its business if it is to compete effectively in a global market. The proposed merger of DT with Telecolm Italia, (threatened by a hostile takeover bid by Olivetti), will if accepted by all parties, create Europe's largest telephone company with 350 000 employees and $69 billion of sales. At the time of writing the regulatory hurdles looked enormous. The rationale for the scheme looked to be a defensive merger, in order to do together what they could not alone. This seems to draw its inspiration from old style monopoly togetherness, rather than a long term vision to exploit the technological advances, which are changing the nature of telephony. A merger between DT and Sprint in the US would seem to make more commercial sense.

In a first for Europe Sweden and Norway merged their state owned telephone companies Telia and Telenor with a view to selling 32 per cent of the equity in the new company before the end of 1999. Before the share offering Sweden will own 60 per cent of the combined business while Norway will hold 40 per cent and its headquarters will be in Stockholm with an international division based in Oslo. After the initial public offering of shares each country will hold 34 per cent of the equity in the new company. As cutting costs will inevitable feature as part of the rationale for the merger heavy job losses can be expected from the current roster of 51 000 employees.

## After the concert

In the world of old-style telecommunications giants BT, privatized for over a decade, looked nimble in the early 1990s but alongside WorldCom it looked positively old-fashioned by 1997. To BT MCI looked modern, progressive and full of zest, but in the new US context, and compared with WorldCom, it looked slow and tired. The MCI and BT merger represented two old-style telecommunications companies seeking an old-style alliance while WorldCom represents the opportunistic flowing together of various technologies thrown up by rapid progress. Companies like WorldCom represent the next generation: fast moving, amorphous and unpredictable, something of a metaphor for the telecommunications business as a whole. This is a world where the likes of BT, DT, France Telecom and NTT of Japan look increasingly clumsy and out of place. However, the giants are slowly beginning to adapt, to forge alliances with the new boys on the block and to respond to the competitive pressure. The new century will see many more new entrants doing interesting things with that which to many of us is still something of an abstract concept – telecommunications traffic. Already new intermediaries, who do not have to invest in costly infrastructure, have sprung up to buy spare capacity to sell on to the public at discount rates and to develop Internet protocol (IP) telephony to enable voice communication over the Internet. The telephone infrastructure once developed to secure the widest possible opportunity for point-to-point voice communication is now a global grid onto which all kinds of services can be hung. At some time during 1999 data volumes will overtake those of voice traffic on the majority of the world's communication networks.

The saga of consolidation and mergers among the world's fixed-line telecommunications operators is just warming up and will not be over until a lot of fat shareholders have sung. However the most recent round of mergers, de-regulation, privatizations and technological advances has left us with some colourful graffiti with which to speculate.

1. The Internet is tearing up the rules of traditional telephony just as it is in the distributive components of many other businesses. World growth in traditional telephone lines grew sedately from 450 million lines in 1987 to around 750 million in 1996, at an average of 33.33 million lines per year while the number of Internet host computers grew from around 100 000 in 1987 to 16 million in 1996, at an average rate of 1.77 million per year with the biggest increase of 7.5 million occurring in 1996.

2. The sheer speed of the telecommunications revolution still plays to America's strengths while the rest of the world struggles behind.

3. New companies with expertise in Internet technology are gamely challenging the traditional telephone companies and their number looks set to increase.

4. The slow progress of de-regulation in the US is acting as a road-block to outsiders such as BT who, although they want to act quickly, may suffer (ironically given the business they are in) by operating at too great a distance from the centre of the action.

5. Within the US the technology is mutating rapidly and bypassing the regulators.

6. The chief thrust of strategy within global telecommunications is temporarily shifting. The turmoil and volatility of the US market has disrupted what it means to be seeking global alliances; the focus of change in telecommunications, for the short-term at least, has shifted from creating world-wide alliances to competing in the US domestic market.

7. Voice communication looks set to become a subset of data communication with voice calls routinely travelling across networks designed primarily for data, as they do on the high capacity networks that link many US, UK and Canadian universities.

8. Data networks are clearly not now the sole prerogative of the old telecommunications providers and the aggressive stance taken by new entrants wishing to develop them could severely threaten their most valuable income streams. Revenues for data traffic are growing by 30 per cent annually compared with voice traffic growth of just 7 per cent annually. However only the old dinosaurs have the scale and the financial muscle to take up innovative technologies and employ them across broad swathes of the market-place. They will not be able to resist technologies that revolutionize service and cut

costs but they will have a good shot at assimilating them at a controlled and evolutionary pace rather than as the full-scale assault on their citadels that so many commentators predict.

9.   Big customers want a limited number of global service providers with uniform products. As revenues from multi-national companies are crucial to the future profits of the industry those telecommunications providers who secure the business of the top 5000 multi-national companies by offering them a 'one-stop-shop' will emerge as the winners. The strategic value of networks will mean more mergers to ensure control of telecommunications assets around the world.

10.  The segmentation of the wider customer base will require substantial on-going capital investment alongside a steady decline in the tariffs that customers are willing to pay. The potential upsurge in demand, especially from business users, will put call charges under intense pressure.

11.  Alarm bells are already ringing over the slothful progress of pro-competitive initiatives in the US, the EU and the WTO and so we can expect regulation, as well as market forces, to continue to play a key role over the next few years, including some re-examination of the rules of the game. The arcane system of international settlement rates that still allows some countries, including some of the world's poorest, to charge inflated prices for completing an international call is likely to be one area that comes under scrutiny. Seventy-two countries, representing 90 per cent of the world's telecommunications traffic have committed themselves to the WTO agreement liberalizing trade in telecommunications services but many will be slow to act and the quality of telephony offered across the globe (as in AT&T's problems with its WorldPartners project) will remain patchy, irritating and frustrating for some time to come.

12.  The large number of mergers, including those still awaiting regulatory approval, in the telecommunications industry is a powerful example of how technology can speed the removal of barriers, which to many lay people already seemed artificial, between markets. Once perceived and operated as separate businesses – wired, wireless, local, long-distance, cable television, telephone, information and entertainment – all of these services can now be brought together by technology. The market is beginning to recognize this

and is bringing the companies together so that they can offer customers a comprehensive 'service' rather than simply one form of conduit.

13.   The speed of technological change in the international call arena can be gleaned from the changes inherent in the make-up of the kind of cable that we are now able to lay across our oceans. The first trans-ocean fibre cable was laid just 12 years ago with a capacity of around 40 000 simultaneous calls. The new fibre-optic cable being laid across the Pacific Ocean will be able to handle eight million simultaneous calls. Such changes in the order of magnitude of call capacity (together with call anywhere from anywhere satellite technology) will transform the landscape of international communications in the new millennium but they require some very deep corporate pockets to ensure delivery.

The big story of the last four years was how the twin forces of technology and competition were changing the landscape, however slowly, of the communication industry within individual countries. Now the same two forces are redefining communications between countries.

Use of global communications by the world's largest companies is growing by 19 per cent a year. Use by small and medium sized companies is growing even faster – about 25 per cent. And consumer demand for international voice and data services is increasing by 20 per cent a year. In fact, traffic between countries is increasing twice as fast as traffic within countries themselves. Overall what is now a $40 billion market will grow to $200 billion in a few years. [4]

A third force is the power of common standards as represented by the IP standard for Internet communication. This force is still in early childhood but it will offer both opportunities and threats to the established telecommunications companies. New players like International Discount Telecommunications (IDT), who have gained a million customers in just two years for their IP telephony service, are pushing back the mysteries of international telecommunication. By piggybacking on excess capacity, they can offer cheap international calling through a regular telephone as well as a via a computer link. Whatever happens to such 'upstarts' in the long term they have shown that international calling can be cheap and still return a profit, and they will have added a little more stress to the chain holding down the old telecommunications' grip on high-cost international calls.

## Cellular wars: old and new world standards

Schoolchildren in Hong Kong, where 40 per cent of the population have a mobile phone, half of the pedestrians on Helsinki's streets, students and women travelling alone have all found the mobile phone an invaluable link with business, family or friends when they are on the move. Although decreasingly as they become more common, the mobile phone has also attained something of a reputation as a fashion accessory, poseur's prop and attention grabber. In strange public displays of multiple connecting young people insist on sharing their half of an intimate phone call with complete strangers in the street while noisy executives on trains similarly share their high-pressured lives with others who would rather sleep. Young people particularly like the mobile phone – their lives are mobile, and it has the joy of advertising a personal, rather than a family, number. A mobile phone number is a liberating piece of data about them rather than a mixed-generation household, and once hooked (like students and their first bank account) they will stick with the mobile habit. If pot, sex, and rock and roll were the liberating themes of the 1960s a mobile phone with a messaging facility has become the liberating force of the 1990s.

Finland takes the prize for having the highest penetration of mobile phones in the world (currently around 57 per cent of Finns have a mobile phone) and all the Nordic countries are expected to have a penetration of at least 50 per cent by the end of 2000. Finland however is predicted to continue its lead (can it just be because of Nokia?) and is expected to achieve a 100 per cent penetration (that works out at more mobile phones than people) by the year 2003.

The mobile phone is still in its infancy. The miniaturization of the microchip still has some way to go before it reaches its physical limits, and its role at the centre of a new generation of portable communications devices looks set to become the battle-ground for the next round of corporate wars. The success of Microsoft's early operating system as a standard for PCs and the open TCP/IP standard for Internet communication clearly shows that common standards quickly lead to the point where exponential growth starts to take off while incompatible standards hold back a large installed base of products. Yet in the world of the mobile phone we have the situation where Europe adopted the GSM standard in 1991 followed by over 100 other countries including Hong Kong and Australia, while the US has doggedly stuck to the NADC standard.

Despite all the evidence that incompatible standards cause customer confusion, reduce competition, hinder economies of scale and damage long-term profits this old incompatibility of standards could continue into the third generation of mobile communications. The EU and US seem to be having some difficulty agreeing on a global standard for the 'code division multiple access' (CDMA) technology that will be at the heart of the next generation of mobile phones. Due to arrive in 2002 and known in the industry as 3G (third generation) the US and the EU are currently sponsoring different 'versions' of this technology and a 'negotiated settlement' has not yet been reached. The 3G should be faster and cheaper, handling voice and data calls at very high speed and at far less cost to consumers than the recently introduced global satellite systems (see below). Users of 3G should be able to download graphics from the Internet in seconds, conduct a videoconference and zap video pictures around the world. For those who make handsets and provide networks for mobile phones the stakes are huge. The US has accused the EU of protectionism by promoting a European standard that requires manufacturers to license a version developed by Ericsson and Nokia. The EU responded by suggesting that the US government is being manipulated by Qualcomm, a large mobile phone company whose chief executive is a big donor to the Democratic Party. The Ericsson–Nokia version of the standard is called wide-band CDMA and uses more bandwidth than the US version. The Europeans maintain that wide-band CDMA is necessary if 3G is to deliver the kind of sophisticated multi-media services over mobile phones that future users will be seeking. The US has already assigned some of the frequencies that would be needed for wide-band CDMA to existing mobile services and so are pressing for the adoption of a platform called CDMA 2000 which uses less of the broadband spectrum. They argue that the economies of scale gained from making the standard work globally (i.e. the Qualcomm way) would more than offset the disadvantage of lower bandwidth. EU officials maintain that they are backing a 'concept' rather than any one manufacturer and that the US knew when it assigned the wide-band frequencies to other services that the rest of the world had reserved them for 3G. The International

Telecommunications Union (ITU), an arm of the UN, is charged with setting global standards for mobile services but has been hindered by the refusal of both Ericcson and Qualcomm to license the key patents which would allow its normal standard-making process to move forward. Frustrated, the ITU has set a deadline of March 1999 for deciding on the key characteristics of the 3G standard.

Because of the faster take-up rate of mobile phones in Europe than the US (see below) the frequency used by the current GSM standard will reach saturation in many European countries much earlier than expected and both Finland and Germany are planning to start auctioning radio spectrum for 3Gs in 1999. The industry will eventually find a solution but, given this acrimonious stand-off, it would be idealistic to anticipate a single global standard for G3 in the near future. Notwithstanding the confusion over standards ownership of a mobile phone looks like a steamroller that can't be stopped and over 600 million people world-wide are expected to be using mobile phones by 2002. Market researcher Dataquest estimates that the sales of mobile phones will soar from c. 100 million handsets a year in 1997 to c. 360 million a year, approximately 18 per cent of which is expected to be 'smart' phones that can handle data as well as voice transmission. The market for 3G is expected to include 100 million users by 2005 generating $100 billion in annual business world-wide. This represents a market to rival today's PC sales and there will be tremendous battles for who controls the value in this chain. Although some concerns have been raised about the health risk of microwave emissions from mobile phones so far few studies have been carried out on the long-term effects of prolonged use of mobile handsets particularly as they might affect the neck and the throat. The WTO is conducting a three-year research programme on the effects of handset use and they hope to publish guidelines on mobile phone microwave emissions by 2004.

## For once Europe is ahead

The bidding war between the UK's Vodafone and Bell Atlantic for the San Francisco-based mobile phone operator Air Touch in early 1999 emphasized the consolidation (similar to that going on in fixed-wire telephony) needed to take advantage of the 'telephone number' opportunities in the mobile phone industry. Air Touch was only spun off from Pacific Telesis

in 1994 but had already acquired around 12 per cent of the highly fragmented US market, just slightly more than its nearest rival. Surprising for
a country obsessed with technology the US has lagged behind in adopting
mobile phones, and just as surprisingly it has been European companies
that have taken the big initiatives in this corner of the telecommunications
market. The US invented cellular phones but they did not implement them
well. They were slow to shift over from analogue, access and reception
varied widely between regions, they did not have national licences and
prices stayed high for far too long. In Europe it has always been common
to charge the caller making the call to a mobile phone while the US
retains the 'mobile user always pays' billing system under which mobile
phone users are charged for both receiving and making calls. Such a system
hardly encouraged US users to hand out their mobile phone numbers and
mobile telephony is perceived as an expensive option even though prices
are now falling. Thousands of mobile phone licences have been granted
in the US to groups ranging from telecommunications giants to corner
stores, creating a market that was so fragmented that it was almost impossible to control. At the beginning of 1999 the penetration of mobile phones
in the US was around 24 per cent, up from 22 per cent at the start of
1998. By contrast the UK, a slow mover in European terms, began 1998
with 14 per cent market penetration and ended it with 22 per cent and
many commentators now believe that a penetration of 40 per cent is
achievable in the UK by the end of 2000, at least two years earlier than
previously thought.

But competitive pressure is beginning to have an impact on the US
mobile phone industry. Air Touch, McCaw Cellular and Sprint have begun
what they hope will be a market transformation in the US. They are
offering national tariffs – in some cases offering one-price calling right
across America – together with more reliable and widespread reception
zones which they hope will stimulate a European-type growth rate. AT&T
encouraged some of this opening up of mobile telephony by launching its
'Digital One Rate' letting consumers make calls all around the US for the
same charge, upsetting the industry's convoluted price code. Now AT&T
is also offering a service whereby customers pay the same ten cents per
minute for all long-distance calls whether made on a wireless or a fixed-
line telephone.

Handsets that can handle more than one technical system are also
being introduced in the US and many believe that the Universal Mobile

Telecommunications System (UMTS), the next generation mobile phone technology soon to be introduced into the UK, will also become the standard in the US. The UK government plans to auction four UMTS licences during the latter part of 1999 with the new services coming on-stream in 2002. The UMTS system promises high speed Internet access, video phones, Email and E-commerce while on the move from a handset no bigger than today's mobile phone. The pre-pay, no contract, buy a phone in a box, no credit check, one-off purchase deals offered in the UK at many retail outlets, including supermarkets and convenience stores, just before Christmas 1998 saw an explosion in UK sales. If the short-term loss of revenue can be sustained by the mobile phone companies such a marketing approach will feed a great expansion of mobile phones in the poorer countries of Europe like Ireland, Italy, Greece and Portugal. Vodafone paid £37 billion for Air Touch ($60.3 billion) and the joint company, to be called Vodafone Air Touch, will begin its life with operations in 23 countries and a controlling position in 12 of them. The joint company is worth c. £67 billion, making it the largest mobile phone company in the world and the world's fourth largest telecommunications company after AT&T, MCI–WorldCom and NTT. The UK's BT comes sixth after Deutsche Telecom.

That a UK mobile phone company's capitalization could overtake a national institution that has always dominated telecommunications in the UK may seem incredible but it is a sure sign that the old rules no longer apply. Prior to their deal Vodafone and Air Touch kept coming up against each other as bidders for licences in Europe. Thus Air Touch's great attraction is not so much its western US mobile operations – where Vodafone could add nothing to Air Touch's existing coverage – but its European presence which accounts for about half of its business. Air Touch has built up a network of mobile phone licences and joint ventures throughout Europe and has the best European network outside Vodafone – put together the two companies cover nearly all of Europe and look a bit like the Microsoft of the mobile phone world. In the US MCI–WorldCom has no mobile phone division as yet and is likely to want to rectify this gap in its portfolio over the longer term.

The UK has some aggressive players in the mobile phone market and it may see some more consolidation in the near future. Currently there are three main competitors to Vodafone: Orange (whose largest shareholder is Hong Kong's Hutchinson Whampoa) who really started the aggressive retail marketing of non-business mobile phones in the UK, Cellnet (currently owned by BT and Securicor but soon to come into the sole ownership of BT who have secured government approval to buy Securicor's 40 per cent stake) and One2One (partly owned by Cable and Wireless).

The US accounts for more than 90 per cent of the most visited Internet sites and about half of all Internet users but its mobile phone world has been slow to develop. Europe on the other hand, slower to take to the fixed-line Internet, has been powering ahead on the mobile phone front. Home to two of the world's largest mobile phone makers, and now to its largest mobile phone company, Europe is in pioneering mode, simplifying standards and now encouraging the purchase of pre-paid talk time over the counter. It may seem hard to imagine now but the future of talk is mobile and the same factor that's driving big take-up rates, i.e. falling call charges, will inevitably squeeze margins and force even greater efficiencies among those hoping to carve out a slice of this huge market.

## Karen's question

On her holidays in the Bahamas in 1985 Karen Bertiger asked her husband Bary, an Illinois-based engineer for Motorola, why she couldn't call home on their mobile phone. It was a question that has been asked by many people many times since. During late 1998 Iridium, a consortium of Motorola, Lockheed Martin, Sprint, Germany's Veba AG and a Russian Space centre, handled their first calls from the $5 billion low-earth orbit satellite system that answered Karen's question. The low orbit, around 1500 km above the earth, is important because such satellites are easier and cheaper to launch and they weigh less. Also because the satellites are closer to the ground they can run off comparatively small battery packs using smaller antennaes and, vital for voice communications, signals can go up and back with no perceptible delay. The downside is that more of the satellites are needed to cover the earth's surface and their expected life of 5 to 10 years is shorter than that for the older models occupying the higher altitudes. Circling in orbits 760 km above the earth, 66 Iridium communication satellites bounce cellular calls from one to another and then beam the datastream down to one of 12 earth-based 'terrestrial' gateway stations from where it hops about between the networks of around 100 cellular licensees. The latter are a necessary middle stage for the Iridium project; it originally planned a sky-to-ground system that would have cut them out, if its service wasn't to fail in high-rise urban environments where its high paying customers might be out of a satellite's line of fire.

Piggybacking on terrestrial cell-phone networks which use different standards (see above) means that Iridium phones need different plug-in modules depending on which side of the Atlantic the call originates. So when you buy a phone it comes with either the NADC or the GSM standard with the option of buying a $500 module to cover the other one. Even an 'anywhere' satellite service would quickly be brought down to earth if it couldn't resolve the incompatible standards problem. Iridium has had other problems – mainly software glitches of one sort or another and the need to develop a production-line approach to satellite manufacture and testing – in its quest to make the 'anywhere' satellite phone a practical and popular means of twenty-first century communication. Iridium took 13 years to develop, it is first in this field (it has even been issued with a universal dialling code +8816, effectively classifying all those satellites as a separate country in telecommunication terms) and it is expensive. Iridium launched a massive advertising campaign to develop market awareness of its service towards the end of 1998. Despite its high cost it hopes to get some first mover advantage by signing up the global executives, whom it sees as its main target, a year or so ahead of the launch of any similar service by its competitors. Once caught it hopes that those first and most eager customers will balk at ditching their expensive handsets for a rival unit even if the price of the rival's calls is cheaper. Soon after opening up for business Iridium added Claircom Communications, the second largest provider of telephone communications to commercial aeroplanes in the US, to its range of high-rise telephony. Through some 100 000 in-flight phones on 1700 commercial jets Claircom's link with Iridium will facilitate the sending and receiving of calls in the cockpits and the cabins of both commercial and private aircraft.

Despite the capital costs of securing entry into this 'dial from anywhere' world Iridium will face competition from a number of other providers and the earth's atmosphere is beginning to fill up with a lot of satellite hardware. San Jose-based Globalstar, with its partners France Telecom, Daimler-Benz Aerospace and Vodafone, hopes to be in the business of 'anywhere' telephony by late 1999. They are building a rival constellation of 48 low-atmosphere satellites operating from 1400 km altitude that is purported to be less complicated than the Iridium system. Rather than building intelligent satellites that can route calls between themselves as Iridium has done Globalstar's satellites will act as simple relays with all the complex processing done at 60 ground stations. This will cost only half as much to launch and set up as the Iridium system. Globalstar's handsets (provided by US partner Qualcomm) are expected to cost just over a third of what an Iridium telephone costs, but to begin with they will also only operate in a few key countries. A Ukrainian-built rocket carrying 12 Globalstar satellites suffered engine failure in September 1998 and although insurance will cover the cost of the $190 million payload restoring the lost time as Iridium signs up customers is another matter.

Another potential competitor is London-based ICO Global Communications. This company is owned by some of the world's biggest national telecommunications companies including BT and Deutsche Telekom and is building on the ICO system developed by Inmarsat to extend the GSM standard to satellite telephony. ICO Global hopes to launch its service sometime in 2000, but with only 12 satellites including two for backup. Fewer satellites are possible as they will operate in a 'medium-earth' orbit higher than those of Iridium and Globalstar but there is a trade-off between financing fewer satellites and minor delays in telephone conversations. ICO ran a half-page advertisement in a UK national newspaper in early 1998. The headline, printed over a large picture of an eye with the world as its cornea and a satellite hovering over it, read:

> By the year 2000 International Travel will be possible in the blink of an eye.

It then went on to emphasize how this wonder would be delivered by employing only 400 people.

> Blink your eye and one of our satellites could have dealt with 4500 calls to anywhere on the face of our planet. ICO is taking mobile communications technology to a new level by using 12 state of the art satellites to link people any time, anywhere on the planet – on land, at sea or in the air – with high quality digital voice, fax, data and message services. A project backed by $2 billion from 59 leading telecommunications and technology companies in 51 countries and all this with just 400 staff world-wide. [5]

## The mobile Internet

The possibility of a fast satellite link-up offering 1.5 megabit processing across the Internet at less than a tenth of the cost of an earth-based digital pipe is an attractive prospect for companies who currently have to pay around $1000 a month for such a service. One consortium hoping to offer low-cost Internet connectivity through a mobile device via satellite is Teledesic whose investors include Microsoft, Saudi prince Alwaleed bin Talal, cellular pioneer Craig McCaw and Iridium's 20 per cent stake holder Motorola. Teledesic has so far only launched a test satellite; it needs 288 satellites to cope with its massive data transmission needs, but it promises download rates as fast as 64 Mb per second which would be some 2000 times faster than most of today's modems. Skybridge, a venture of France's Alcatel with Japanese friends Sharp, Toshiba and Mitsubishi Electric, also plans to deliver fast Internet connections via 80 satellites to the world's more populated areas by 2001 while a private firm from Missouri called Angel hopes to do something similar, by bouncing signals off squadrons of high-altitude aeroplanes circling above metropolitan areas, by 2000. Yet another scheme, being developed by Washington-based Sky Station who already holds the necessary frequencies from the US FCC, envisages bouncing Internet services off huge blimps tethered 14 miles above large cities.

Satellite telephony has been slow to develop because in 1965, assuming that satellite telephony would always be a luxury and if it wasn't it might threaten their existing telecommunications monopolies, eleven nations handed Intelsat a virtual monopoly over the satellite business. Only in January 1998 did the World Trade Organization bow to the inevitable and open the earth's skies to satellite competition. Strange as it may seem to those of us who don't want to be in touch all of the time the market for satellite-based services promises to be vast, and like many other services operating at the top (luxury) end of a spectrum, very profitable. Like the first cold beer vendor on a hot beach Iridium hopes to satisfy the pent-up demand for its service among those nomadic elites prepared to pay top dollar for the first 'anywhere' service.

The range of technologies being explored in the wireless Internet arena is literally mind-boggling. However, fixed digital telephone lines and cable modems will soon be cheaper and better and it is unlikely that most urban citizens will choose dizzy pilots, blimps, or satellite connections over these or the faster cellular phones as they roll out. But commentators have always underestimated just how much we desire access to mobile communication. In 1982 there were only 43 000 people using mobile phones in the US and the most optimistic forecasts envisaged that number only increasing to around 900 000 by 2000. An estimated 40 million people used a mobile phone in the US at the end of 1998 and, as the US moves from a regional to a nationally-based mobile system the number will grow even faster. In the end it is likely that a range of satellite options from highly flexible to quite flexible will be on offer and how each is taken up will simply depend on what level of service individuals and companies want and how much they are prepared to pay for it [6].

## A number for life and a portable device for everything

Telephone users in developed countries can usually take their telephone number with them when they move house but the promise of a single telephone number that works wherever we are and irrespective of the 'kind' of telephone we are using, must be one of the most desired features of modern communications. The reality of a telephone number for life that can be used from a home telephone, a mobile phone or a portable communications device capable of a much wider range of functions cannot be far away. Business users could undoubtedly profit from the simplicity of access that a one-stop number provides but the details concerning how families deal with the allocation of such numbers could provide some fun. During late 1997 Logica, a software house in the UK, forecast that by the turn of the century 5.1 million Europeans will collectively spend around £2.7 billion per year via mobile commerce using a new generation of digital mobile phones. Putting its faith in its research and hoping to get in early to meet the anticipated demand Logica launched 'M-Commerce' – a suite of services to support mobile commerce in alliance with over 100 GSM operators world-wide.

Theirs is just one of a range of initiatives being taken by software companies to try and anticipate the next wave of communication mania and Europe's mobile hardware providers are also keen to ensure that they get some of the action. Nokia's 9110 communicator, a second-generation device about the size of a fat mobile phone with a flip-top computer screen capable of composing faxes, sending and reading Email and surfing the Internet, is a sign of the features that will be crammed into the small handset of the future. Similarly Alcatel, a large French telephone company, has been marketing a mobile phone called 'One Touch Com' which incorporates all the functions of a palm-sized organizer, such as an address book and scheduler, in a hand set small enough to slip into a pocket. The mobile phone as an intelligent, multi-purpose device is clearly in prototype mode in many parts of the world.

## Symbian or Microsoft?

The battle for the hearts and minds of those seeking the all-singing, all dancing, portable agent looks likely to be fought out between two rival consortia. One is mainly European-based and includes three firms that currently account for 70 per cent of the global sales of mobile phones; the other is US/Microsoft based, utilizing all the clout of Microsoft's Windows compatibility. Microsoft has formed an alliance called WirelessKnowledge with American mobile phone company Qualcom to produce the hardware and software to enable mobile phones to connect to the Internet and to stake a claim for its MS Windows CE operating system to be the operating standard for the next generation of mobile communications. Meanwhile PSION, a manufacturer of small personal organizer computers in the UK, has formed an alliance called Symbian with Nokia, Ericcson and Motorola to transform their digital personal assistant technology into a comprehensive communications tool. Symbian hopes to combine the experience of PSION in developing small, hand-held computers using its own (not a Microsoft) operating system with the experience of the world's three leading mobile phone makers to produce the ultimate in portable electronic communications.

The mighty Microsoft will of course pursue its own alliance with its usual vigour and market savvy. Policemen in Derbyshire in the UK already use Windows CE in small devices attached to mobile phones to communicate with the national police computer while out on the road. The facility to transfer data between mobile and fixed devices for all kinds of personal and field operations is seen as a huge market by computer makers, software developers and telephone companies. It is not easy to predict the standards that will come to dominate this valuable hybrid industry. Success for the Symbian group, all big players with a lot of financial muscle, could mean that the portable communications device of the future actually breaks out from the Microsoft womb. It could go either way. Handheld computer makers could offer devices with Symbian software in the hope of making them more appealing to customers with mobile phones; or the mobile phone industry could beat a retreat and adopt Windows CE to ensure that their devices link up easily with existing PCs.

## A mobile phone? That will do nicely

The mobile phone as a credit card may seem strange at first thought. However when you associate a mobile phone number so precisely with a person (perhaps adding a couple of digits known only to them) there is no reason why this number can't be used to make purchases with the charges appearing on their telephone bill later. At Helsinki airport there is a coca-cola machine that will accept a mobile phone number instead of a coin. Dial in your number and a can of coca-cola drops out, the cost appearing in amongst your call charges. They also have a car-wash in Finland which you can operate without leaving your car: dial 1 for wax and 2 for no wax.

Unique telephone numbers, in association with other identifiers, offer a perfect vehicle for some lateral thinking in the charging business. What with software companies wanting to be telephone companies, telephone companies wanting to be computing companies and everyone wanting to discover how to make money over the Internet a mobile device using a unique number that acts as a credit card to pay for the services that it dials up doesn't look so far-fetched. Perhaps Visa and MasterCard will be looking to put their badge on the intelligent mobile devices of the future or, better for them, to put intelligent mobile devices on to a credit card? The ubiquitous plastic that we use in lieu of money is after all just a 'carrier' – it is the unique number that is stored and recognized for being OK or not OK.

The greatest cost in the charging business is in the billing system. Those who already have experience of billing and already have a large clientele to bill can easily include other charges on a monthly statement. Gas and electricity companies competing in the UK market to undercut each other after de-regulation in 1998 basically cut costs by consolidating or re-structuring their billing arrangements – the gas and the electricity continued to flow down the same pipes and wires that it always had.

Turn a mobile phone into a computer with a unique code and the possibilities look endless. Mobile or fixed, intelligent or basic, the telephone has generated an accelerating range of responses in both our business and our personal lives. From freephone numbers and 'call centres' to the tyranny of the pager, the fax and the answer machine, the telephone has adapted itself to our insatiable desire for speedier and more convenient communication. Its new clothes are probably not anything like its originators expected but then technological evolution has never been easy to predict because the environment in which it operates is always changing. The coincidence of change between the social and technical domains, or even between different technologies, e.g. one needing the other before it can accomplish something that we want, is a mystery that is not easy to predict beyond 10 or 20 years. Almon Strowger, just seeking to even up the playing field to bury the dead in 1905, could not imagine the playing fields that his invention of the dial telephone eventually helped to even up. In 1912 the Wright brothers would have had difficulty imagining Concorde or a stretched Boeing 747, let alone a passenger making a telephone call home from one.

## The new sweat shops

Just over 30 years ago the AT&T 'invented' the idea of the 'freephone' number. This has developed as one of the world's most useful marketing tools. Just sitting there in printed advertisements, mail-shots and in TV advertisements, much like the more recent W3 address, its object is to work hard at growing business by encouraging that freephone call to buy or discover more about the product or service on offer. Apart from 'new' 'free' must be one of the most potent words to put in front of another word in any marketing context and, in a classic example of the synergy between competing forms of communication, freephone numbers are often distributed on paper delivered to homes by the postal service. Many homes now receive two or three items of such 'junk' mail, mail-shots, catalogues, freepost return cards, etc. everyday and their rubbish bins are full of the paper to prove it.

Over the last five years we have witnesses new ways of selling old services by telephone. Banking, insurance, catalogue purchases, cinema tickets, groceries, CDs, T-shirts, holidays and computers are now all accessible by telephone thanks to the availability of virtual money as represented by a unique number and an acceptable expiry date. Cold-calling by house decorators, double gazing salespersons, credit card companies, telecommunications operators and those offering free holidays from heavily disguised time-share companies represent the semi-criminal end of the telephone sales spectrum. They have played their part in prompting a range of colourful responses and coping mechanisms from domestic telephone users, most of which can't be printed here.

As banks and building societies close branches they are increasingly replacing the expense of manned counters with cash machines, supported by the telephone and the Internet for more complex transactions. To cope more effectively with telephone purchases and enquiries companies that do a lot of business on the telephone now often set up their own internal call centres or buy in the services of agents working from big call centre warehouses. In the US around 3 per cent of the workforce is now employed in such and the business is growing by around 40 per cent a year in Europe. In the UK it is similarly growing by more than 40 per cent a year, with 1 in 10 of all new jobs being related to telephone sales or enquiries. It is expected to reach 1 per cent (c. 240 000 jobs) of the UK workforce by 2000. Given this kind of growth the regional economic development agencies in the UK now compete as hard to get a call centre set up on their patch as they used to do for a new plant from Honda or Toyota. To cope with the anticipated demand for training in the skills required to organize these people-stocked warehouses the UK's Open University now offers a course for call centre managers. The first UK centres in the 1970s tended to be set up within 60 miles of London. In the 1980s the South West, the Midlands and Yorkshire became favoured locations and the 1990s have seen a positive move to the North East, Scotland and Wales. These moves, though driven primarily by cost, have been made possible by a more robust and flexible telecommunications network.

Airline ticketing is one of the most active telephone services and in the late 1980s British Airways (BA) employed 900 people at Heathrow selling airline tickets by telephone. But a more reliable telecommunications network allowing enquirers to call at local rates or to use freephone numbers from any part of the UK, allied with smart switching that allows calls from busy lines to be redirected automatically to less busy centres, has facilitated a significant dispersal. BA now has centres at Newcastle (600 jobs), Glasgow (450 jobs), Manchester (430 jobs) and Belfast (270 jobs) [7]. Generally call-centre staff working outside the south-east of England are paid much less and they tend to hang on to their jobs, thus reducing the company's training and assimilation costs. Less than 5 per cent of BA's regionally based sales staff leave every year compared with the 35 per cent who churned over when most of them worked at Heathrow. In gross employment terms dispersal is often accompanied by other cost-saving measures and the net loss from one location is often greater than the gains made at another. In the 1980s BT employed 10 000 people handling directory enquiries, most of them in London; now the total number of staff spread around the UK, all located outside London with some working from home, is only 4000.

As we would expect telecommunications companies are big in the call centre business and BT is one of Europe's largest operators. BT is moving on from only handling inbound calls to launching outbound, or pro-active, operations from six new telemarketing centres at Warrington, Glasgow, Belfast, Bristol, Newcastle-upon-Tyne and Doncaster at a total cost of £100 million and with a total staff of 3500 'agents'. Most of these will be employed part-time and about half of them will be supplied by external agencies in order to give BT maximum flexibility in coping with the peaks and troughs of demand. BT already employs 12 500 'agents' in its existing inbound call centres to handle billing queries, fault reports, operator services and calls for sales of equipment such as fax and telephone answering machines. The Merchants Group, a management consultancy, has built a 450-seat communications centre at Milton Keynes in the UK that services 43 countries and offers 'agents' speaking 25 languages. It is one of the most advanced communication centres in Europe, taking more than 250 000 calls each month on behalf of clients from financial services, technology, utilities and the pharmaceuticals industries who have outsourced their call centre operations.

Achieving effective integration of the technology is a major and expensive challenge for those setting up call centres as the required economies of scale, until recently, precluded anything smaller than a 150 seater operation which required some very complicated connections between telephone, computers, switches and software. Now with 20–30 seat systems becoming available the call centre is coming within the reach of the small to medium-sized company but getting the best technology is still essential. People represent 65 per cent of the cost of a call centre and if callers cannot get through to 'agents' because of blockages in the system their time is wasted and customers are lost. As is often the case with developing new technologies, to solve local problems BT hopes to sell on around 50 per cent of its call load balancing and networking software, developed by the US company Genesys, to its corporate networking clients to help recoup some of the costs.

Call centres tend to employ women and students, often as part-timers, and they spread themselves around a bit to prevent the kind of spatial competition that might drive up the price of cheap female labour in any particular region. As telecom costs fall competition from overseas call centres will grow. Ireland is currently marketing itself aggressively as the 'call centre of Europe' and has attracted several American firms (that old US/Irish link again!). Call centres, however a company dresses them up, will always have the look of tidy sweatshops. Answering telephone calls all day can be stressful with many people talking simultaneously at rows of computer terminals. Staff working at careline centres set up to handle customer complaints, like those at the Lever careline who handle customers' questions about the company's foodstuffs and cleaning products, can find their day particularly tiring. In the UK HMV Direct, the telephone-based branch of the high street music store, takes some care over its recruitment, looking for people with good communication skills (they conduct the first interview over the telephone) and a passion for music. They believe that their low 4 per cent staff turnover compared with an industry average of 10 per cent shows that their selection techniques work.

Unfortunately very few companies invest in people development at call centres, at least at this stage of their evolution. Many corporations see their call centres as a form of cheap distribution, always looking for the lowest costs per call, rather than increasing value. Too often the managers of such centres are measured and rewarded on the basis of driving down costs rather than reflecting on how they can invest in value. If the customer only has the chance of interacting with the company via the telephone then whoever answers the phone *is* the company and how their request is dealt with generates a memory just as lasting as any exchange across a desk or a counter. A better name for these information production lines might be 'customer centres' – after all it is where the organization collects all the information about customers, their preferences and the success or otherwise of the products or services it offers, as well as picking up some information and comments on competitors' products on the side. Investing in some training to tap better the collective knowledge of the people who work the telephones would be a good idea as they will know more about customers – how they feel and what they want – than anyone who sits reading printouts away in the back office. The proliferation of call centres naturally leads to a search, like the BBC in the 1930s, for the right accent, one with which we will all feel at home:

> '. . . one that is mellifluous, friendly and makes you feel like reciting your credit card number. In America it is believed that the inhabitants of Omaha have the ideal accent, and the city has benefited from an influx of jobs in 'call centres' which do everything from selling insurance to diagnosing computer faults. In Germany the Hamburg accent wins. And in Britain the evidence is mixed. A soft Scottish voice is often held to denote reliability, and a recent study claimed to show that people thought that a Birmingham accent conveyed criminal tendencies. [7]

Now we know why Irvine in Scotland is such a popular place for establishing call centres and why so few are springing up around Birmingham.

## What no answer?

Despite the hi-tech sophistication of the exploding call centre idea many businesses have not eradicated the frustration of no one being there when we want to make that all-important contact. Ring up any service provider, particularly a telecommunications provider, and the odds are that you will have to plod through a series of numbers to be offered a range of services whose descriptions only rarely fit the one that you want. Where they are not corporately funded freephone numbers these 'touch-tone' time-hungry hierarchies provide a boon to telecommunications companies everywhere. A Co-operative Bank survey published in the UK in November 1998 discovered that office workers are spending upwards of 45 hours per year plodding through a hierarchy of numbers and listening to music before talking to a real person. The same survey found that having to listen to country and western music while waiting on line was often the last straw for even the most patient of UK enquirers, nearly always prompting a quick end to their attempt to make contact. After all the plodding the survey revealed that often the caller didn't ever get to talk to a real person but was greeted by a computerized voice that just gave out their place in the queue. Rather than telling callers their position in a queue, which offers little by way of precision in regard to how long the caller still has to wait, smarter companies could organize themselves to give out the times when the assistant/s will be free to take calls?

The telephone as home-based sales counter has come of age and is doing good business despite the frustrations occasioned by its use in some arenas. The Internet as a virtual sales counter is beginning its advance towards doing good business. Its frustrations will be different from the telephone and from those we experience over today's slow networks but we should be in no doubt that there will be some country and western music somewhere in the works.

## What no message?

After some time away it is now common that our first port of call on arriving home is to press a button on an answering machine or call up our answering service to note down any messages that have been left for us. It is always a mixed blessing – no messages at least means no crises anywhere, but it might mean that our place in the great web of human connectivity has moved too far towards the back burner. If there are messages we can be disappointed if they are just confirmations of appointments or family members reminding us of an errand or other job. Like 'waiting by the telephone' the answering machine has become something of a repository for our hopes and dreams, particularly during complex personal transactions. In the absence of an answering machine citizens of the UK can dial 1471 to discover the telephone number of the last person who called them; in the US dialing 1471 provides the caller with the numbers of *all* those who rang and how many times. In the UK one half of the population is voraciously checking 1471 to see who telephoned while the other half are dialling 141 before ringing a number to stop it being discovered later if no one answers first time.

'. . . when the three of us found out about 1471 Sharon said she was dead against it, considering it exploitation by British Telecom of the addictive personalities and relationship-breakdown epidemic among the British populace. Some people are apparently calling it upwards of 20 times a day. Jude on the other hand, is strongly in favour of 1471, but does concede that if you have just split up with or started sleeping with someone it doubles misery potential when you come home: no-number-stored-on-1471-misery, to add to no-message-on-answerphone-misery, or number-stored-turning-out-to-be-Mother's-misery. [8]

Although taken from the fictional diary of a thirty-something single girl obsessed with finding a partner, who when contemplating the US facility shudders at the thought of her multiple calls to an indifferent boyfriend being exposed, like all good satire it reveals uncomfortable truths about ourselves. Although the telephone has been an unreserved boon to mankind it has its fair share of sadness and alienation. Because it is so easy to pick up a telephone and make contact a disinclination or failure to make time to connect over the telephone is often interpreted as a serious act of rejection. They for whom such absentmindedness is just a part of their frantic lifestyle, or simply a long-standing refinement of indolence, are amazed how seriously their forgetfulness can be rated when it comes to telephone expectations.

## Can't live without it

Expecting or dreading a telephone call is just one aspect of the huge story of the social impact of the telephone. So much of the daily communication that we in industrialized countries take for granted is based on it, depends on it or stems from it. Indeed so many of our transactions, appointments to make transactions and our feedback from transactions involve the telephone that it would now be difficult for us to imagine a world without it. And yet a large portion of the world's population have never used one and even in developed countries a significant minority of people don't have personal access to one. For them a telephone call involves an excursion to a friend's house or to a telephone box and is something special. The huge installed base of telephone users means very little to them as they are not part of it, nor are they part of all the other agendas that the conquest of space and time by telephone facilitates.

## Dial M

We don't usually involve the telephone in our murder plans but in Alfred Hitchcock's film *Dial M for Murder* a man uses a telephone call to his house to bring his wife to a place where a confederate is hiding to murder her. The telephone call elicits the desired effect but the murderer fails to overcome his victim and is killed by the struggling wife wielding a pair of sewing scissors. The husband's alibi, that he was at a dinner with friends at the time, is supported by his having made a previous telephone call from the restaurant to his office. In the 1998 remake of this film entitled *The Perfect Murder* the husband dials his wife from one (secret) mobile phone to bring her to the killing point while his other (known) mobile phone is set up to make a long call to a computerized financial service. In the first version of the story a telephone call, as well as instigating the attempted murder, was cited in support of an alibi; in the second version a call from a mobile phone to a computer *was* the alibi. Although the first version, made in 1954, was a far superior film the 44-year gap between it and the second had made the telephone the star – an intriguing metaphor for the central place that it, together with computerized sources of information, now claims in our lives.

## References

1.  Haywood, T. (1995) *Info-Rich – Info-Poor*. London: Bowker Saur

2.  *Investors Chronicle*, 31 July 1998, p.90

3.  'Telephones from Toledo to Tierra del Fuego'. *The Economist*, 12 December 1998, p.96

4.  Armstrong, C.M. (1998) 'It's all coming together'. In *The World in 1999*, London: The Economist Publications

5.   *Daily Telegraph*, 5 Feb 1998

6.   I am indebted to an excellent article titled 'E.T. – Phone Home' by Declan McCullagh in *Time*, 23 November, pp.52–55, for much of the company information used in 'Karen's Question'

7.   'Call centres: a nation of telephonists'. *The Economist*, 1 November 1997, p. 36

8.   Fielding, H. (1996) *Bridget Jones' Diary*. Picador

CHAPTER FIVE

# Wires, beams and modems: the Internet

## Part one: birth, early life and the corporations

A new kind of relief; that warm feeling you get when you receive an Email that you don't have to answer.

### From APRA to asset

Hardly a day now goes by without some mention of the Internet in some medium or another, including of course the myriad of celebrations of itself within itself. Almost all TV, magazine and poster advertisements now include a W3 address and many newspapers and general interest magazines include features on 'best sites' or 'site of the month' as well as directing readers to the delights of their own site. The Internet is a network of networks that can be accessed from anywhere that has the use of a telephone line, a fibre optic cable, spread spectrum radio or satellite communications. Initially developed in 1969 as a project within the US Advanced Projects Research Agency and initially known as APRANET, its origins lay in the desire of APRA researchers to share the files held by other scholars on distant computers. In this research environment early inter-networking developed alongside a range of other ideas and technologies, e.g., queuing theory, packet switching and electronic mail, each of which added a valuable component to the improved utility of the electronic networking jigsaw. In those early days academics used the new network for electronic mail, bulletin boards, news groups, sharing software and drawing down large files of statistical information.

The current structure of the Internet still reflects its 'no central control' evolution with no one body owning or controlling the use of it. Something like a cross between the PC and citizens' band radio its rules are made and policed by the users or, more precisely, by those users who are active enough to want to make rules and police them. New users, particularly commercial users, do not always find it easy to comprehend the de-centralized, freewheeling and somewhat anarchic nature of the Internet. On the other hand academic users, always more at home with anarchy than organization, see the growing intrusion of commerce as a mixed blessing which, while massively extending the range of content available, could also lead to calls for a more secure and a more cost-conscious, central control regime.

There is little doubt that the Internet is becoming both a strategic communication asset for many existing enterprises and the inspiration for completely new forms of enterprise, as in e-commerce, e-lancing and particle marketing. A growing army of 'intrapreneurs' will influence its shape and structure over the next decade in ways that will be quite different from the current uneasy co-habitation between business, academe and computer science. Whether a 'grown-up' Internet will lose all the innocence of its youth or, like a 1960's radical mellowing into late middle-age, it will retain some of its old anarchy it is too early to say. Like all evolving technologies it will change and some of those changes will inevitably bear the stamp of corporate intervention in all its many guises, including some that we haven't seen yet.

## The new Penny Post

On Rowland Hill's retirement as Post Office Secretary in 1864 the UK Prime Minister William Gladstone said of Hill's creation of the 'Penny Post', that 'his great plan ran like a wildfire through the civilized world'. Up until 1840 in the UK the addressees had to pay for all letters turning up at their door. Rowland Hill's mother, anxious and poor, once had to send him out to sell a bag of clothes to raise the three shillings needed to pay for a batch of letters. In 1837, after an indifferent response to his ideas from the then postmaster general, Hill published his ideas in *Post Office reform: its importance and practicability*. This report pointed out that postal rates had now soared above most people's means and should be reduced to a flat rate of 1 penny per letter. Hill contended that each letter cost only a fraction of a penny to deliver whether it travelled 100 miles or to the next town as the overheads – sorting, stamping, mailcoach maintenance and the wages of drivers and guards – were the same for every item irrespective of the distance travelled.

In many ways long-distance telephony on the cusp of the millennium is in the same situation as the pre 1840's postal service. Charged for by distance and duration long-distance calls are priced at premium rates and many domestic users, fearful of the mounting telephone bill, balk at making many intercontinental calls, and when they do they tend to keep them short. The Internet by contrast is the new 'Penny Post', using the one flat-rate price of a local telephone call to connect to anywhere in the world. In the US a local call is often either free or very cheap, so that relatives and friends scattered across north America or on the other side of the world and who have Internet connections, can chat forever on Email without worrying too much about the cost. With the increasing availability of real-time talk software, which is poor quality at the moment but improving all the time, the possibility of mimicking a long distance telephone call poses a real threat to the telecommunications operators in the very domain where they have created their most profitable margins.

The old postal service was in the grip of sedate conservatives who could not imagine it changing in any way. The Post Office secretary at the time, a Colonel William Maberly, told a Parliamentary Select Committee that Hill's ideas were 'fallacious, preposterous, utterly unsupported by facts and resting entirely upon assumptions'. He also pleaded that it would take the Post Office 50 years to recover from such loss-making lunacy. On the first day of the Penny Post, 10 January 1840, 112 000 Penny Post letters were sent throughout Britain, three times the national average. The rest of the year saw postal volumes double to 140 million items, tripling in 1841 to 208 million. The floodgates had been opened and nearly everyone who could read and write could now afford to send a letter. The social and economic impact of this move is probably not easy to quantify but a myriad of benefits over and above cheap communication, including much improved commercial contact and incentives to gain basic literacy and educational skills, were carried on its back. The following quote from a 1997 report issued by the International Telecommunications Union compares the culture that lies at the heart of the Internet with that of the telecommunications companies, a comparison not unlike that which might have been made between the old and the current versions of our postal system:

> The Internet grew out of the dynamic young and unregulated culture of the computer software and networking sector. The telecommunications industry is more sober, highly regulated and moves at a slower pace. [1]

## Growing! Growing! Growing!

In mid-1997 a joint UUNet Pipex/*Internet Magazine* pamphlet, produced as a beginner's guide to the Internet, heralded the following (now very old) 'Internet Facts':

- There are one million Web users and 2.7 million people using Email in the UK.
- Of those online 66 per cent are male, 75 per cent are employed and 90 per cent are between the ages of 18 and 44.
- Nearly 23 per cent of UK business executives are online.
- The number of Fortune 500 companies with Web sites will double in 1997.
- The total number of Web users is predicted to rise to 50 million in 1998 and pass the 200 million mark by the year 2000.

A short *Financial Times* piece in September 1997, reporting a UUNet 'multicasting' initiative to improve the efficiency of publishing over the Internet, noted that such initiatives were needed to cope with bandwidth traffic which it noted was doubling in volume every 90 days. In February 1998 *The Economist* reported that the number of Web sites worldwide had risen from 55 million to 230 million over the year to October 1997. The same report noted that the density of Internet hosts per head of population is growing fastest in Scandinavia, particularly in Finland (c. 99 hosts per thousand people) and Norway (c. 66 hosts per thousand people); Britain was well down the list at around c. 16 hosts per thousand people. At this rate there could be more Finnish Web sites than Finns who, as with mobile phone use, tend to top the charts in the assimilation of connecting technology.

Low telephone charges obviously encourage Internet penetration and, except for Denmark, are partly the reason for the busier Internet scene in Scandinavia than in Germany for instance, where telephone connection costs are at least twice as high. English as a strong second language also helps, given that the majority of Internet content still comes from the US. The American concept of a 'free' or 'nearly free' local telephone call when extended to the rest of the globe should catapult home-based Internet use into the big league although European telecommunications operators are likely to resist this for as long as they can.

Notwithstanding the high cost of a lengthy local call in the UK the UK's *Mail on Sunday*, quoting an NOP Research Group survey, reported in March 1998 that the number of Britons accessing the W3 had quadrupled over the past two years to 4.3 million. They used it mainly for Email and 'leisure' – whatever that might be. The same research highlighted how some employers were getting worried about employee's use of W3 in the workplace for time-wasting fun, including accessing pornographic sites and playing games. BT was one employer cited as having banned the 'improper use of the Internet at work', while 48 per cent of IT managers in UK companies with over 500 employees were said to have taken action to restrict employee's use of the Internet to prevent abuse. The survey went on to highlight how susceptible we are to advertising on the W3 with 32 per cent of people who had seen an advertisement on the Web in the previous four weeks of the survey having made a related purchase either online or from a shop. Regular Internet users send fewer letters (31 per cent of regulars sent out less mail), make fewer telephone calls (24 per cent used the phone less), spend fewer hours watching television (21 per cent watched less) and read less newspapers and magazines (11 per cent said that they read less). None of this is really surprising given that people in work who can afford to use the Internet will also be those with a limited window of leisure time. As this time, despite our optimism about what the end of the century would bring in terms of an improved work/leisure balance, does not seem to have grown in quite the way we expected, it is obvious that time spent accessing the Internet will be at the expense of time we would have allocated to other diversions.

When it comes to purchasing across the wires those that feel it safe to do so currently buy computer software and hardware, books, cars, toys, CDs, CD-ROMs, independent holidays, videos and magazine subscriptions, with clothes, package holidays and electrical goods trailing some way behind. Internet commerce is currently a hotly discussed issue but as UK media planning and buying firm Western International disclosed in July 1998 many people are still fearful to buy over the Internet. Two thirds of the 3000 people surveyed said they would be interested in buying from a simple TV form of access but were worried about security and convenience. Of those surveyed 68 per cent said that they feared that their credit card numbers would not be safe, 58 per cent thought delivery would be too slow and 79 per cent worried about high prices. By the end of 1994 around 3 million people used the Internet in one form or another. By 1998 this had grown to 100 million people and over 100 million Emails were being sent every day.

A variety of projections of Internet use in 2005 suggests that it could encompass as many as one billion users. There is something about numbers that both captivates and comforts all Internet commentators and enthusiasts. Like the number of people who drive cars, own washing machines or videos, Internet statistics are rolled out as a sign of both massification and virility, shrieking the 'don't be left out' kind of message that is inherent in so many published statistics.

## Never mind the width what about the quality?

Handy as they are in giving us a guide to the penetration of the Internet all such data need to be taken with a hard disk-full of salt. It is time to move on now from simply counting connections and servers to learn a little bit more about 'why' people use the Internet and 'how' it impacts on their lives. Surprisingly the 1997 claim that 'nearly 23 per cent of UK business executives are online' doesn't seem very impressive for a technology that they must have been told more than once that they couldn't live without. That 'nearly' is all the more poignant since many 'registered' Internet users within big corporations, although notionally warm, ambulant and connected to a hole in the wall, are often dormant rather than active users particularly if they are over the age of 50. Note how much Email to executives is obviously answered by their secretaries or assistants or doesn't get answered at all. Of course the latter phenomenon is time-limited and as younger Email users get older they will remain active users, only stopping to sigh over how much faster connections are 'now' than when they first used it in the 1990s.

However accurate or inaccurate the number of users on a particular date there is no doubting the rapid march of the Internet on many fronts or the speed and ingenuity with which those involved with developing new products for it have responded to the gathering force of its wave. One of the characteristics of that ingenuity is the shorter and shorter time-scale of innovation among internet companies in order to retain a competitive edge. However, we should also step back a bit and recognize that to the uninitiated some of the 'major' developments in browsers, search engines, modem speed and the like are no more than they would expect from a technology that they have repeatedly been told offers them easy and unlimited access to infinite stores of information. Indeed many people expect much more by now. Having honed their own biological browser and search engine to a high pitch they find the keyboard discipline, uncertainties of access, poor ease of use, lack of organization and the time-consuming false trails of the Internet tedious and unfulfilling. Those of us who have embraced the step-by-step improvements as they came along with alacrity are prisoners of memories of the even cruder facilities that we once had. Those without such a history come to it with much higher expectations of specificity and convenience than it currently accommodates and often wonder what all the fuss is about. Of course we know that it will change; nothing that relies on a keyboard for access can become a commodity. Even with a TV-like remote control the steps will need to be reduced by a factor of four or five before families sit before their interactive digital TV/computer for a night's 'surfing'. Even then a communal reading of text from five or six feet away is unlikely to prove very attractive. It is chastening to remind ourselves of these things. As impressive as the Internet story is, it is not yet for everyman – indeed it may require another decade of development before the swapping of Internet stories in the pub becomes commonplace.

The Internet has grown rapidly over the last five years, having spent the previous 24 years quietly developing at the hands of enthusiasts and researchers. No sudden explosion this – more a slow 'big bang'. For the pioneers those 24 years was a time when they enjoyed membership of a club of clubs, where they connected with like-minded others to help, aide and abet each other, to have a bit of fun and to revel in the erudite pleasures of an elite, almost secret, network of global communications. The pre 1990s part of their story is well documented; some of the more recent highlights are noted below.

## 1992–1994: Father Tim and Brother Marc

There have been many 'seminal' moments in the life of the Internet wave, some of which are included in the selected chronology at the beginning of this book. Early 1992 was the time that the first 'killer' application, Tim Bernners-Lee's World Wide Web hypertext software, entered the public domain and this has to be recognized as a key moment. Armed with the ability to click on one 'hot' heading to lead to another it created the opportunity for a new and now the most sizeable part of the Internet, the W3, to grow and blossom. Tim (Old Father Web) had created a big new room on the Internet but getting into it required a different kind of front door if it was to appeal to more than just nerds and geeks. During September 1993 Marc Andreessen and others at the National Centre for Supercomputing Applications at the University of Illinois released a W3 browser called Mosaic. This, the second 'killer' application, enabled people using the W3 to apply the same kind of 'point and click' graphical manipulation that Apple had introduced in the early 1980s and which was later taken up by Microsoft in their more widespread but clumsier Windows operating system.

The back end of 1994 became the time of the browser, the time of online services chasing browsers and the time when Microsoft almost woke up. In October of that year, just six months after they had formed Netscape and building on Andreessen's work on Mosaic, Jim Clark and Marc Andreessen posted the first version of their Navigator browser on the Internet free to anyone who could download it. The 'give it out free' strategy which they started on that day has become a part of the new economics of the Internet and a marketing ploy that Microsoft with its deeper pockets would emulate later. Netscape's idea was to get its application loaded on to as many computers as possible so as to become an Internet standard. Achieve that and everyone else, including Microsoft, whom everyone wants to beat, would be left way behind. Once the product was established in users' hearts and minds, more refined versions could later be sold to individuals and licensed to corporations, all building on the familiarity which had once come free. Netscape's timing was perfect. The growing numbers of Internet users were hungry to explore the connectivity that W3 gave them. In 1993 the number of commercial sites available on W3 was only around 50 but this had exploded to nearly 10 000 by the end of 1994 and Navigator offered the friendly interface that John Doe wanted.

In Redmond, Seattle browser technology was not yet a priority at Microsoft who, just like the paradigm-locked IBM of the past, still saw themselves as kings of 'stand-alone'. This was a mind-set that, for a brief moment on the computing time-line, was to generate another of those computer industry 'if only' folk stories, if such a young industry can have folk stories. In the autumn of 1994 Microsoft held talks with two browser companies Booklink and Spyglass, the latter holding the rights to the still popular Mosaic browser. But Microsoft, following its usual 'pay-once' policy, refused to offer royalties to Booklink who quickly found an alternative home at the then rapidly expanding America Online. By this time Microsoft had set up their own browser development team but they would not have their own browser ready for six to twelve months, it certainly wouldn't be ready to bundle in with the all-important launch of Windows 95. In December 1994, after much angst, Microsoft signed a deal with Spyglass for Mosaic and this was duly incorporated into Windows 95. In 1996 the Internet made the front pages of the tabloids. Web site addresses began to appear in product and service advertisements and at the end of television programmes, both the print and audio-visual media were running regular features and documentaries on the Internet and ordinary people without a computer started asking each other what a modem was. It was also the year in which one 'sleeping giant' woke up to tackle the threat of an aspiring one.

## 1996: bombing the Internet

In 1995 on the 7th December (the same date as the surprise attack by the Japanese on the US Pacific fleet at Pearl Harbour in 1941) Bill Gates, Chairman and Chief Executive of Microsoft Corporation, addressed a meeting of analysts and media people in the Seattle convention centre to declare war on Netscape. Microsoft, though now awake, had been dragging its feet over the Internet. As a supplier of operating systems and software applications for PCs that generally stood alone, it had watched the growth of the Internet and Netscape in particular with the bemusement typical of the near monopolist who, prisoner of a particular mind-set, sees its hold on that monopoly slipping away. 'Stand alone' was giving way to 'stand together' and Microsoft, although incorporating Mosaic in its software, had not quite yet worked out the potential size of this new force. Connectivity was starting to become big business and Microsoft, for once, was on the outside looking in. Netscape's Navigator browser was looking like the next Windows with the potential to supplant the traditional 'Windows-inside' operating system in favour of one that could be squirted down wires in infinite configurations. Recalling the words of the Japanese Admiral Yamamoto 'I fear we have awakened a sleeping giant' on the day of Pearl Harbour, Bill Gates declared a full mobilization of his troops to fight on a new front. With a 1995 market valuation of $70 billion, sales of $6 billion per annum and a workforce of over 19 500 Microsoft was a software-supertanker that needed to pilot a nimble turn-around. But it would now start to re-orientate and all new Microsoft projects would be pointed in the direction of the Internet. During 1996 Gates backed his words by initiating a supreme effort. Dumping some sacred projects and dipping into $1.5 billion from the company's 'rainy-day' pile (it had hardly ever 'rained' for Microsoft) he re-focused one of the greatest bands of knowledge-workers in the world on cracking the Net.

In the spring of 1996 Microsoft unveiled its Internet Explorer 2.0 which was poorly executed and just as poorly received; it obviously needed much more work. All effort was thus directed towards developing Explorer 3.0 and this was duly released in August 1996. This looked more like the 'killer' application that Gates wanted. Matching Navigator feature for feature it worked well and following the Netscape example it was made freely available to download from the Internet. Promoted in such a way Explorer notched up a million downloads in its first week (Netscape's Navigator was then retailing at $79 per copy) sending Microsoft's share price to a new high and Netscape's share price down, from its high of over $70 to a new low of $35.

Two weeks after the launch of Microsoft Explorer 3.0 Netscape unveiled plans to create a new software company called Navio. As well as Netscape this new company would include partners like Sony, NEC, Nintendo and IBM, with the eventual aim of developing a super-product to take over many of the operating system functions of Windows and to browse local files as seamlessly as Navigator browsed the Web (see below). In a bid to get some 'applications' power into its portfolio Netscape also joined with Sun Microsystems who owned the rights to the highly flexible Net-based programming language Java, which had the potential to include software applications that could compete with such Microsoft products as Word and Excel. The 'Web Wars' were settling into attrition mode – a poker game with high stakes: a massive pot for the winner and nowhere to go for the loser.

Early in 1997 Microsoft issued Explorer 4.0 raising the stakes in software refinement time to half a year and falling. Schumpeter's 'perennial gale of creative destruction' [2] underlining the transience of all monopoly positions was finding its most animated apotheosis in a software industry that he could never have imagined. However his thesis – that all monopolies self-destruct in the face of incessant innovation – was not one that Microsoft was willing to accept lying down; the 'gale' might be raging but perhaps it could be stopped by employing a bit of muscle. Spyglass, which still holds the rights to Mosaic, the original Web browser, decided that it couldn't take the heat from the accelerating competition between Netscape and Explorer. The company boldly turned its attention to developing software that would enable users to access Web pages and send or receive Emails from the non-PC, new generation devices, e.g. special TV sets and smart telephones, that many commentators expect will now take over from the PC. Its new mission is to establish itself as the premier provider of browsers for this arena; however the market for these devices has yet to materialize and, despite some success with Motorola and General Instruments, Spyglass is currently struggling to secure profitable licensing revenues for its technology. Netscape's browser had raised the spectre of the PC operating system becoming a commodity with all the added value (that Microsoft had so ruthlessly exploited) residing on the Internet. This vision, of dumb computers connecting to intelligence and rich resources outside their plastic cases, was an anathema to a company whose wealth was based on the 'control' of all the functions that had, up until the early 1990s, occurred inside a box.

## Justice and the free market?

In early January 1998 Netscape shocked the markets and its supporters when it announced that it expected losses of around $87 million in its fourth quarter of 1997. The share price plunged 21 per cent and Netscape looked very mortal. Since then Microsoft's share of the browser market has soared from only 2.9 per cent at the end of 1995 to over 49 per cent by August 1998. Netscape's one time 80 per cent share of the market had slid to 63 per cent by the end of 1996, sliding further to just under 48 per cent by August 1998. Since the end of 1997 Microsoft had been fending off charges from the US Justice Department that it was using its monopoly power to insist that all computer manufacturers install its browser on their machines as an 'integral' part of its Windows 95 operating system. In December 1997 a US judge issued a preliminary injunction forcing Microsoft to make available two Windows applications to manufacturers, one including the browser and one without, and to remove the 'Explorer' icon that automatically appears on the computer screen when a user starts the Windows system. Microsoft promptly offered a two-year-old version (antique by software standards) of Windows to any manufacturers who chose the 'without' option and the latest version of Windows to those who stuck to the Explorer 'within' version. The US Justice Department and many in the computer industry regarded this as an arrogant contempt of the court ruling. In January 1998 a slightly humbler Microsoft agreed that, for the time being, i.e. until the full hearing of the primary case over whether or not it had violated the 1995 anti-trust decree, it would 'hide' the 'Explorer' icon in the Windows 95 system without removing the software. After all its new Explorer 4 browser would still be 'within' the operating system whereas the user would have consciously to buy or download Netscape.

This phase of litigation against Microsoft ended on May 12 1998 when the US Appeals Court ruled that shipment of Windows 98 could proceed as planned. However six days later the Department of Justice, joined by the attorneys general of 20 states, brought a new suit against Microsoft alleging a much broader range of monopolistic business practices. These included barring business partners such as hardware manufacturers and Internet service providers from distributing or licensing non-Microsoft products, unlawfully tying products together (such as Internet Explorer) with Windows and using its monopoly of the PC market to try to monopolize the browser market. In addition the states' suit alleges that Microsoft used illegal tying to promote its Office suite and Email package Outlook Express. This wider anti-trust case began its hearing in October 1998 with the Justice Department's opening statements being made beneath a three-metre-high, computerized video monitor hosting a larger than life image of Bill Gates. The US Justice Department was clearly putting Bill Gates front and centre as the force behind Microsoft's plans to dominate the world technology market.

## First mover advantage: the virtuous circle

During this flurry of litigation Microsoft has argued that it has the right to continually enhance its operating system in response to customer needs and that it is being unfairly penalized for fulfilling the American dream – i.e. being successful. Monopolies tend to get to where they are by being 'too' successful and distorting markets by their power. The spirit of the American dream, as Standard Oil found during the early part of this century, is to celebrate success as long as it leaves other dreamers with a bit of space and being dream-greedy is not good form. If it had been Apple Computers with its minuscule 8 per cent of the market bundling in a browser with its operating system the same questions would not have been raised. It is Microsoft's dominance of the PC operating system market that makes it look like the bully in the schoolyard. Over the last decade Microsoft's strategy, facilitated by its huge cash reserves, has evolved to respond to competition on three levels. First denigrate all non-Microsoft innovations; second seek to incorporate them if they look threatening; thirdly dominate them to remove the threat. It is this attitude in association with its market-place power that has built it up into a 'hate' figure among its industry competitors. All technologies manifest increasing returns from adoption. The more a particular technology (e.g. Microsoft, Intel, Cisco, Yahoo) is adopted the more experience is gained in their use, thus the more research and development effort is devoted to them and the better they become. This effect is particularly dramatic in the case of 'network' technologies such as telephony or the Internet where the utility of the technology to one user is very much dependent on how many other users are connected. The networking economy is one that attaches value to plenty rather than scarcity.

> This means that early adoptions – achieved for whatever reasons – may give a particular technology an overwhelming lead over actual or potential rivals as that technology enjoys a virtuous circle in which adoptions lead to improvements which then spawn more adoptions and further improvements while its rivals stagnate. Technologies, in other words may be best because they have triumphed rather than triumphing because they are best. [3]

By getting into hi-tech markets first companies can soon come to dominate them, impose price controls, block entry by others, stifle innovation and use their dominance as leverage into other related areas – they gain what regulators call 'first mover advantage'. Shapiro and Varian [4] have called this 'positive feedback' – the tendency for technology winners to take most, if not quite all, of new markets, and they describe a 'tipping effect' when one technology emerges as the winner giving its owner the opportunity to lock customers into particular technologies.

This advantage is driven by being first and by being taken up by a large population of users but it is also a mixture of two bigger questions. The first of these is the question of 'network externalities', i.e. do free-market forces guarantee the success of the best products in hi-tech fields, as it does in other areas of commerce? Or does Schumpeter's 'gale' turn into a puny draught once a hi-tech product has such a large installed base that it becomes the de facto industry standard from which consumers dare not stray? Secondly, and possibly the most important, does achieving such a position allow hi-tech companies to leverage this advantage to expand quickly and easily into other related markets, dominating them in the same way and doubling or trebling their influence? Microsoft truly dominates the current PC world and it has sufficient cash reserves to take on and crush any new entrant. Its former market valuation of $70 billion, which seemed so vast when Bill Gates targeted the Internet in 1995, had multiplied 3.7 times to $260 billion by 1998, overtaking General Electric as the US's largest company by market valuation. Given that 'paper' valuations of companies can ebb and flow, measuring a monopolist by profitability might be a more useful guide to their 'predatory and exclusionary' practices. In 1998 Microsoft's net profits of $4.5 billion were greater than those of all the next 49 biggest software companies put together. When the US Attorney-General Janet Reno suggested that she might seek to fine Microsoft $1 million a day for their non-compliance of the 1995 'consent decree', one San Francisco radio commentator noted that if Bill Gates were to pay it personally he would not run out of money until 2095!

Microsoft's relationship with Intel, the near monopoly supplier of microchips to PC manufacturers, is also cosy and mutually reinforcing, if not always harmonious. When Intel was involved in development work on Internet and operating-systems software that would rival Windows Microsoft asked it to stop and, rather than alienating its most important business partner, Intel halted the work. 'We caved', Intel's Any Grove later told *Fortune* [5]. Microsoft has always been suspected of implementing operating system code changes in its own brand of applications before releasing them to other software manufacturers.

Clearly Microsoft's position in the PC world is one of a monopolist owning the rights to an industry standard which it builds on and modifies in a way that imprisons customers caught up in the legacy of their installed base and it uses this advantage ruthlessly. My favourite Bill Gates joke:

> How many Bill Gateses does it take to change a light bulb?
> None: he calls a meeting and makes darkness the standard.

captures the way much of the world sees Microsoft and its determination to impose its will wherever it can in order to retain its grip on the PC market. Microsoft often defends itself by pointing to all the other successful applications that turned into failures proving that securing a dominant market share is no guarantee of on-going success. But Word-Perfect, dBase and Lotus 1–2–3, all of which lost out to Microsoft products, were all software applications. They had to run on Microsoft's operating system because it was there and Apple, the only other competitor operating system in the PC world, would not (big mistake) license its product to other computer manufacturers. Building Internet Explorer into its operating system clearly extends the hand of Microsoft deep into the bowels of 90 per cent of the world's PCs and while not actually instructing us to use it, its role as the 'default' option almost dares us not to.

Integrating software applications with the operating system is really only an issue because of Microsoft's dominance of the latter in the PC world. In a few year's time when the networked PC and its hybrid the 'thin client' gain more acceptance the distinction between an operating system and an application will begin to look like a quaint part of computing history. Oracle, a leader in database technology, has a mission (see below) to eliminate the computer operating system by mixing 'operation' and applications into one seamless whole. Late in 1998 Oracle agreed to an arrangement with Sun Microsystems to combine its industry-dominant database software with Sun's networking technologies to create business systems that can be used in E-commerce Web sites and corporate information. By mixing Oracle's popular database software with the core functions of Sun's Solaris computer operating system the new operating system becomes 'invisible'. We can expect to see an acceleration of moves to merge operating systems with applications over the next few years, all in the name of seamlessness – not to mention clipping Microsoft's wings.

## More engine choice

Our problem is that where we are now, and where we will be in the near future, is 'Windows World'. We don't see, with Microsoft standing at the door, how we will get out of 'now' or, if Microsoft continues to hold the keys to the near future, how it 'long' it will dominate long term. If 90 per cent of all the cars in the world, however different they looked from the outside, could only run with one engine made in Tokyo or Detroit, new engine initiatives would be springing up all over the place. But we do not overlay one engine on another and we do not need a particular engine to drive things like wipers, heaters, lights and air conditioning; we 'drive' Windows because, for the time being, it drives everything else. The PC world could do with more engine choice but such a high percentage of the players are tied into the current standard that moving across to try out other options, e.g. Sun's Java technology, seems too much of a risk. To paraphrase a common saying of the 1970s in relation to IBM: 'no one ever got sacked for buying Windows'.

This is just one of the 'market freedom' versus 'regulation' issues that the contradictions (i.e. rapid innovation alongside a huge installed base of legacy systems) in networking technology will continue to throw up. John McCain, the Republican who chairs the US Senate committee overseeing competition in US cable TV, once said, 'I strongly oppose regulation but I don't oppose regulation as much as I oppose unregulated monopolies.'

Monopolies come in many different forms but their aim is always the same: first to dominate the market and then to exclude others from it. The best outcome from the US Justice Department's action against Microsoft (the case is still going on at the time of writing), as with their suit against IBM's dominance in the 1970s, will be to discourage Bill Gates from exploiting his present dominance to delay the next stage of the computer revolution. We may have to accept that the occasional breaking up of monopolies, although time-consuming and hard to do, is a normal phase in the hi-tech business cycle. Companies gain first mover advantage, they become more powerful, they buy up or destroy competitors, they seal their partners' lips with ruthlessly tight contracts and they wield their power to take over other markets. Eventually competitors complain, regulators get restless and a big showpiece case is held in the public domain. Past break-ups suggest that the divorce can often inject a new lease of life into the separate parts. AT&T was forced to spin off its regional telephone lines as Baby Bells and Standard oil was chopped up into Mobil, Exxon and others, and these smaller companies have flourished. However the pendulum seems to be swinging back towards consolidation in a number of industries including oil and telecommunications.

With the benefit of hindsight we can see that the 1970s ruling forcing IBM to share key technologies with rivals and to break up some of its businesses actually improved its chances of survival. Opening up its technology broadened the market for products that in the end it controlled. The ruling made IBM realize that it could not now run the market all its own way and that it had better shape up. It became, temporarily at least, nimbler and more aggressive and eventually spread into the completely new support operations that it is now managing with great success.

Bill Gates says that Microsoft does not stand in the way of innovation and at one level he is right – anyone can write applications to run on Windows. The Internet is too big for one man or one company to dictate what its future might be. But while the main gateway to it is the PC, Bill has his hands firmly on the keys and that may just be enough to inhibit those who would like to explore new territory or to enter from a completely different door. It is often said that a policeman on a street corner never knows how many crimes he may have prevented by just being there. Similarly with Windows inside 90 per cent of the world's PCs we will never know just how much innovation it is stifling by just being there. Biodiversity is a clarion call of the ecologists who wish to preserve a world where nature's great panoply of creations is allowed to flourish. 'Compudiversity' could be the clarion call of software developers who would like to try new stuff without it having to 'fit' in with Windows. Even those who write applications for Windows say that they do not have sufficient access to the crucial Microsoft codes that marry the applications to the Windows software. One result of the anti-trust case could be that the court could order and then supervise the sharing of Microsoft's application–programme interfaces (APIS), thus ensuring a level playing field for all programmers who want to write for Windows.

## No life inside: the network computer

Netscape was joined in the battle to break Microsoft's grip on the computer industry by another colourful player who had earlier predicted the death of the PC as we know it, and who was just as keen to see 'Goliath' get a poke in the eye. During mid 1995 Larry Ellison, the clever eccentric at the heart of database supplier Oracle, announced that the $500 network computer (NetPC) would soon replace the need for a complex piece of hardware full of dedicated software. His view was that cheap, simple machines should soon be able to draw their intelligence and power from the Internet without the need for 'much inside'. He also believed that after 15 years the PC had become too complicated and expensive to reach new markets and, more whimsically, that 15 years was about the right time for the technology to shift gear and throw up cheaper and simpler solutions. At that time the mandarins at Microsoft, again taken a bit by surprise at the credibility and support with which Ellison's ideas were greeted, reacted to these speculations defensively. They insisted that the PC, with its unbeatable economies of scale, continued to harness and integrate the innovative powers of an entire industry rather than a single company and that it would continue to prove the most appropriate and flexible individual node of an expanding Internet.

Since that time Microsoft has conceded that their will be a place for the NetPC which would, of course, continue to utilize Microsoft software somewhere at its heart, wherever that heart may be. In May 1997 Gateway 2000 became the first big PC manufacturer to start selling NetPCs aimed at the corporate market. Microsoft soon promised a 'zero administration' software for such machines, the 'zero' being a promise of an 'eventual' zero, not a current possibility. In May 1997 they also announced the 'Windows terminal standard' that would make it easier for cheap and cheerful desktop machines to display any Windows software that might be running on a central computer. While ahead on prophecy Ellison's Oracle proved to be slow on delivery as new NetPC machines using Oracle's own software were late arriving in the market place, the first ones only arriving during the summer of 1997. However Oracle maintained its desire to offer a real alternative to Microsoft by buying up Navio, the spin off company initiated by Netscape, whose main thrust was to integrate Netscape's Web browser technology in hitherto non-Navigator consumer-electronic devices such as TV set boxes and games machines.

Netscape and Oracle have been joined by Sun Microsystems, the makers of powerful workstations and servers, in the anti-Microsoft lobby. Sun is important for the Java programming language that it launched in 1996. Initially seen as a way to enhance Web pages, Java was soon hyped as the new 'killer' application. Its great advance was that it was an 'open' system, i.e. platform-independent, and small programmes written in Java, called applets, could be distributed over the Internet and downloaded to run on any computer, be it running under a Windows, Unix or Macintosh operating system. The Java 'virtual machine' is like a computer within a computer and building it into most Web browsers means that it can adapt any Java programme to run on any kind of operating system. In theory this means that software developers could write their programmes once – 'write once, read anywhere' is the claim from Sun – without having to start all over again for different operating systems. The source code of Java can be licensed and downloaded for evaluation; the specifications are freely available and anyone can voice an opinion to influence changes to the technology. Most of all customers who purchase or build applications using Java technology can run them on any operating system: i.e. they have a real choice.

As presently constituted Microsoft's business model allows neither openness nor choice in the same way. As if to add a second front in the struggle with the software demon Sun Microsystems sued Microsoft in early 1998 claiming that it had violated a 1996 licensing agreement by fiddling with Sun's 'open' Java code in order to create a version that would run only on Windows. Microsoft replied that its alterations were only for the good of the consumer since they made Java programmes run better on Windows and then counter-sued, claiming that Sun itself had broken the 1996 contract by introducing a new Java dialect that did not run as well as the old one.

As always there are lots of grey areas. When it comes to altering Windows Microsoft treats even a proposal of change by a third party as high treason whereas Sun has been known to be more indulgent with other software firms, like IBM, that failed its Java compatibility tests. In November 1998 a Federal Judge in San Jose, California, in a preliminary injunction, ordered Microsoft to stop shipping its 'special' Java and to re-write it to make it compatible with the Sun original. Microsoft was also ordered to make it clear to software developers that its Java code is incompatible with Sun's version of the operating system. This minor setback probably did more damage to Microsoft's gung ho psychology than to anything else. Losing is not something that Bill Gates sees in his stars. Losing in public to its old enemy Sun, whose cherished aim is to replace Windows with the son of Java, while Microsoft was busy defending itself against the Justice Department in Washington, was definitely not in the game plan. Lawyers could never have dreamed of the lottery win that disputes over the ownership of intellectual property in the form of computer code and software parameters are set to shower on them, as the fingerprints of each new process pass from one entity to another.

## Sustainable development

Ellison's original idea of the NetPC has not been taken up as fast as many industry watchers expected and while the $500 PC may be still some way off, it does not seem as far-fetched as it was in 1995. Home-based computer users however will need a lot of convincing that all the applications that they use every day can be squirted down to them reliably on demand across the Internet with less trouble than having it stored on their very own hard disk, despite its occasional glitches and bugs. The advantages for companies and big corporations seem more convincing: one set of operating software held on an easily maintained in-house server, less need to 'attend' and service individual machines, easier access to glitches and less opportunity for users to mess about with the system, etc. – just like the advantages that the old centralized 'computer centres' used to enjoy when they provided access to all the organizations' information from juggernaught mainframes via dumb terminals!

But systems managers are notoriously conservative and few will be willing to give up their familiar Windows software in favour of a yet-to-be-proved Java-based system just to get less tampering and easier maintenance, and anyway they can get a lot of networking functionality out of the slowly improving, if bloated, Windows NT. The NetPC has opened up the old debate about user control versus MIS control in organizations, centralized versus distributed systems, desktop power versus inexpensive access and individually-owned information versus the active sharing of mission-critical information between workgroups and enterprises. Interestingly electronic networking in organizations, seemingly such an inherently decentralizing force, might yet bring power back to the central systems managers. They may seek to convince the management that a dozen or so departments all buying devices which suit their particular needs is incompatible with the standards needed for effective networking irrespective of local needs. Also their constant reminders to CEO's about network security and the vulnerability of the various databases held in the system could, in some settings reinforce a fortress like approach which limits departmental freedoms to innovate. Some central standards are necessary to facilitate effective networking but without hospitality to some trickling upwards of imagination from users centralization tends towards a lowest common denominator approach that satisfies no one and stimulates the inevitable growth of parallel, patchwork solutions at departmental level. The oft' repeated mantra of 'we must listen to what the users want' sometimes rings hollow in the world of corporate networks as systems managers, cheered by the move back to central control, seize the opportunity to mandate, rather than cooperate with the users of the system. These issues are not likely to be resolved by blockbuster, once-and-for-all solutions. Most organizations move from one investment in IT to another gradually and always with one eye over their shoulder. Legacy systems (see Chapter 8) can hang around for a long time and there is growing resistance to the 'must get the latest whistles and bells' culture which has dominated the last two decades of computer marketing.

As the NetPC's promise has dithered so the original idea about what a networked device is has got fuzzier. Indeed all the signs are that as a generic name it will not now mean very much. However the concept of a 'thin-client' – a device with only some very particular stuff 'inside' – looks like just the kind of hybrid to emerge out of the PC/NetPC debate in the short term. Such a device would be more tailored to the user, and concomitantly users would have to show more confidence in specifying their needs a little more precisely than they have done. For this effort they would gain the comfort of faster processing for the applications that they use every day while drawing down the whistles and bells that they use only occasionally from a network. The idea of sustainable development, which originated among the agencies dealing with third-world self-determination, is fast being appropriated by those who procure IT for both large and small organizations and the common standards of the Internet are helping them in their mission. The Internet is driving what kind of screen-linked device we will want/need in the future. All the evidence (what a hostage to fortune that word 'evidence' is) is that we will use a wide range of devices, many of them of the 'thin-client' type, for general applications alongside a wide range of application-specific devices for fast, reliable service in particular domains. However difficult it is for us to contemplate the forces for change are now so strong that 'Windows World' as we know it is a time-limited advantage for Microsoft.

## Portal, portal on the wall . . .?

America Online's successful bid for Netscape Communications in November 1998 provided a slight breeze of change across the Internet landscape. Associated as it was with an important side-deal, to give Sun Microsystems licences to market Netscape software to corporate clients, it created a new competitor to the 'portal' services of companies like Microsoft's MSN and Yahoo. This new troika is particularly keen to develop user-friendly gateways for the devices other than computers, such as television-set-top boxes and pagers, that they believe we will be using more and more in the future. Repeat usage is the key to attracting advertizers to the portal and Netscape, despite its battles with Microsoft's Explorer browser, has impressed industry observers by its direction of around five million people a day to its Netcentre site. Before buying Netscape AOL earned most of its revenue from its 14 million subscribers; by adding these to Netscape's Internet audience AOL hopes to gain more access to the kind of advertising and commerce revenue that a popular gateway now attracts. The 'portal' is a refined Internet gateway that, as well as facilitating access to the Internet and its wider 'free' information world, instantly showcases a range of retail and other services in addition to the advertising banners that are now a common feature of Internet sites. The aim is to offer lots of interesting and difficult-to-ignore features that the operator hopes users won't be able to resist before leaving the gate to explore further.

This mixture of service provider, search engine and shopping facility requires partnerships between hitherto separate business models. Key brands will be sought out to front these portals, much as developers of retail sites seek to sign up key brand names for a project before they go ahead with a shopping centre or a mall. Banner headlines, special offers, competitions and free offers will all be part of the portal's charm and we can expect to see a process of mergers and consolidation within the Internet industry to provide the kind of one-stop shop that media and telecommunications companies are also seeking to provide. The latter, of course, are already part of the Internet industry with telecommunications and media companies already owning or taking stakes in Internet-related companies and the portal could be the place where they all come together.

Just to prove that consolidation is not the sole prerogative of telecommunications providers the AOL and Netscape merger was closely followed in early 1999 by the purchase of Excite, an Internet portal service, by @Home, a company that provides high-speed Internet access over cable TV in the US. The loss-making @Home has access to a potential market of c. 60 million cable users although only around 330 000 of these are currently 'live' Internet users. @Home hopes to add Excite's audience of 20 million people who have a personalized Web page on its site to its own subscribers whom it will now direct to Excite's range of services, plus those using AT&T's service. AT&T owns 40 per cent of @Home and has an alliance with it to promote its WorldNet Internet service. It will be much easier for AT&T to move these customers seamlessly over to @Home's broadband/Excite service. The deal is particularly important to Excite giving the company access to the new market for high-speed, broadband Internet services across cables that facilitate much faster communication of data, audio and video material.

These two mergers underscore the growing competition among leading Internet portals to establish a dominant position prior to the Internet taking off as a more popular source of information, entertainment and consumption via digital TV. AOL (CBS provides it with news), Yahoo (does some cross-promotion with News Corporation), and Microsoft's MSN (joint venture with NBC) have established themselves as global Internet brands. This is forcing second-line competitors such as Excite, Lycos (merged with USA Networks' home shopping and retail operations) and Infoseek (43 per cent owned by Walt Disney and relaunched as 'Go') to look for new partners. The 'portal' hunger has to be fed from a variety of sources and it looks like a handful of big portal sites will dominate this part of the Internet world in the early years of the new millennium.

Until recently most of the interest in expanding the role of portals came from traditional media businesses buying a foothold in the new medium, e.g. Disney taking a stake in Infoseek and NBC's 19 per cent stake in Snap. However the valuations of Internet companies have reached such astronomical proportions that very few non-Internet companies can afford to buy into the sector. The dilemma for the traditional media companies, who produce and distribute content, is that they have learnt that every 25 years or so a new way of distributing content emerges. If they fail to invest early as it begins to roll out, as they discovered with cable, they live to regret it and so they cannot afford to be left out whatever the price. They have at least one ace they can play. The main barrier to entry on the Internet is getting noticed; this is something that the old-style, slow moving media companies know something about and can bring to the party of bright young things running the new Internet companies. The economics of the Internet are still evolving but combinations of regional telecommunications companies, Internet service providers (see below), portal companies and Internet retailers all joining forces to share marketing expenses in order to get a slice of the action looks like a model that will run for a time. The evidence of effective returns from advertising on a 'big' portal is not readily available yet. Although FirstUSA, a credit card company, paid $90 million to Microsoft's MSN to secure an exclusive advertising deal some commentators believe that advertising on smaller, more focused, Web sites, as well as costing less, may also score a much better hit rate from being better targeted. US consultancy Forrester Research, who is generally quite bullish about the future of commerce on the Web estimates that only about 0.07 per cent of total US advertising revenue currently goes into Internet sites and that this is unlikely to reach 5 per cent by 2005.

## The New ISP: branded and free

At the time of writing many home-based users of the Internet subscribe to an Internet service provider (ISP). By paying a subscription they have unlimited access to the Internet through the provider's many modems and big servers as long as they can pay their telephone bill. Sometimes like AOL the ISP offers access to 'other' services from which it derives income and sometimes the fee structure is related to time spent online. This model of providing an Internet service now looks to be time-limited as new entrants to this market begin to offer a free ISP service almost as an adjunct to other, notionally unrelated, services. In September 1998 the UK electrical retail group Dixon's began offering free access to the Internet by giving the 'connection' software to its Freeserve ISP free from its high street shops. By the end of 1998 they had given away 900 000 connections. Given that, at that time, the UK had just under two million home-based Internet accounts this was an impressive take-up rate which, after only 16 weeks of operation, made Dixon's the biggest Internet service provider in the UK. The 'Freeserve' challenge was a big blow to America Online (AOL) who painstakingly had taken four years to build up their UK customer base to 550 000.

Dixon's makes its money from Freeserve through a combination of advertising revenue, help-desk charges and a share of the call charges (its telecommunications provider is Energis) incurred while online. This last income stream is a new business model that looks to have a lot more mileage in it while European telecommunications operators continue to charge for local calls. However it is also a source of revenue that is currently being reviewed in the UK by Oftel, the telecommunications regulator. Two other ISPs, Internet Technology group, and Easynet were quick to follow Dixon's lead. Both these groups have links with telecommunications providers and they will generate income in the same way as Dixon's but they plan to link up with other partners, probably in the traditional media, to help them with the current high costs of publicizing 'free' services.

VIP, a part of ICL who provide brand-customized Internet access services, facilitated the Dixon's launch and provides a similar package to any business that wants one. At the end of 1998 around 1200 potential clients were talking to VIP about setting up as an ISP in a similar way to the service launched by Dixon's. These included retailers, football clubs and other major companies. Towards the end of 1998 VIP facilitated the launch of an ISP service for US retailer 'Toys Я Us' who distributed well over 250 000 of its 'Internet access' CD-ROMs before Christmas 1998. Such a business that specializes in toys and computer games has a ready-made audience for an Internet gateway, an audience that is young and yearning to be Internet savvy as well as a brand name which carries all sorts of warm signals to potential users of its service.

All of this suggests that the traditional subscription ISPs, if they are to stay in the straight ISP business, will have to differentiate themselves more clearly by offering better back-up services, greater reliability and other forms of added value. The move to free and branded ISPs looks similar to what happened to credit cards in the 1990s. Once upon a time in the UK there were only two or three credit cards charging whatever interest rates they wanted. Now there are more than 50, many of them branded, e.g. Ford, GM or Alliance and Leicester, or promoting an affinity of some kind, e.g. for a charity or a service link, or simply as a novelty as in the Frank Sinatra card. Many of these new cards offer much lower interest rates or allow their users to accumulate points or cash to use on future purchases and, although taking off slowly, it is now much more common for people to switch from one credit card to another to get a better deal.

As other well-known brands jump onto the Internet bandwagon by offering free gateway/content ISPs customers may also switch more readily between them to identify with a brand that better suits their lifestyle. Leading UK high-street retailers like W.H. Smith, Tesco (Tesco.net), Virgin and Electronics Boutique are all looking to capitalize on their retail brands the Dixon's way. Tesco's move is part of a strategy to mirror its bricks and mortar business in cyberspace by creating an online retail outlet linked to free access to the Internet. As well as groceries it will also sell a large range of household and 'lifestyle' goods through a deal with the German owner of the UK's Grattan catalogue who runs the world's largest mail order business. Unlike Dixon's 'Freeserve' which is open to anyone Tesco.net users must also hold the supermarket's Clubcard. As there are 10 million of these in circulation this should be no hindrance to Tesco building up a loyal Internet following.

Free ISP services using cheap local call charges will clearly interest more people in the Internet and, who knows, those that sign up for a free service may soon, as at Tesco, get bonus points or air miles for time spent online and for any purchases made. BT's free Internet service is called 'ClickFree' and offers a free connection with the possibility of low local call charges. Although obviously designed to capture new subscribers ClickFree is also aimed at those BT customers who use one of its current call discount schemes which would mean being able to connect to the Internet at less than the normal local call charge. BT has also linked up with Value Direct to give its ClickFree users the ability to shop online for products at lower prices than are available through other services. As noted above the buzzword in Internet land, for the next year or so at least, is 'portal' and retail brands who offer a free ISP will be keen to enlist non-threatening partners to join them to help defray costs and spruce up the portal doors with a bit of variety.

## Cable and new friends

The embryonic portals being developed and tested on the Internet are an important precursor to the kind of front-ends that companies will need to develop in order to attract visitors to Internet sites via digital television. The layout and user-friendliness of 'front-pages' as accessed via a PC can be tested and refined before the big push to family TV. In the US the cable companies have dominated pay-TV for years and the regulations applied to them have ebbed and flowed, first tighter and then looser, as the industry lobbied effectively or as the political will changed. Since the Telecommunications Deregulation Act of 1996 the regulatory climate has been at the looser end of the spectrum and the price of cable TV for the consumer has rocketed, prompting 'snails move faster than competition in the cable industry' comments from consumer groups. In the UK cable, though growing, is currently the weaker player and it is BSkyB, half owned by that old buccaneer of the skyways Rupert Murdoch, that controls both the main sources of programming, including a desire to own the nations favourite (and richest) football team Manchester United, and the main subscription channel.

Like Microsoft, with its legacy of control over PC operating systems, cable TV in the US and BSkyB in the UK profit from the kind of first mover advantage noted before. Such an advantage, in arenas where the capital needed to come up with competitive technology runs into billions of dollars, seriously deters new entrants. The race to digital television in the UK at the end of 1998, between BskyB and OnDigital, saw BSkyB straining every muscle in its corporate body to get started first. By offering a substantial discount if consumers also took the telephone link which enables easy pay-per-view at a later date they hoped not only to gain a first mover advantage but also to secure future revenues by making it much more expensive to sign up if buyers didn't take the telephone link.

The concept of a regular payment for each service called down the Internet or accessed via digital television is a mouth-watering one for all delivery systems and all content providers. If they prove attractive to consumers such income streams offer a dream ticket to all those involved. It might be just a few cents per transaction but multiplied by millions, every day and every year, it beats the hell out of one-off sales. Microsoft also has its eye on those millions of cents' worth of repeat business and it is rich enough to buy or invest in whatever distribution technology it feels might prove useful to achieve it without the need for immediate returns. In May 1997 Microsoft bought WebTV, a company that makes software to convert television sets into primitive Internet terminals. Microsoft had already established a joint venture with the NBC television network, and in June 1997 it invested $1 billion in Comcast, the US's fourth largest cable television operator which owns a 50 per cent share in the US home-shopping network QVC. In early 1999 Microsoft moved across the Atlantic and invested £300 million in NTL, the UK's third largest cable TV company and it is widely expected that this will be followed by a partnership with NTL to boost its high-speed voice, video and Internet services. Later in 1999 Microsoft, as part of a complex deal with AT&T, purchased MediaOne's 30 per cent stake in UK cable operator Telewest showing its growing determination to be at the forefront of the rapid development in the cable industry.

All this re-positioning by such a software heavyweight gave new hope to the once moribund US cable industry whose billions of dollars of investment had thus far reaped little other than serious debt. Things would have been even worse for the US cable industry if its satellite competitors, unlike the position of BSkyB in the UK, had not been weak, broke and fragmented. However some recent consolidation in the US direct satellite broadcasting (DBS) arena could change the landscape. In 1997, to the cable companies' delight, their erstwhile *bête noire*, Rupert Murdoch, wanted to sell the assets from his failed US satellite venture to Primestar, the second biggest satellite operator in the US. The Justice Department blocked this deal because Primestar was owned by the same cable companies who were delighted by the move and who were unlikely to support the kind of vigorous competition between satellite and cable that was needed. Thus thwarted Murdoch sold his business, comprising a valuable broadcast licence, an uplink station and some satellite capacity, to his old rival EchoStar, the third biggest and fastest-growing direct broadcasting satellite company in the US. At the end of 1998 DirecTV, the biggest satellite company in the US, merged with United States Satellite Broadcasting (USSB) and in early 1999 the cable companies threw in the towel and announced the sale of Primestar to DirecTV.

With two much bigger players, DirecTV and EchoStar, satellite competition with cable now looks more promising. But the statistics suggest that it will be a hard slog. US cable companies have 65 million subscribers while DBS has only 10.6 million. DBS is growing at 26 per cent a year but even if that rate of growth continued every year it would still take eight years for DBS to overtake cable's 65 million subscribers and the cable companies, busy rolling out digital cable across America, are unlikely to stand still and watch. One solution for DBS would be to team up with its enemy's enemy. Local TV stations in the US are beginning to go digital, and people will need set-top boxes to receive the signals. DirecTV hopes to negotiate with these local stations to sell customers a box that is able to receive both types of television signal – satellite and local terrestrial – a Trojan Horse that, if it caught one in a big way, would really raise the competitive stakes. At work corporate Americans often enjoy high-speed direct connections to the Internet while at home most of them churn through the copper wires like the rest of us, so any alliance that gives them a fast cable connection from home will be an attractive option.

The emergence of new partnerships between intelligence, content and distribution, though not always an instant success, during some 1990s experiments, has been a hallmark of the last decade and this will gain momentum during the first years of the new century courtesy of the generous hospitality offered by digital engineering. The coincidence of digital television with greater cable penetration in the UK also offers the possibility of faster Internet connections, more bandwidth and all kinds of opportunities to interact with the media. One of the great un-knowns is just how 'interactive' the current population of 'passive' TV couch potatoes will really want to be.

## It's been a ball so far

Since the development of Mosaic in 1993 every one involved with the W3 has been having a ball. The share prices of Internet companies like Amazon.com and Yahoo have shot through the roof prompting predictions of an Internet share bubble that must eventually burst. Most (pure) Internet companies have attracted investment from private shareholders in the US who want to make a quick buck and because sentiment tells them that these companies have a big future. Most of these companies don't make any profits at the moment, Amazon.Com included. During the current enthusiasm for these shares, and while the bubble lasts, making a profit from the Internet is regarded almost as a sign of low ambition and poor foresight – the future potential is the thing. At the end of the 1990s a profitable Internet company looks to be something of a contradiction in terms. The corporate battles over the Internet have been intense because all the signs are that it will eventually support a wide range of different 'service stations' along its many routes as well as increasing in importance as a medium of contact between individuals and institutions. Currently it is a diverse melting pot of actual and experimental services supporting scholars, schoolchildren, businessmen and the casual surfer without interference from a central control room. Its 'footprint' is not limited to the rotation of the earth and it can deliver information directly to a customer or potential consumer without mediation. The downside is that it needs special equipment (getting cheaper all the time) for access and its impact is currently restricted by the small 'pipe' of twisted pair telephone lines that most of us who connect to it from home still have to use. The 'big-pipe' future of broadband connections is not too far away (two years for the US and five years for the UK) and Forrester Research [6] forecasts that by the end of 1999 2.2 million households in the US will have a broadband connection. Two million of these will be using special modems designed to work on the cable systems that currently carry television signals.

> Forrester reckons that one in four online homes will have broadband access providing an 'always on' capability and speeds at least one hundred times faster than today's digital modems. Although the cable operators must spend heavily to upgrade their networks, it is clear that their new two-way digital fibre is a better platform for high-speed Internet access than the copper wire that the telephone companies still use for the last mile of their networks. On the back of this huge potential, the previously dull cable companies have become fashionable investments. [6]

Where do we, the potential users, figure in all this? Are our dreams for the Internet the same as those of the telephone and cable companies, software producers, search engine providers, advertizers, modem producers etc? Sometimes is the not very profound answer. All technology destined for mass/home use starts off complicated and expensive and gradually passes through several phases until it is much cheaper and simpler to use. Those who use the Internet extensively today have got used to its little foibles and by being active in voicing preferences and requests for modifications they play a part in encouraging changes that meet their requirements. Some of this feedback will become embedded in the kinds of browsers and search engines that we are offered in the future but those who don't use it now and yet who may pick it up, via say digital television, may still find the access devices complicated or counter-intuitive. They will certainly not be keen to use a keyboard and, heresy of heresies, they may find that there is not much out there for which they would want one.

The arrival of the free connection, from whatever source, like cheaper international telephone calls, will encourage more use particularly among younger members of any connected family. However I feel a bit like Colonel Maberly (see above) and his 'fallacious, preposterous, utterly unsupported by facts and resting entirely upon assumptions' when I contemplate the Promised Land of 'interactivity'. Try as I may I cannot envisage a world of citizen 'interactivity' at a distance of five feet or so. Choosing from a large menu of TV programmes, yes; paying to see recent film releases, yes; children locked into hours of computer games, yes; but constantly ducking and diving around a television set in search of 'interactivity', no. Maberly eventually had to eat his words and I may have to eat mine but I see the promise of interactivity as a very mixed blessing that will be driven mainly by marketing and sales forces rather than viewer participation or citizen engagement. In the UK the 'interactive' elements of the different digital television providers are currently planned to be small-scale and whatever 'facilities' there are will be exclusive to each service. This will have to be remedied early on in the life of digital TV if interactivity is to become a regular, rather than a marginal, feature of household life.

In the US the Justice Department versus Microsoft may not be the trial of the century but it could be the trial that ushers in a turning point in anti-trust law for all would-be monopolists of the next century. It took 13 years for the now 109-year-old Sherman Anti-trust Act to defeat IBM and Microsoft did not go gently into court on this occasion. However both the judge and the Justice Department say that they plan a Blitzkrieg rather than a war of attrition in this case so that it should all be over by mid-1999. If the Justice Department wins it will have to decide how to punish Microsoft without punishing the whole of the computer industry as well. Whatever the decision the fall-out will be just as important as the judgement. The contestability of monopolies in the hi-tech world of computing and the Internet is not easy to foresee although it may seem so in Microsoft's case. There is still not enough evidence available to measure how well-established companies might stand up against the 'gale of creative destruction' in the roller-coaster world of the ICTs.

Other amalgamations like that between AOL and Netscape, the adoption of the Red Hat Linux operating system by Compaq (supported by Intel and Netscape) and the growing use of Sun Microsystems' Java by programmers are just three developments that, in coincidence with others, could change not just the dimensions of the playing field but whether or not there is one. In November 1998 *Time* produced one of those popular 'top fifty' lists of the movers and shakers of cyberworld. Here the co-founders and chairpersons (only five out of the 50 were women) of companies like Microsoft, Sony, AOL, Intel, IBM, Yahoo, Apple, Dell and WorldCom were each 'written up' in about 300 words to explain their importance and justify their place in the list [7].

A hundred years ago a list of railway and steel making companies would look very different from the much smaller one put together today. A list of automobile makers made just 30 years ago and compared with now would reveal a similar contrast. Industries change both in size and impact over time and, despite claims that the ICT industries are different, they will also change, not beyond recognition, but in their richness and reach and in the role they play in our lives. In 30 years' time consolidations and mergers among the ICTs of today will throw up some mixtures that would surprise us now and in 100 years' time the whole electronic networking landscape will look very different. If we compare the life-span of the Internet to a human's this chapter has been about birth and babyhood: lots of tests to ensure that the system actually works, plenty of injections to boost the immune system, a lot of checking and sensing of the environment by chucking stuff around just to see where it lands, quite a few teething problems and a regular quota of messy disputes. Early childhood is where the Internet is now and so we should not be surprised to see a lot of experimentation, some shocks for the parents, a few bumps and grazes and the occasional stealing of someone else's apples. The next chapter looks at some of the school reports we can expect before graduation.

# References

1.    International Telecommunications Union, 1997

2.    Schumpeter, J. (1954) *Capitalism, socialism and democracy*. London: Allen and Unwin

3.    MacKennzie, D. (1996) *Knowing machines: essays on technical change*. London: MIT Press

4.    Shapiro, C. and Varian, H.R. (1998) *Information rules: a strategic guide to the network economy*. London: McGraw-Hill

5.    'Demonizing Gates'. *Time*, 2 November 1998, p.61

6.    'Broadband bottleneck', *The Economist*, 7 November 1998, pp. 109–110

7.    Just for curiosity's sake the five women in *Time*'s list were Ann Winblad (Venture Capitalist), Shelly Day of Humongous Entertainment (educational software), Deb Triant of Checkpoint Software Technologies (security and credit checking), Mary Meeker of Stanley Dean Whitter (technology stock analyst) and Aki Maita of Bandai Co. (who came up with the Tamagotchi electronic pet idea)

# CHAPTER SIX

# Wires, beams and modems: the Internet

'The Internet is fast becoming a global auction market and could comoditise most markets for products and services'

Ed Yardeni (1999), US economist.

## Part two: childhood and the e-word

All of the corporate and entrepreneurial activity set out in the previous chapter is serious and frantic because of certainty and uncertainty. Everyone is certain that the Internet, in one guise or another, holds the key to many new commercial, recreational, news and educational possibilities but no one is quite sure what the dimensions and user take-up of those possibilities will be or how they would make money from them. Those companies that live by the Internet, those that hope to live off it and even those that eventually might die by it cannot afford to be left out. Yet many of them have no idea how it might benefit their business except that the potential audience is said to be bigger than their wildest dreams. Their Internet world is very much one where the users are seen as customers rather than individuals seeking knowledge and enlightenment. Indeed they hope that the Internet will help them to define 'customer' in a much more precise and focused way. The non-commercial side of the Internet, the posting of information to inform and illuminate for the sake of informing and illuminating, is also growing fast and every schoolchild and student now knows that the answers to some of his or her questions lie out there somewhere in cyberspace. Government and International agencies, e.g. OECD, WHO, UN, UNESCO and EU, now make many of their reports and much of their statistical data freely available over the Internet, as do companies and amateur site-builders who guide each other around their own and other sites of interest. Politicians, princes, political parties and pressure groups have all taken to the Web to promote their ideas and to show themselves as they would like to be seen. The Internet is young and future developments may not resemble anything like the way it is used and promoted today but some interesting pointers are emerging from its colourful childhood.

## A warm embrace from the brotherhood

There are clearly signs that the conventional media – TV, radio and news-papers – are being cast in the role of Internet promoters. This is because they have an interest in utilizing it themselves, as an adjunct to selling their conventional products, and because news about what is happening on the Internet, e.g. novelties, crime, censorship, gossip and revelation, is difficult to separate from the medium itself. The latter phenomenon will be time-limited in that once we've heard that 'an Internet posting today revealed. . . .' a few more times it will begin to lose some of its novelty. A number of specialized magazines like *Wired*, *.net*, *INTERNET* and *Internet World* feed on the hunger for Internet understanding offering information on the latest developments, new sites and gossip about the Internet. TV companies are increasingly presenting programmes about the Internet, both of a 'what does this mean for life on earth?' and the more practical, 'what is it and what can you do with it?' variety. Also the youthful Internet, like digital television, BSkyB, Disney, Time Warner and other media companies, is often 'the' news as in the 'millions of dollars that new Internet companies are being valued at' and 'what you can do with it now' type stories. Traditional publishers have also been lucratively swamping the world with books about the Internet. The irony of so much paper to help explain electronic networking cannot have been lost on the suppliers of a medium so often threatened with extinction by the onset of an electronic Ice Age.

The Internet is becoming a part of the brotherhood of media that feeds on and off each other in a myriad of different ways. TV documen-taries, Internet magazines, radio interviews and movies that integrate the

Internet and the use of Email in their plot all help to popularize and explain it. Digital television with its two-way telephone link will soon begin the oft-proclaimed convergence of the computing, television and telecommunications industries bringing the power of the Internet to the masses. With a digital connection we will be able to spend our time fiddling with set-top boxes that can give us home-shopping, pay-per-view, our own choice of angles during a football game and any Internet page that we care to look at from five feet away. No one really knows how all this will pan out. Although some pundits anticipate that digital convergence will be the most transforming moment of the new century, just using it to grab our attention for more advertising could end up simply giving us a new definition of boredom.

## The attention grabbers go digital

All media are in competition for our disposable time and those who try to market and sell their products and services using the Internet face the same 'how can we secure their attention' challenges as those who wish to sell by TV, radio and newspaper advertising. We are now thoroughly used to content arriving in conjunction with advertising so the flickering banners that proclaim cheap flights, virtual bookshops or cheap software on Internet sites and search engines are as easy for us to ignore/respond to as those of other media. One gripe of many W3 users is that the banner-headline advertisements which run along the edges of many Web sites increase their telephone costs by taking too long to download. Of course Yahoo, Excite and other Internet companies rely on just these components to make their money and so they have little sympathy with personal telephony costs which, in the US at any rate, are free or very low. However in Europe local call telephone costs can still end up being quite expensive for serious Web users.

A piece of UK-developed software called Adfilter may be a sign of the help to come in regard to this problem. This software enables computers to filter out automatically any type of advertisements on Web sites; it thus speeds up connection times to sites with just one advertisement by an average of 50 per cent and those with two or more by 75 per cent. It uses 12 methods to detect if a graphic is 'foreign' to the page and so is likely to be an advertisement and it works in just the same way when installed on a corporate gateway to the Internet as it does on a home PC. It is not the kind of innovation likely to appeal to the fragile online advertising industry in the UK whose revenues for 1998 are estimated at £15 million but which are forecast to grow to around £480 million by 2002.

In the past the trick has been for the advertizers in all media to be clever, to 'be there' but not to overwhelm us. Digital television in conjunction with the Internet will offer all kinds of new possibilities for the attention grabbers. Integrating marketing and sales with content is a seductive idea and there will be some crass examples of this kind of cross-fertilization before it all settles down. While watching a TV drama we may press 'text' to obtain further information but if all it does is to tell us that 'the electric kettle Charlotte is using in this episode is the fast boiler now on special offer from Haywood Electrics' we are unlikely to call up the text very often. Some indicator during the running of TV advertisements, such as a whirling icon in the UK, will indicate to viewers that they can obtain more information via a click on a button. This will reveal a short menu of options: perhaps a free brochure, perhaps just to 'bookmark' the site to return to it later, perhaps a screen full of text about the product or perhaps an opportunity to arrange a test drive or an in-house demonstration of something. In the hugely popular television 'novellas' of Brazil it is not at all unusual for a brand of car, coffee, whisky, shoes or clothes to be given some extra close-up treatment as the story progresses. But in Brazil the audience has long been aware that the sponsors behave in this unsubtle way, and they have come to understand what is happening during lingering shots of static clocks and dressing gowns and so the subterfuge is slight. In the UK and Europe sponsorship of TV programmes, dramas and 'premier' film slots is now well-established and clearly labelled but digital television will make the demarcation easier to blur. Sponsorship can now be embedded in the proffered objectivity of a documentary or the content of a drama watched by audiences who are not used to recognizing or analysing such links. The depth of the partnership between the sponsor and the content may not be made known as explicitly as it has been in the past and audiences may require some help in disentangling it. A star system in programme guides could help: five stars and the programme can be written off as just one big advertisement, while one star could indicate that the content is almost sponsorless.

## Your story, their database

The post-modern remote control will become the key to a world of shopping and consumer information. We will be able to watch a pop concert then press 'interactive' for details of the band's records or the range of T-shirts on offer (complete with order form). We can watch a football match and then move on to the club shop to buy a scarf or to request more information about the players, again all while 'the heat is on'. After watching a holiday programme or travel documentary we can visit the sponsor's 'easily accessible' Web site to get more details or possibly book a holiday. There will be no need just to envy Inspector Morse as he relaxes in the pub drinking his pint of beer – just a click and you can be at the sponsor's Web site to order a home delivery six-pack of the same.

The aim will be to match advertising broadcasts to consumer preferences much more precisely than before and parents will be an obvious target. Children's programmes, already heavily marketed via supportive merchandising, will be able to offer books, tapes, life-like models, etc., from their programmes at the click of button and that 'must-have' latest craze doesn't even have to wait for a trip to the shops. Imagine the impact of a personal message to 'little Florence' inviting her to share a secret moment in Teletubby land. Television advertising already varies during the day to reflect what marketers call 'day parting', hence the plethora of 'funeral insurance' advertized on daytime TV. Digital will enable this to be done with much more precision via the central monitoring of consumer preferences. We dial up to show an interest in something and we end up in a category; we do it again and we get rated as a perfect target for similar goods and services. All of this precise information-gathering about consumers, and the 'particle' marketing that it facilitates, looks like a nightmare for data protection bodies and groups concerned about personal privacy. However the truth is that this kind of information agglomeration has been going on for a long time by all kinds of agencies and our responses to it have been weak. Indeed to gain access to many pages of stuff on the Internet we have gladly filled in electronic forms telling newspaper and magazine publishers a good deal about ourselves, so we can't really say that we're surprised when they use it. A recent US opinion poll discovered that 80 per cent of Americans believe that they have 'lost all control' over personal information. In Europe, where the state has always been intrusive but often reassuringly inefficient in handling the information that it holds, privacy of personal information seems to be a non-issue [1]. Personal privacy is now a lost cause in databased economies and much of the corporate involvement in digital television is unashamedly based on their desire to gain access to more and better information about customer preferences. A lot of information about our lives is collected, without our permission, by government agencies in the name of the public interest. They also use electronic networking to share it between them. If we don't want to add to the stores of intrusive information kept about us we should avoid giving it up voluntarily to private entities for trivial reasons (see Chapter 9).

## Jennicam and novelty

We can expect a continuing stream of novelty productions to appear on the Internet and to make headlines in the conventional media. One such was the Jennicam Internet offering from the US that delivered new photographs of the same girl's bedroom refreshed every two minutes 24 hours a day. Twenty one-year-old Jennifer Ringley was captured online sleeping, kissing her boyfriend, doing her make-up and playing with her kitten. At its height the Jennicam Web site was accessed over 100 million times a week and Jennifer offered a subscription service where 6000 'regular' viewers paid £10 a year to watch her nearly every move. The UK got its own 'Jennifer' in February 1998 courtesy of Bravo, an American-owned satellite television channel. The company said that it wanted a girl who was driven by a desire for fame but not a professional actor. The 'star' gets £50 per week for half a day's work responding to Email messages but her screen time is unpaid.

Whether a living history, a work of art captured on camera or just a window for voyeurs with a sad Internet addiction Jennicam will take its place along with weddings, supposed first sexual encounters, births and bizarre family albums as Internet novelties that will come and go. They are part of the culture of an emerging medium and we should not worry too much about what they mean for life on earth. All new media generate novelty; some of it will entertain us and some of it may cause us to despair about the preferences of our fellow human beings. As with the initial responses to commercial television in the UK during the 1950s, fears about the death of culture (in this case as represented by the gravity of the BBC) usually prove to be greatly exaggerated. Humans enjoy a bit of trepidation mixed in with the launch of a new medium but once it is established we eventually accept it and move on to indulge in new fears about the drop in 'standards' promised by the even newer media that are said to be just around the corner. It is now well established that commentators in old media enjoy urging us to worry about the potential pitfalls of new media. Worry sells newspapers and trying to work out what we should worry about next is part of the old media survival kit. Like their obsessions with the sexual orientation of politicians they eventually catch up with public opinion and discover that we don't rate these things quite as much as they think we do. Generating some despair about the impact of new media will always be with us and so it will be with the Internet in its novelty stage.

One aspect of the novelty scenario is the W3 fight-back by the famous who, whatever they try to do to correct stories about themselves or their families, have their words and actions mocked and disparaged by the tabloid press. The solution to the dilemma of how to 'get their voice heard' is now at hand via a W3 page of their very own. Live chat shows on the Internet can be the equivalent of the Feeding of the Five Thousand (in that a lot of people are reached with minimum effort) as George Michael's question-and-answer session about his arrest for lewd conduct in a Los Angeles lavatory and Tony Blair's gruelling question-and-answer session in April 1998 proved. Noddy, Saddam Hussein (the first world leader to celebrate his birthday online), The Rolling Stones and Michael Jackson, who used the Net to discuss divorce rumours with his fans, have all discovered the joys of an unmediated right of reply. This is ersatz democracy in action: the illusion of immediacy behind the protection of an electronic screen and, like the number of sites dedicated to the 'X Files', they look set to proliferate as a vehicle for 'my side of the story'.

## Not in front of the children

The intelligentsia often join the religious censors in societies in bemoaning the arrival of media that reach large audiences, particularly children. Children are regularly used as the touchstone by which we should test and critique any new media and the Internet, like television now and in the past, will be regularly subjected to the 'damage to children' test. However all the children I know seem much better informed, even by bad television, and have a much stronger sense of popular culture and how other people live, than children did in the pre-television 1950s. Indeed television has helped the barriers between different social classes and races to become more penetrable just as it has helped children achieve a greater psychological understanding of the world inhabited by adults. Seeing adults more realistically may make children more anxious but perhaps it also makes them wiser and less easy to manipulate.

There are many things about current affairs and contemporary life that only television can show and so to set out deliberately not to watch TV is to be cut off from a large slice of contemporary life and to be ignorant of a lot of what is going on. What the masses like is (literally) vulgar and so vulgarity is (by definition) what they will choose if they are free to do so, in television as in anything else. Vulgarity is part of the price that we pay for freedom. The Internet will throw up a lot of vulgarity and if we lived in Iraq, China, Afghanistan or Singapore we would probably be 'protected' from it. Over the last 50 years children in the West have, on the whole and aided by a bit of parental advice, learned to cope with and choose from a growing range of media offerings. They now live in a multi-media society and they will incorporate the Internet into the tapestry of their lives as they have done with other media innovations without suffering any serious harm. After all, as we have learned in the UK over the past few years, it has not been the confections of the media but real, live, dysfunctional adults, sometimes protected by the secrecy bestowed by authority, who have committed horrors on children. They succeeded in their perpetrations not because of media encouragement but because society still does not take children at risk seriously enough to check out adult behaviour behind closed doors. No media has depraved and corrupted children in the way adults operating in real space have, but it is always a useful distraction to blame media sex and violence while turning away from the reality.

This is not meant to be taken as a blanket approval of bad television or bad Internet content – there is much to be critical and vigilant about – but this vigilance is our own responsibility not that of the nanny state or those who would set themselves up as 'filters' on our behalf. Some big Internet players are already deciding that they won't allow certain material to flow via their service. Yahoo, one of the most popular search engines, has decided to exclude some content, e.g. how to make a bomb, how to blow up a building and all child pornography, from its database and we can expect more of this self-policing from the larger

Internet gateways in the future. Anthropologists maintain that societies tend to establish initiation rites that reflect their priorities, e.g. memorizing scripture in a religious community or making one's first kill in a hunter gatherer community.

In the US the Child Online Protection Act (COPA) of 1998 requires Internet purveyors of pornography to require some proof of adulthood before allowing access to their Web site. Chief among the acceptable forms of proof is a credit or debit-card number. As any new college student knows the credit card sign-up table is as common an introduction to campus life as booze and pot but now, along with a few flight discount coupons, it comes with the right to download pornography from the Internet. Most college students cite establishing a good credit record as their reason for getting a credit card but since the COPA it has also become de facto legal proof of majority, a kind of secular bar mitzvah. Visa and MasterCard surprisingly find themselves defining manhood and womanhood (i.e. if you have debt) and as Internet bouncers for those who don't make the rite of passage (i.e. can't be trusted with debt).

The spectrum of media content will never be even-handed between high and low culture; it will always be a messy mix that will keep us talking forever and so it should be. Who can agree on what is important or relevant in news coverage or on what is good and what is trivial drama? The world's media will never make a living by only appealing to the intelligentsia or the church. There is a lot of valuable content on the Internet posted by both commercial and non-commercial organizations and just like every other medium we have to take responsibility for seeking out what kind of entertainment or enlightenment we want. It is as easy not to click a button on a mouse as it is to turn off a TV.

## News and gossip

The Internet has clearly established itself as the quickest way to disseminate both gossip and hard news around the world. The Clinton Presidency, mainly via Al Gore, has championed the Internet in the naïve way that politicians do when seeking words to describe what they don't quite understand, seeing it as the superhighway that, foreshadowing the death of distance, would pull the world together in an electronic global village. It was thus doubly ironic that it should be the medium used to trigger Clinton's public disgrace, although we should not forget that it was those old-fashioned spool tape recorders and their incessant recording of all those gritty conversations in the Oval Office that accelerated President Nixon's eventual resignation. We can only imagine what any White House CCTV cameras would have captured in the Clinton case. After *Newsweek* pulled its early story on the Monica Lewinsky affair it fell to Internet gossip-columnist Matt Drudge to stir the pot. Alone in his bedroom in Los Angeles, he trickled out a succession of sordid details about Clinton, cigars and gifts via his 'Drudge Report' Web site, to millions of Internet users and there was nothing that the White House could do about it. As his site grew in popularity hard information was often leaked to Drudge by conventional newspeople whose publications were loath to print the more pornographic parts of the allegations (ironic again that in the end this was left to the Government Printing Office).

What Drudge had to say, as fact or fiction, was avidly perused by netizens all over the world who in turn posted his musings on to other newsgroups and the global domino effect was complete. Producers working for conservative radio stations in the US, particularly in the conservative and Republican South, would check out the Net daily for Clinton tales and have them read to their audiences prefaced with paltry 'taken from the Internet today . . .' disclaimers. The Internet as gossip sheet is here to stay and our challenge, as with so much information on the Web, is how to validate and cross-check it. Validation takes time and we are unlikely to want to spend hours checking one story against another. Eventually validation corners of the Web will emerge where we will be able to clarify the value of information. Until that time we need our friends and other media to test the information for accuracy and authenticity and report the results to us. We are used to handling partial truths and keeping an open mind about most news stories so information on the Web is really no different in that respect from conventional news media.

## Starr and Gripe

The House of Representative's decision to disseminate the Starr Report on the Internet, via 'Thomas' the House server, as the fastest way to get the facts to the American people saw the Internet come of age as a news medium. It had been used before to report on events such as the wonders of our galaxy as seen by the Hubble Telescope and to report the Louise Woodward judgement (delayed for an hour because of a power cut), but this was the big one. Rapidly digitized and made available for the entire networked world to read, and of course print out, the Starr report claimed a ferocity of attention. At the time conventional news media, TV and newspapers always prefaced their own coverage of the case by declaring that 'the report would soon be made available on the Internet'. Fearful that the volume of interest in the report would be so great that the network might crash the House of Representatives eventually decided to publish the report on several Web notice boards to ensure public access. Releasing the Starr Report on the Internet made all journalists equal, for a day at least, the only advantage going to fast readers. CNN, overwhelmed by the sheer volume of material cascading down to its computer screens, and lacking any alternative strategy to handle the speed of its delivery, decided to televise the report as it appeared with a correspondent reading the text straight off a screen. All the usual editorial standards and filters usually employed by journalists evaporated in the face of getting the story out fast. Presented with this instantaneous, raw, unfiltered information the role of the news editor was handed over to the American people who were left to decide what was worthy to print and what was not. Back in 1996 the White House had acknowledged in its so called 'Food Chain Report' that the Internet had wrested news from the manipulating hands of the President's own spin doctors and that this was the ultimate vindication of their musings.

The gossip-driven nature of the Internet is one of its great attractions for late-night surfers, and the powerful 'whistle-blowing' (see Chapter 8), 'grand-exposure', 'read-all-about-it' feature of its culture is an area which is only just beginning to be recognized by the more conventional news media. Everyone with a modem can be a tabloid journalist and they don't have to fear a 'stop-that-story' telephone-call from Rupert Murdoch. This feature of the Internet, non-validated and uncorroborated as it often is, is clearly modifying the relationship between authority, power and citizens among the vocal online population. Juicy Internet stories are picked up and re-packaged by the traditional media making them available to the great mass of people who never click on an icon. Information about what is going on inside companies, industry sectors and among individual investors now appears on many bulletin boards affecting company share prices and forcing CEOs and executives to make statements, confirmations or rebuttals on a regular basis. Much of the information disseminated in this way is unreliable and often turns out to be wrong but

there is so much of it that only a small percentage needs to be correct
to attract wider attention.

## SOS

In corners of the world where free speech western-style is suppressed
Internet bulletin boards offer their participants the opportunity to talk
about governments, ministers, corruption and abuse of human rights in
ways that they could never do in public or even among their own families. The drip-feed impact of news and entertainment via television that
enabled citizens in the communist regimes of Eastern Europe to observe
the lifestyles and opportunities of western capitalism was one-way.
Nonetheless it is often credited with helping to destroy the images of the
Dickensian state that were repeatedly promoted by communist governments. The Internet by comparison offers the opportunity of rapid
two-way traffic. Not only 'gosh, what a great time you guys seem to be
having, we want some of it' but also 'you would never believe what is
going on here'. This is bound to have an affect on those regimes where
secrecy and misrepresentation of external events continue to be the focus
of their propaganda. While traditional media magnates like Rupert
Murdoch may bow to the wishes of a regime like China's and exclude
material that they don't like from their satellite broadcasts in order to get
licences for now and in the future the Internet has no such restrictions.
As the dissemination of information about the fate of individuals during
and after the Tiananmen Square massacres of June 1989 showed the
Internet can send information about the fate of individual protestors
around the world faster than any other medium including CNN.

In November 1998 Anwar Ibrahim, Malaysia's former Deputy Prime
Minister, faced charges of corruption and sodomy in Kuala Lumpur. While
the Malaysian newspapers obediently followed the government line a
variety of Anwar Web sites put forward the alternative view that these
charges were trumped up as part of a high-level conspiracy to neutralize
a political rival. The Prime Minister of Malaysia Dr. Mahathir Mohamad,
another big Internet fan, must have had some doubts over his previous
enthusiasm for a 'wired world' as the world read this unstoppable alternative scenario. Paradoxically Anwar Ibrahim's claim that he was a political
prisoner would have been well reported in the west by conventional newspapers and TV but not in Malaysia. There the Internet, acting as a local

rather than an international newspaper, was the principal source of alternative information about his beliefs and claims of legal manipulation by the government.

A contrary picture emerged in Serbia during 1998. There the poor economic situation for the majority of people meant that access to wider satellite and Internet news coverage was restricted to a wealthy minority while the government of Slobodan Milosevic continued to sack university professors and close newspapers and radio stations in a political purge to stifle free speech. Web politics are unlikely to shake the foundations of corrupt or violent regimes overnight or to bring down corporations accused of pollution or evil working practices in poor countries. But their drip-feed of topical and up-to-date information into other media can build up a head of steam that is difficult to contain. The Internet as gripe sheet, putting forward alternative views to those promulgated by 'official sources' everywhere, is now well established in rich economies. Official government Web sites, however nobly intentioned, usually carry the stigma of 'not to be trusted' while unofficial, maverick sites are seen as places where the true situation will be revealed. Again, if we are sufficiently interested, we will learn to read between the lines of all the forms of Internet-speak just as we do with other media.

## E-commerce: sex and Mickey lead the way again

E-commerce is a generic term that can cover almost anything. All transactions across the Web that involve exchanging products and services for money come within its scope. The UK government's definition 'using an electronic network to simplify and speed up all stages of the business process, from design and making to buying, selling and delivery' seems to cover most of the angles. Aware that things move fast in Internet world OECD ministers from the developed world met in Ottawa during October 1998 to begin the task of forging some broad principles for regulating E-commerce.

> When radio was introduced to the US mass market in 1922, it took 38 years to build up a base of 50 million listeners. TV hit the market soon after the Second World War but managed the same total by 1964. Most observers reckon that the Internet went mass-market in the US less than five years ago. It has 50 million users already. The

OECD reckons that within five years up to 15 per cent of global retail sales could take place over the Internet. Include transactions between businesses, and estimates of the value of the market in the UK alone by 2001 range from £1.7 billion to £6 billion. [2]

The first great moneymaker on the Web was an old business – sex. Hard and soft pornographers have always jumped at the chance to sell sex using each new medium as it proves popular and sometimes, as with the Betamax versus VHS tussle, it may even help one form of medium to triumph over another. Satellite, video, CD-ROM, telephone, floppy disc even – they have all been put to use by a sex industry that is ever on the lookout for new outlets to complement their paper-based productions and the Internet offers them a near perfect vehicle. It is confidential, the unmarked brown envelope comes down the wires to adults sitting comfortably in private. It can be three-dimensional, it can be tailored to the predilections of individual subscribers as in 'please wear the red hat', it accepts all credit cards over encrypted pages, it can be constantly refreshed and distribution is about as cheap as you can get.

These same qualities are also attractive to non-sex commerce. The customer can be watching the Toyota, Mercedes or Chrysler pages unmediated and undisturbed by interruptions from anyone else. He or she can check out specifications, see the vehicle from different angles, read reviews and specify colour, engine size, upholstery and price range. At the moment a dealer (telephone number, fax and address supplied) will have to be contacted for a test drive but it could all be done without leaving the house until the dealer arrives outside with the model of choice. Choosing a flight, picking a rail itinerary and booking hotels are all examples of the kind of personal, unmediated transactions that are now popular on the Web. In June 1998 Disney purchased a 48 per cent stake in Infoseek, then the fourth largest Web-based search and directory firm, with the aim of marrying Infoseek with Disney's own Starwave to build a new-style portal to the Web. The object will be to create a simple to use 'family' front door to the Internet with universal navigation, registration and passwords all supported by a unified customer service centre. The customer will only have to log on once but all the information collected concerning their preferences will be applied throughout the Web site allowing easy access to all the products in the extensive Disney family from Mickey to the Lion King. Disney promises all kinds of customization that, as well as making people happier, will also make life easier, e.g. a front page that notes the bad weather in your town and suggests 'things to do with children when it's raining'.

Before its latest push to centralize all its offerings around one 'front door' Disney had already run a number of successful Web sites. Disney.com which provides news about movies, TV shows, videos and software attracts some 550 000 different visitors a day and is regarded as the number one kids' site on the Internet while family.com is available for parents seeking advice about the care and feeding of children. From its shop.com Web site it offers 2000 Disney-related products which on a typical day makes a level of sales equivalent to five bricks-and-mortar stores. Disney already runs the number one online sports site, ESPN's Sportszone, which records close to one million individual visits every day, while its Blast.com monitored content and chat for kids online service, which costs $5.95 a month, ranks number two after the Wall Street Journal in Web revenue from paying subscribers. Disney has been quick to see the Web potential for sales of its branded goods and a great deal of E-business is being carried out in the area of retail sales, more examples of which are noted below.

## Business to business

A lot of E-commerce is of course invisible to consumers. Company-to-company sharing of commercial information via the Internet is now widespread. This is particularly true with regard to inventory whether from supplier to producer or from producer to sales point. The Italian firm Benetton has long since substituted information for inventory. Sales from their outlets around the world are collated daily at a central point and this information is used as the basis for manufacturing decisions rather than holding stock made in advance which may not fit the preferences actually being declared by customer at all the Benetton outlets worldwide.

Information about customer preference collected on a daily basis like this is a potent weapon in the hands of skilled respondents. Boeing now buys its computers online from Dell as a matter of course. Dell not only builds computers to specifications ordered by its customers in this way but it also uses the Internet to inform them about current developments and solicit feedback to help develop the products that users say they want. Cost savings of up to 25 per cent can accrue from paperless sales of this kind and Dell's great competitor Compaq, normally a supplier via conventional retailers, has also begun selling some of its computers directly over the Internet. According to research by the Gartner Group, business-to-business trade over the Internet is growing even faster than E-retail with $15.6 billion worth of such trade being executed over the Internet in 1998, and this is expected to grow to a massive $175 billion by the year 2000 [3]. Some of this increase will be fuelled by the growth in cross-border online commerce in Europe that will follow the introduction of the Euro. This will make such transactions more attractive by enhancing price transparency and eliminating expensive currency exchange expenses.

All stock-holding is expensive for companies and the more pro-ducers can fine-tune the information flows back to them about customer preference (a bit like the old Japanese idea of 'just in time' deliveries to auto factories), the leaner, fitter and more competitive they can be. There is still a long way to go before this feedback loop is universal. Even some large retailers who use EDI (Electronic Data Input) and EPOS systems to collect information on sales often fail to make the whole five yards. In these enterprises the direct link to the supplier is still spasmodic and customers, who are becoming more critical of delivery failures, complain that supplies of popular lines are not replenished fast enough. They have heard about fast electronic networks helping to keep the shelves full in other stores and they wonder what's gone wrong when the shelves are empty in theirs.

## E-retail: groceries and slippers

All companies are nearing the time when they will have to compete on the assumption of information symmetry, i.e. that everyone knows the differences between the price and quality of products and services on offer at different locations. Greater access to information for everyone means that markets are becoming closer to being 'friction free' and all the intermediaries that live off skimming the cream from that friction have finite futures. Symmetry of information is not yet in any way total in all markets in all places but customer knowledge is growing fast and the Internet is playing a part in this. The UpMyStreet Web site constructed by consultancy firm Aztec Internet in the UK to show its clients how to get the best out of the Internet allows online comparison between areas in the UK based on house prices, schools examination performance, council tax levels, ambulance response times and crime clear-up rates. Once the name of a town or the postcode is entered it automatically compares the house prices with the national average or those of a second nominated area. This 'demonstration' package could prove a godsend to estate agents but the same kind of software is now being used to compare second-hand car prices, insurance quotes, airline ticket prices, share prices and prices of CDs and books and more categories are joining them every day.

No area of Internet commerce has had more publicity than its antic-ipated potential for retail selling. Personal banking services, Internet shopping and buying and selling equities are all now well established on the Internet. This area will grow rapidly as people begin to trust the encryption that protects their credit card details and start to mix their shopping habits between real and cyberspace. The mix will vary signifi-cantly between economic groups and within the same groups, depending on the desire to exercise a range of not always predictable preferences. Sometimes the desire to handle and compare stock on the ground is important; at other times it is not. Sometimes the desire to spend time in and around shops is strong whereas at other times, particularly given the winter climate in some places, it is not. When we know exactly what we want and it is just a question of getting it rather than shopping for it, the Internet/WebTV will be the medium of preference for those in the top quartile of national income groups. Internet shopping is only likely to take off among a wider range of economic groups when it becomes as easy to access as using the remote control of a TV set.

Four years ago the April 1995 issue of *Smart Money*, a US magazine dedicated to personal business, ran a story called 'Will we ever leave the house again?' The gist of this piece was how easy it was for a marketing executive, 3000 miles away on a business trip in Charlotte, South Carolina, to complete her weekly shopping at the Peapod Grocery Delivery in San Francisco where she lived over the Internet. She got back home at 6pm and the delivery van arrived 35 minutes later with her weekly order of groceries. The store held a personalized list of her weekly shop online (which she could call up and amend) and, most importantly, they held her credit card number on file so she did not have to give it over the 'unpro-tected' telephone line in real time.

As the graphics used on Internet shopping pages become more attractive, access codes get simpler and credit card transactions become safer, the Internet will become the world's biggest market for people in work who declare that they have less time available for the look and feel of shopping in 'real space'. What these world-without-legs shops are selling, more than anything else, is convenience. They allow those who can to cruise the cyber-malls at any time of night or day, without a screaming child in their shopping trolley. They let them shop without having to hunt for a parking place in the rain, without having to queue at a check-out and without having to get dressed to go out. A few clicks on the mouse get you into the store and it doesn't matter that you are still wearing your slippers. Many traditional retailers already sell from selections made from general and speciality catalogues sent through the post. A hybrid version, a classic example of mixing paper-based information, W3 ordering and postal delivery, is to select from a paper catalogue and order via a W3 page. The W3 catalogues are often cluttered and confusing at present but they will get better. If the ordered product is made up of atoms rather than bytes it will still require some form of postal service to deliver it. Postal services around the world show no decline as Email increases, indeed with faster, overnight guarantees etc. they seem to be expanding everywhere. It may be easy to send picture postcards across the Internet but postal volumes at Christmas seem to have been unaffected by the small number of festive greetings sent down wires instead of via the usual envelope. As Internet shopping grows so will the postal deliveries of goods ordered across it and, as is often the case, an old medium profits from the widespread adoption of a new one. The Internet itself may be almost pollution-free but some of its direct spin offs won't be. Retail via the Internet will give a boost to delivery companies, and also to van suppliers as more vehicles will be needed to deliver the goods ordered across it.

## What happened to the fax machine?

Unlike postal services the fax machine could find itself a victim of an alternative Internet solution, as it is now common for many PCs to come bundled with fax software that can operate via the computer's modem. Barely used 20 years ago the analogue fax is now a common consumer of all the paper that the paperless office was going to do without. Offices around the world often have reams of faxes pouring out on to their floors awaiting attention. In 1997 companies around the world spent $60 billion sending faxes, a massive 40 per cent of all corporate telecommunications expenditure, and a large company can easily run up $13 million a year on fax transmission alone. However, although many individuals now often send documents created directly on computers as faxes via the Internet most companies have been slow to recognize the double advantage of not only missing out the paper bit but also being able to use local call charges, to send faxes anywhere in the world. A 1998 study by Mercer Management Consulting suggests that nearly 10 million analogue fax machines are purchased every year to join an installed base of around 60 million worldwide [4]. Buried in organizations' telephone bills fax charges have been a largely hidden cost but companies are belatedly waking up to Internet faxing. By 2000 as much as 10 per cent of all corporate telecommunications will go over the Internet, compared with less than 2 per cent now, rather than through the voice network. Low-cost Internet voice telephony is less of an attraction to companies as the quality is so poor but data networks actually transmit faxes with better quality than voice lines. Such a take-up rate will have a dramatic effect on both the makers of analogue fax machines and the telecommunications industry. Over the next couple of years traditional long-distance carriers could see as much as $13 billion in revenues shift from their networks to the Internet [4]. Those telecommunications companies whose merger and acquisitions binge has brought them Internet providers, e.g. WorldCom/MCI and AT&T/TCI, or like Deutsche Telekom who are busy investing heavily in Internet telephony, will be hit less than those who, like the five Virgins at the biblical wedding, turn up with no spare oil for their lamps.

## Books lead the way online

Amazon, the biggest supplier of books across the Internet, spotted the great synergy between atoms and bytes when it opened for business armed with the biggest electronic catalogue of books in the world. It has no need to invest in high-street shops that can only store a few thousand titles, theft (always a serious issue in bookshops) from virtual bookshelves is difficult and it does not have to hold any stock. By dealing in such large quantities Amazon also offers reductions in the prices of large numbers of selected titles and it costs very little to add new sections to its W3 pages. Amazon already offers separate sections on award-winning books, book reviews, lists of bestsellers, music CDs, computer games, videos and audiobooks, all without having to lay a brick. As with Microsoft in 1996 many book retailers, well established in real space, are now waking up to the threat from virtual suppliers and recognizing that their long experience in selling to customers who come into a shop should help them in taking the shop to the customer. After two years of watching Amazon grab a big slice of their market share in the US, Barnes and Noble set up their own Internet bookshop in 1997. In the UK W.H. Smith's £9.2 million purchase in mid-1998 of The Internet Bookshop, the UK leader in online book sales, quickly added a virtual outlet to their traditional high-street presence.

Internet book sales are tiny at the moment when compared with the number of books sold from traditional sites. However the Jupiter Communications consultancy predicts that online books will account for 6 per cent of the UK market by 2003 while the Corporate Intelligence on Retailing consultancy forecasts that within seven years worldwide Internet book sales will total £450 million [5]. Amazon's success took Barnes and Nobel, Bertelsmann and many others in the book business by surprise. This was just the kind of surprise that Internet ventures have tended to have in many areas but, if there is such a thing as a learning curve, we should hear less about such surprises in the future.

Publishers have long harboured a desire to sell directly to customers and German publishing giant Bertelsmann's Books Online (bol.com), launched in Europe in November 1998, made it the first big publisher to compete directly with booksellers on the Internet. Bertelsmann's great, and very profitable, strength lies in its book clubs. They supply over 700 000 volumes to 25 million members daily making Bertelsmann the world's biggest bookseller. The club members' address list and purchase histories facilitate highly targeted recommendations for further reading and other promotions. Amazon, without being a 'club', also knows what its customers are buying and welcomes them with some personal recommendations. The Internet plus some friendly graphics have thus re-created the community, clubby atmosphere that Bertelsmann first created in the 1950s. Bertelsmann was going to launch BooksOnline in the US as well as Europe but it decided instead to buy 50 per cent of Barnes & Noble's Internet venture, paying $200 million for it in October 1998.

The Barnes & Noble site, despite several re-launches, was poorly laid out and signposted. Bertelsmann, in its partnership with AOL and Compuserve in Europe, has online experience that it can bring to bear on the problem. Amazon will not be easy to beat. It has signed up 100 000 associates on the Internet (popular sites and search engines) who channel potential buyers to its own site and they are only likely to defect for a much better deal. Amazon has also announced plans to set up its own Internet bookshops in the UK and Germany. It's a great irony that the sale of paper-based products should prove one of the keenest battle-grounds in the early days of Internet commerce.

Perfumes and personal care products may not be far behind. The Body Shop, which has suffered some severe losses in the US (it lost nearly £5 million in 1997), plans to sell its products on the Internet, further deepening the disagreements it has had with those running its franchises there. The franchise operators complain that customers won't bother to go into a shop if they can buy the product off the Web, over the telephone or off TV. The company replied that by using the Internet it can attract many new customers who are nowhere near a Body Shop store and who would thus have been unlikely to visit a franchise operation. The Body Shop, who has now bought out their disgruntled US franchises, have no plans to launch this service in the UK where Internet access is currently too small to justify it. House insurance, home contents insurance, life insurance, travel insurance, car insurance – indeed any type of insurance – is now easily found on the Web where comparisons can be made between the quotes from half a dozen or more companies quickly and without leaving home.

## Retail: but not as we know it

E-retail is here to stay and, in the short term, will undoubtedly grow into a significant market sector for those old established retail businesses who seize the challenge quickly enough and for new E-based business ventures that will shake out their winners and losers in the usual way. However in the long term the idea of 'retail' as we currently define it is set to change dramatically with wider Internet usage. In the past, with a few exceptions, producers stuck to producing, wholesalers stuck to accumulating large stocks acquired at big discounts from producers and retailers bought stocks from the wholesalers and invested in display space to sell on to consumers. Each player knew their place and although we always knew someone who could get stuff cheaper than retail price this was small fry in the great scheme of things. The Internet offers producers the chance to sell directly and cheaply. It offers the 'old' wholesalers the same opportunity and it threatens the nature of 'old' retail in that now many people can act as retailers, 'putting up' attractive display spaces that can reach millions of customers at low cost and without laying a brick. Record producers and book publishers will tread carefully at first as they will not want to be seen to be breaking their contracts with third party suppliers but the floodgates will eventually open.

A serious aim of all electronic networking has been to empower the individual by releasing them from the grip of middle-persons so that they can deal directly with the source of products and services. For a variety of reasons, including the tenacious retention of their mysteries by the professions, liberation of the individual in this way has been slow to materialize at the higher end of the service spectrum. The Internet will do away with some intermediaries but, contrary to popular belief, it will also provide opportunities for a new breed of broker and middle-person. These new cyber agents will bring together on a Web site the offerings of a number of suppliers of, say, insurance services, they will collect your details and then calculate the one that would be best for you given your particular circumstances. Brokers who can manipulate the wealth of information locked up in perhaps 20 suppliers of a service and match it to an individual need over the Internet will be able to extend their reach rather than become extinct. Dialog, via its Planet retail site, offers a free and easy to use price comparison service across a range of products while, more specifically, Compare.Net offers a free online buyer's guide that allows users to compare features between more than 10 000 brands of stereo receivers. Thus brokers who only offer the same limited range of options that they peddle from their office will lose out.

Whatever the eventual impact of the Internet in other domains buying and selling across the wires is here to stay as is a serious re-definition of what it means to be in retail. Classified advertisements 'centres' are springing up across the Internet as are Internet auction sites like UK-based QXL and California-based eBay who provide a base for selling and buying just about anything. eBay started its virtual flea market in 1995 and by the end of 1998 had sold more than 45 million items through 165 million bids. It holds one million items on its auction list at any one time ranging from computers to baby clothes and picks up 25 cents for a listing and a small percentage of the sale price. This site also provides customers with references (from other customers) on every trader operating on the site. Too many bad references on a trader's profile means that business migrates elsewhere.

These kinds of sites may be breaking down national borders but borders still matter, as tax differences between countries can be significant, and governments will lose out on VAT and import duties if large volumes of goods and services can be 'imported' from low-tax countries. The OECD believes that retail sales across the Internet will be worth about £120 billion by 2000 and has set up a committee to study tax losses which it believes could seriously affect 29 governments which are currently losing about £8 billion a year in unpaid revenues. The shopping mall created a revolution in the 1970s and 1980s defining not only how we bought things but also how we spent our time. Cathedrals of consumption they became an essential part of a new car-based suburban culture claiming our time and shaping the way new communities were planned and changing the landscape and economic foundations of many older ones.

E-retail is about building a new car park and (partially) petrol-free culture of convenience and speed. In the early years its impact will be restricted to those who have the educational background and the economic resources to access it. Later the TV 'catalogue' will bring it to a wider audience and only then will we be able to assess if it will leave the malls as empty as they left the small town shop. The Gartner Group estimates that by the year 2000 global online consumer sales will reach $20 billion, an increase of 233 per cent over the $6.1 billion of sales made in 1998. Charity Web pages explaining their work and extending a cybertin have found a new corner to stand on while, at the other end of the spectrum, gambling is now carried out over the Internet and this is destined to become big business, particularly in countries where gambling is illegal. The thrust supersonic car project of 1998 that aimed to break the sound barrier over land kept people informed of their progress via a Web site which, on the days they were attempting to break the sound barrier attracted 2.5 million visitors. When the project ran out of money, just before they were about to make their final record-breaking run, they used their W3 page to appeal for cash and raised over £320 000 in just 10 days and in doing so probably changed the nature of this kind of sponsorship for ever. Business-to-business trade, all kinds of retailing, money-raising for charity and sponsorship, auctions, sex and gambling – all these are up and running now and the range of Web services is undoubtedly going to explode over the next few years. You don't have to be a cyber revolutionary or technological determinist to accept this. It is just the natural migration of trade and commerce to the cheapest and most profitable conduit.

## E-vacancies/the hiring fair

In the nineteenth century groups of agricultural workers in the rural counties of England, as in Hardy's Dorset, used to make their way to the hiring fairs held in market towns. Here they would wait around in the market square for potential employers to come and have a look at them in the hope of employment. Much agricultural work was seasonal and a man may have offered himself as shepherd in the spring and a thatcher in the autumn; flexibility was the key to keeping the wolf from the door. This was the poverty side of free-lancing. The hiring fair of those days was not unlike a slave market in the US or the Caribbean during the early part of the same century. Itinerants, tinkers, jobbers, fruit and vegetable pickers, men waiting at dock gates in the hope of being picked for a day's work – all these groups have enjoyed the 'flexibility' of advertising themselves for work by their physical presence in a market place.

The Internet offers a new breed of itinerants, this time offering knowledge, intelligence and talent rather than brawn, the opportunity to put themselves up for sale without leaving home. The electronic dockside now comes to the worker, waiting at a screen, to offer him or her employment. Though hardly neon-lights stuff it is just the sort of nuts and bolts facility that can make a significant contribution to the economic life of those nations where much information/knowledge work no longer requires daily attendance at a place. Spatial prerequisites are still strong in developed countries but more work is increasingly done in a mix of work and home space and this will accelerate with the onset of greater bandwidth and a more robust electronic networking infrastructure. The examples are growing fast. The WWW.topjobs.net Web site complete with colourful globes advertising 'top-job' vacancies in a selection of countries also provides access to vacancies in a range of large corporations and the public sector. The IT division of UK recruitment group Reed Executive now only accepts applications from candidates for computing and other

IT jobs over the Internet and this medium looks set to be the hiring fair of choice for IT professionals in the future. Many national newspapers and professional journals also post their recruitment advertisements on the Internet (usually some hours before they appear in print), as do large companies of every sort. It will not be long before students applying for higher education in the UK will be able to post their applications for colleges and universities on the Internet, and indeed just about everything that requires the filling of a form can be transferred to it.

Most of the current cases of hiring in this way are still adjuncts or extras to printed media, extending the audience and offering a new dimension to their customers. This has happened faster than most of us would have thought. Access to the technology in schools is moving fast, access to the technology at the kind of workplace where a high level of information processing goes on is increasing but access to the technology in job centres and blue collar work environments is growing much more slowly. The likelihood is that 'machine operator' type posts are unlikely to be advertized in this way for some time although some late-night television channels do offer job vacancy services of this kind. Home access to the Internet is still limited in the UK – around 14 per cent of homes have access compared with around 40 per cent in the US – and is predominantly centred around the white collar/professional household. When access to the Internet comes via a more user-friendly TV set, perhaps as part of the expansion of digital television, the opportunities for employers to reach more economic groups will expand. When this happens the Internet hiring fair will really have something to contribute to job mobility and employment among low-income groups. The unemployed suffer from the asymmetry of information more than any other group. If the wide variety of blue collar vacancies within a region could be distributed via the Internet and presented at job centres detailing their precise requirements, their location and their rates of pay it would add a valuable new dimension to job seeking. Applications could be made, with support from staff if necessary, and sent off to potential employers straight away while advisors and applicant were still actively engaged with each other.

## E-lancing and Tupperware

Working from home, sitting before a computer screen writing, designing, translating, editing, generating computer code or anything else that can be squirted down a wire without losing its meaning, is heralded as being the great liberator of the professional freelancer. A return to the cottage industry paradigm of the nineteenth century mixed in with the techno-logical possibilities of the twentieth – a neat blend of both pre- and post-industrial behaviour. As with the hiring fair the home worker for much of this century was predominantly a poor worker, earning poor wages with poor (often non-existent) job security and no trade union protection. Today many examples of this low-pay home working continues, e.g. seamstresses, envelope fillers, soft toy makers etc., and it has now been joined by data inputting, record creation, word processing, telephone sales and all kinds of boring key-stroke labour.

We must not assume that electronic networking is always about the high-end knowledge worker sending in his or her invoice after completing a rich and fulfilling assignment (see Chapter 3). There are many levels of home working and some of them will be exploitative. However this is not to decry the potential that the Internet offers for bright entrepreneurs at all the levels in between. One enterprising woman in the US now racks up sales of between $100 and $300 each week selling Tupperware over the Internet via 45-minute online 'parties' without leaving her home. The scope for online parties for all kinds of products like lingerie, cosmetics, motorcycle and car accessories must be quite large and no doubt the 'adult' end of consumer preference will be even larger.

There are many stories of young computer enthusiasts developing new software, posting it on the Internet and inviting other programmers to download it, test it and use it for free in exchange for nothing but feed-back. Such communities of the highly motivated and like-minded devoted to solving a particular problem are seen by some as the basis of a new paradigm for the way work will be done in the future. Malone and Laubucher [6] are enthusiastic about the possibilities of e-lancing and a bit like Handy and his 'portfolio of work' see the liberation of individual talent emerging as a positive spin-off from the downsizing/outsourcing habits of cost-conscious corporations.

> All these trends point to the devolution of large, permanent corpo-rations into flexible temporary networks of individuals. No one can yet say exactly how important or widespread this new form of busi-ness organization will become, but judging from current signs, it is not inconceivable that it could define work in the twenty-first century

as the industrial organization defined it in the twentieth. If it does business and society could change forever.

The temporary self-managed gathering of diverse individuals engaged in a common task is being offered as a model for a new kind of business organization that, when in full flow, will form the basis for a new kind of economy. The fundamental unit for such an economy would not be the corporation with its layers of managers, budgets, meetings and reports but the individual. Tasks would not be assigned but carried out autonomously by independent contractors who join together in fluid and temporary networks to produce and sell goods and services. When the project is completed and some cash is pocketed the group dissolves and its members sniff out new projects along the wires. I guess that eventually W3 notice boards, heralding the start of a new project and calling on the faithful to join in, will spring up to help them identify jobs and personnel with whom they might empathize.

## E-games

The computer game industry, valued at many billions of dollars worldwide, has been the mother of many computing innovations in terms of chip development and 3-D graphics production and it is constantly working at improving the look and feel of the environments that they want their customers to inhabit. At the moment most games are bought on CD, loaded on to a PC and played by one or two people on the same machine. Many such games now often offer multi-player capability over the W3 extending the range of players and opponents. However most 3-D games require programmes that can run into many megabytes and this is not really downloadable over the Internet using a home modem. So although the game can be played across the Web each player still needs to load the original game, or more specifically the 3-D engine on to his or her PC as the game server, so that game publishers and retailers need not shiver too much yet!

But as the cost of connectivity falls the numbers of people downloading games from the Internet will rise and the computer games market will inevitably have to change and adapt to cope with it. Traditional games like bridge, chess, cribbage, backgammon, Monopoly, even golf can be played on the Internet and require less lines of code in their Java applet to deliver a reasonable performance. A house-bound bridge player can join a Web Bridge Club by signing up and downloading the software to join say 10 000 other members in 130 countries. The players, insomniacs all, can play at any time of day or night and they can both interact with the card play and chat with other enthusiasts in real time. They can have a regular partner based in Canada or an occasional one from Brazil to play opponents in Holland or Moscow or anywhere else where someone is wanting a game.

## E-improvement and metadata

Up until the middle of this century it was not unusual for successful soldiers, politicians, writers and diplomats to pay tribute in their autobiographies to the 'free' lending and reference libraries of their youth. They would remember and praise the peaceful haven, the Aladdin's cave, and the helpful librarians who guided them through it, in an almost hushed reverence. Today public libraries still change people's lives every day and many budding writers and politicians are still making their first contact, though in a much less reverential way, with the ideas and knowledge that shaped the past and forged the present in public and other libraries. When they come to write their autobiographies they may not now pause to praise a particular place as a source of youthful inspiration, but if they do they will include a much wider range of 'places' including the Internet.

The Internet is developing both as a massive source of information to support schools, undergraduates, higher-level research and the personal research of individuals engaged on a variety of projects, and as a conduit via which educational materials can be distributed very effectively. Conventional universities and colleges are using the Web to give their students effective access to administrative information, course and programme outlines, lectures, notes and guides to further sources of information. American universities have been in the vanguard of this kind of programme distribution. The implications are great. Many agencies can now claim to have a 'university' loaded on to their computers offering a server-to-screen service in whatever subject a distant student might want to study. Universities and colleges may have the sole right to validate undergraduate and postgraduate courses but the Internet will facilitate an explosion in the kind of student-funded, part-time education that they also provide but which lies outside this monopoly. Many private traditional

distance learning programmes around the world have gained accredita-
tion from professional bodies for what they do and there is no reason
to expect that those who provide all or part of such a course over the
Internet will not eventually mature enough to deserve the same sort
of recognition.

The world of work is now often far too demanding for managers
to let many of their staff take time off for formal study during a working
day. Such students attend night classes or follow distance learning
programmes that they accommodate around home and work routines.
The Open University in the UK, along with other distance learning agencies around the world, has pioneered distance learning and now offers
courses at every academic level. Imitators will use the Internet to
distribute educational materials to paying customers, to accommodate
their busy schedules and to help them as and when they require help
rather than limiting them to an institution's opening hours. The free market
in further and higher education has hardly begun to use the Internet; when
it does start using it to sell courses 'going to the tech' will never be the
same again.

The academic world is only just beginning to wrestle with the potential of the Internet as a course delivery medium but it has notched up
quite a lot of experience of the Internet as a 'library' whose mystery can
gradually be exposed by the current range of crude search engines. The
Internet is a cataloguer's nightmare and so to avoid bad dreams catalogue
records have been given a new name in Internet-speak – Metadata.
Metadata are data about data, data that describe an information source
and provide access to it. A number of schemes are being developed to
produce metadata for Web pages and other networked resources
including the Dublin Core which provides a set of simple headings (title,
creator, subject, etc.) as descriptors which are placed as catalogue information in a <META> tag at the top of the Web page. This tag is invisible
to the user but as long as it is expressed in the correct format it can be
picked up by the automated search engines that harvest the Web to find
new pages.

When we call up a search engine like Alta Vista or Lycos we do not
actually search the Web itself but rather a database that they 'prepared
earlier'. If these search engines can be trained to understand metadata
and store it in their databases in a structured way under specific headings
then searching for Web pages could ultimately become easier. The

problem is that if Web authors are left to produce their own tags they may intentionally or unintentionally mislead us as to the contents of their pages. Web page stuffing, where the creators of a site 'stuff' pages with lots of terms commonly searched for on the Web in order to attract search engine attention, is a common practice that could also afflict the creation of metadata by Web authors. One way to avoid biased metadata would be to involve a trusted third party in its production, someone with a kite-mark of credibility, a neutral agent, someone trusted to be objective.

This sounds like a 'come back librarians all is forgiven' call. In the world of scholarly database sets librarians have already been at work on subject gateways in the social sciences and in medicine and they are keen to find a meaningful role for themselves in the wider world of electronic warehousing. The British Library in the UK and the Library of Congress and The Kellogg Foundation in the US have all provided funds for research into how the Internet can be harnessed by librarians. A variety of such projects is in progress aimed at discovering how users react to the Internet, how librarians can mine it more effectively and how academic and public libraries can make it a dynamic part of their overall service provision. The librarian functions as an intelligent mediator between a precise or even a vague desire for information and the mystery of where the 'answer' might lie. The Internet already operates on a number of levels of which the scholastic is only one, but this level requires more than the retrieval of a hundred headings that include the key word if it is to satisfy staff and student research needs. The refinement of searches, the establishment of validated metadata and the creation of notional subject-oriented collections within the Web, annotated and rated by level, all pose interesting challenges and possibly new opportunities for librarians.

## Info elites and W3-addiction

Survey after survey of the W3 has found that most Web users are young males who are regular computer users and who often know more than one programming language. This suggests the growth of yet another division in society – Webbed versus un-Webbed humans. Rich, white, male, northern hemisphere, technical, employed, occidental, under 30 and computer-literate looks like the configuration for a new self-satisfied Info-Rich community that is not too bothered about those operating on the outside. Two decades on from its inception the population of the 'cyber village' still makes it look like a big, middle-class white suburb where access to the Internet is as much a badge of belonging to the already advantaged as a BMW or a private parking space.

As we move from geographical isolation to social isolation it is not difficult to see the information age as something of a double-edged sword. You may live in Silicon Valley, but if you are poor and poorly educated you will only benefit from the Internet second-hand via friends or an institution like a school or a library that has connectivity. This is changing; technology always trickles down eventually, but we should not be blind to the unconscious, unseen, accidental, unplanned but very real inequalities that electronic networking can overlay on existing social and economic differentials. Academics are bad at understanding this. They often receive high-speed Internet access for free at work and just as often, though perhaps a little slower, from homes full of electronic gizmos. As we end the twentieth century there are still enormous structural inequalities of access to computing and communications infrastructures in industrial countries which will not disappear overnight and which, heresy of heresies, could even become more starkly defined in the future. The Internet, powerful as it is, is just another tool for accessing information for pleasure, enlightenment, education, or profit. Added to all our other sources of information – newspapers, magazines, radio, television, networks of friends and colleagues, etc. – it can fill gaps and it can deliver facts, ideas and opinions that we would otherwise never have access to or that we would have to travel a long way to find. But we should see it as that, just another string to our bow, and not one that will satisfy all our needs. It is in transition and it is changing all the time both in terms of the information available from it and the tools available to access and retrieve from it.

There are now a great many ways to learn about the Internet via many different forms of media but, as Bet Midler is reputed to have said: 'If sex is so natural why are there so many books written to tell you how to do it?' You can't get much safer sex than when surfing the Internet, but you can only get to understand the sheer range of information sources which is available, and whether it is worth your while to stay hooked up, by doing it!

The cry from many users of bulletin boards who find themselves locked into lonely screen-watching at 5 am is 'Why am I doing this?'

Another is 'I must get out more'. Internet addiction is a reality for a growing number of people. Many regular users of the W3 use it for a very particular purpose, e.g. checking out the retail opportunities of electronic equipment, playing with Java programmes, talking endlessly with distant 'friends' about bugs and fixes or watching share prices. The share watchers might also buy and sell shares via an Internet share-dealing service and they will make only rare forays into other Web sites and these would usually be related to their main interest, i.e. making money. Such users are notorious Internet addicts terrified that they will miss the latest hot tip on the bulletin board if they aren't logged on. There is probably no cure for such people other than them getting a dog that needs lots of regular exercise. A printout from the British Library's translation of the Magna Carta will certainly help those with difficulty sleeping!

# References

1.   'E-commerce: the commercial revolution'. *Investors Chronicle*, 13 November 1998, pp.20–24

2.   'Obituary, Rick Rozar'. *The Economist*, 17 October 1998, p.142

3.   'Click till you drop'. *Time*, 4 August 1998, pp.40–45

4.   'Telecommunications: is it time to unplug your fax machine?' *Harvard Business Review*, Sept/Oct 1998, p.14

5.   'Twinning Mainz and Seattle'. *The Economist*, 17 October 1998, p.25

6.   Malone, T.W. and Laubacher, R.J. (1998) 'The dawn of the E-lance economy'. *Harvard Business Review*, Sept/Oct 1998, pp.145–152

# CHAPTER SEVEN

# The connecting organization

'Change is not what it used to be'
                    Charles Handy (1989), *The Age Of Unreason.*

## Attending to business: learning to navigate

Citizens of industrialized societies spend a significant portion of their life 'attending' organizations that construct unique operating spaces. In different countries even the same kind of organization, say a car-licensing or a telecommunications office, will operate very differently and we marvel at the range and levels of bureaucracy that different cultures can develop to achieve the same, or a similar, thing. The trickle of north-European standards to southern Europe as part of the EU harmonization project still has to battle against some culturally entrenched approaches to administrative matters, particularly with regard to the continuation of paper-based records and labour intensity. Bureaucracy's many seem to be the same the world over but strong cultural inflexions continue to resist rapid harmonization and these differences will take a long time to iron out and some of them will remain to flavour their systems for a very long time.

       After a while we become knowledgeable about how we should operate in such spaces. We become comfortable, turn up with the right form, stand at the right counter with the right bits of identification; later we even advise others, new to the process, on where in the maze of options they should go. A serious amount of knowledge about transacting with organizations is transferred in this way. Regular visitors to hospitals for instance become knowledgeable about the functions of different spaces and this can make them look experts to those who are fortunate enough to use them only occasionally. Time spent in higher education generates a particular kind of knowledge about how such places work as well as that acquired through participating in the formal programmes. Just 'being there' around animated and lively people doing interesting things provides a new level of knowledge exchange irrespective of how good we are at our studies. A fairly ordinary run-of-the-mill life will see us entering and exiting a wide range of organizations, e.g. offices, schools, hospitals, town halls, universities and colleges, into some of which we may later return to work.

A large part of our acclimatization to 'life as we know it' is through learning about spaces, how they work, what they do and how best to place ourselves within them to get what we want. We use all our senses to navigate simple and complex spaces to ascertain the roles of people within them and the resulting pattern recognition equips us with some useful stereotyping. The receptionist's space is one of the most ubiquitous and most important in terms of first impressions, although it is not always perceived in that way by the hosting organization. Despite the ostensible shift to flatter hierarchies an employee's location within a building is still often a clue to the role they perform – executive suites are rarely located in the basement. Educating ourselves about the operation of complex systems in real space is an important part of our development as citizens. We rarely understand the totality of the things that go on in the many spaces with which we connect but then we rarely need to. The nature, comfort and utility of the space where we work is one of the most important factors in our well being.

## Work and life after work

Work is where we make many of our daily connections. We connect with colleagues, customers, suppliers and a network of formal and informal communication systems set up, in theory at least, to help us do our job properly and meet the objectives of the organization. As a rough guide and assuming a six-hour day for every day we work we spend between

7.70 and 8.30 years of our life at work depending on whether we start work at 16 or 22. Going to work thus occupies a serious minority of our allotted time. But although we spend more of our time out of work than in it work is still a place where we construct some of our most important ideas about ourselves and about other people. Whatever its structure our experience at work usually differs considerably from our experience in our non-work fora. At work we encounter a different discipline and different relationships with authority as well as constructing new meanings for relationships and concepts such as power, sharing, helping and competing.

A world where there was no such thing as work, where some kind of voucher system dispensed wealth by age, height or shoe size and where no one worked in any formal way would be a nightmare to most people. Being 'unemployed' in the western world, irrespective of its economic consequences, remains a social stigma because of the doubt observers harbour as to one's willingness to work. Even the soft version of unemployment, early retirement, despite the 1970s promise that more of us would do it and revel in it, is not regarded by many as a satisfactory destination unless it is turned back into some kind of formal, useful, work-like activity. A response to the question 'what do you do now that you are retired?' that suggests a life of pleasant indolence often leaves the questioner shocked or at least bemused. Surely everybody wants to be doing something worthwhile? Others when retired prematurely often resent it. 'We still have years of work left within us', they cry, 'don't put us on the scrap heap yet.' Of course we will all respond differently to the retirement opportunity but as a lot more of us will be doing it there may not be enough of the old (narrow) constructions of what is considered worthwhile to go round.

Post-work trauma is as much a result of how we think other people expect us to use our time as it is of routine and agenda deprivation. Yet think how many times we found 'hiding' places at work just to get away from the absurdity of some of it. Legitimate and abundant hiding, as in pleasing ourselves whether we do something or nothing, suddenly seems much less attractive. For most of us work is a primary economic necessity that we have to accomplish in order to survive, yet we have added a whole range of other reasons for doing it as well. It is now the way that most of us measure ourselves, fuel our self-esteem and demonstrate what kind of person we are. Our job title sends out all kinds of signals and not having a signal to send out is one of the worst things that can happen to us.

For most of us work still takes place in organizations and most of the world's employers still organize themselves in buildings that proclaim their function, just as they did a 100 years ago. A solicitor's office, a doctor's surgery, an insurance office or an accountant's office all look much the same as they did to Dickens and some of them still operate in much the same way. Visit any manufacturing site and you will be able to pick out the manufacturing block, the administrative block and the executive block. Software firms look a bit different but they have deliberately sought to flaunt the paradox of an unstructured space for some of the most structured work on the planet. It is now almost a mission with them that they should proclaim their 'difference' and look more like a university campus than a place of work. Most of us still physically go to work rather than working from home, although (see Chapters 2 and 3) various forms of home working, such as teleworking, are expected to expand significantly beyond 2000 as telephone companies tariffs fall, telephone infrastructures become more robust and more bandwidth becomes available.

## Work, work, work and then the Cuckoo

From the late 1970s onwards citizens of the industrial world have been drawn into increasingly demanding contracts with their employers. They have been asked to give more and more of themselves to their work both physically by being there and mentally by thinking about it a lot. This contract has created some uneasy choices for people in work particularly in their allocation of time, e.g. between being a good citizen, a good parent and a good employee. The current organizational buzz words of lifelong learning, investing in people, valuing intellectual capital, flexible response times, seeking excellence in all areas of the business and developing a strong customer orientation all seem sensible and benign. But at their heart is the demand for us to give concentrated attention to the ambiguities of markets and commerce via constant refreshment of the intellect in the service of work. Newspaper headlines such as 'Working fathers have little time for family life' are commonplace in western countries as survey after survey reveals the increasing stresses and strains faced by those in work. While relating the impact that his father's death had on him Handy candidly notes how his early search for fame and fortune ate up his time. He describes himself as

> . . . dashing hither and thither, the published author of papers and books, on the edge of the big time, too busy to attend to my family. 'Until I was ten,' said my daughter years later, 'I thought you were the man who came to lunch on Sundays.' [1]

Being all together for lunch at weekends is still likely to be a rare luxury for many families. Once the centre of how we experimented with different constructions of ourselves, grew our confidence and placed ourselves within a small and familiar pecking order, the family and the time we spend with it has given way to other priorities. Many men and women now face serious doubts and anxieties about their identity when they are away from work. They have become more attached and more comfortable with their work identities, as managers, professionals, technicians, etc., than to their home lives as fathers, mothers, sons and daughters, as their self-esteem becomes more and more bound up with what they do and what they achieve at work. Seeking 'respect' for being a caring and loving mother or father is much more difficult than achieving respect and understanding in the workplace where a formal structure, despite its ups and downs, ensures that the role one plays is rarely questioned, contradicted or openly ignored. This is quite different from the fuzzy structures available to maintain an orderly house, managing a voluntary group of affiliates of varying ages and having legal responsibility for the invisible actions of some of them. The way we construct ourselves at work has become much more important to us than the way we construct ourselves within families.

However it is an emerging irony that as the new century draws near the 'my soul belongs to the company store' contract is no guarantee of a continuing pay cheque. We also live at a time when the concept of continuous employment is being put under more and more pressure as organizations downsize or invest in smart technology to replace human labour and intelligence, in order to cut costs and increase profitability. As the home lost its place as a centre for the energy of its occupants the organizations to which they transferred that energy are busy re-shaping and re-structuring themselves in ways which require less and less of it. Thus many middle managers, a favourite target of the downsizers, have

found themselves thrown back on their own resources as the old certainties of working life collapse. Retreating back into families who hardly know
them comes as a bit of a shock. Like cuckoos they can seem too big for
a nest that has grown used to them being somewhere else. The 40 years
of corporate service inside companies, that sometimes ran themselves like
small welfare states and on which an older generation relied to provide
a stable and progressive route through the ranks to a reasonable pension,
have long gone. Even the Japanese are busy re-evaluating their 'jobs-for-
life' culture as their banking crisis deepens and their industrial muscle
declines. The big, vertically integrated structures of the 'old' corporations
are now said to have had their day: 'The age of lumps is gone; the age
of ephemera has just begun' [2].

However attractive the idea of the great corporations cracking up
under pressure from an ocean of agile minnows may seem there is a lot
of evidence to show that many big companies still want to get bigger.
Company consolidations in the media, telecommunications, auto manufacturing, oil and even the new Internet industries continue apace. What
is happening is that big companies are seeking to structure themselves so
that they can act like small ones. True, a lot of them have outsourced
many of their support functions but this is a moveable feast with new functions being absorbed as others are shaken off. The component parts of
big companies, equipped with devolved budgets and objectives, now often
behave like small companies but with the muscle of a big brother behind
them just in case they should need it. The re-invention of big companies
as smaller, leaner, muscular and more focused units in parallel with the
rise of an independent Internet Cyberwarrior class is the idea that looks
set to see us through until the next wave of corporate re-invention.

This is not to say that the kind of unbundling and deconstruction of
the value-chain by digital entrepreneurs, as noted below, is not a serious
force to be reckoned with but they will often innovate and then sell out
to a bigger player to avoid remaining merely a niche service. What is true
is that globalization makes access to the latest knowledge more important in every domain. As the price of communication drops to near zero
millions of knowledge workers spread across the globe are just a cheap
telephone call or a modem away from where their knowledge can be
used to advantage. Thus even service activities that we believed would
always be 'home-based' like shopping, insurance, retailing, booking airline
tickets, etc., might now be handled by workers many thousands of miles

away from the point of final delivery. An urgent software problem can be handed over to a Californian facilities house at 4 pm in the afternoon, just as the American workers there are thinking about going home for tea, without inconveniencing the customer. Later it can be squirted down the line to early risers in Bangalore who will work on it 'overnight' so that the customer gets his or her solution the next morning unaware that it was solved half way around the world without using a 'local' night shift.

The western world's most valuable, and possibly time-limited, advantage is its current capacity to produce ideas. This advantage is currently clearly related to the sheer number of students to which it gives the opportunity to access higher education. The number of college and university students in the US is around 12.5 million compared with three million in China which has a population five times the size. In the face of ageing populations and declining birth rates over much of the western world such a quantitative advantage looks fragile and the development of new knowledge-growing environments that can lift this to a qualitative, knowledge-surplus advantage must be a priority for both western business and academe.

## Working on the connections

Organizations which we work in or deal with as customers grow or decline as demand for their products and services grows and declines but whatever their size they cannot survive without making an effort to connect on a number of levels with a variety of other people and institutions.

1.  They have to connect with customers, suppliers and the regulated world in which they operate. The last responsibility of course varies considerably around the world since, despite the hype, there is no such thing as 'global regulation'.
2.  They have to connect with employees via a range of internal communication systems designed to carry messages about the needs, aims and requirements of the enterprise and to secure information about progress in meeting objectives and satisfying customers.
3.  They may have to connect with the ostensible owners of the enterprise, e.g. shareholders, ratepayers or taxpayers, to explain occasionally what they are doing and why they are doing it.

All organizations thus spend a considerable part of their communal intelligence connecting with a wide spectrum of people and yet the judgement of recent history is that they rarely do it very well. Organizations as diverse as the UK's Royal Family, Shell and Volkswagen have, at different times, failed to get their messages across resulting in confusion about their objectives, suspicion about their motives and damage to their image.

## I.   Reaching out: connecting with customers

As citizens of nations that seek to grow economically by buying and selling products and services in markets we are all someone's customer at some time or other. The way that we obtain information about the options and choices available to us in a market and the search costs in time, effort and money that we have to invest to do it, are two of the most critical factors in the way that we handle the asymmetry of information that accompanies the making of most markets. If we always knew the best options for all the goods and services in which we were interested one supplier would always triumph and the market would quickly give way to a monopoly (see Chapter 6). It is the fact that someone knows something that we don't that generates markets and gives a living to the world's great population of middle-persons. Networking technology is transforming search costs, causing the decomposition of asymmetries of information in many areas and facilitating, at almost zero cost, the purest of contact between buyers and sellers. As potential consumers we are bombarded with information, images and text funded by companies to remind us about their products, to tell us about something new or to offer us a special deal. This particular part of the 'connecting' business is one of the most pervasive and resource-intensive activities in any developed society.

### May I take a few moments of your time?

In the 1950s the sales pitch was epitomized by the growth of television advertising and by the door-to-door salesman selling brushes, insurance or the *Encyclopaedia Britannica*. The sales force was one of the most effective ways of instigating a 'rich' encounter. Everything could be explained on a sofa or around a table. Rubbish could be vacuumed up off the floor, different insurance policies explored and sold on the spot (or mis-sold as they often were in the UK) and the delights of a series of cookery books displayed close to the kitchen where they might be used. The communication of such rich information (whatever its quality) required time-consuming encounters with a small audience, often of one, which added up to perhaps no more than 20–25 actual pitches being made in a single day. Such a high cost was regarded as necessary if the product was going to get into homes and be aided in its dispersal by word of mouth.

These rich encounters were supported by the less rich but widely viewed poster sites, TV advertising and mail-shots that reinforced the more intensive work of the salesperson. A company's marketing mix thus became a balance between 'richness' and 'reach'. Richness was expensive and touched only a small number of customers but it offered a lot of information that could be manipulated in response to questions. Reach was cheap, it got to many more people but, by its very nature, it was one-way, brief and transient. Evans and Wurster [3] have suggested that the boundaries of the modern corporation are now being set by the economics of exchanging information in association with universal standards of communication which at almost zero cost allow an extension of reach with negligible sacrifice of richness. They provide a number of examples, e.g. retail banking and classified advertising in newspapers, to show the vulnerability of traditional value chains to new entrants who might choose to cherry-pick the profitable 'information' bits that could be digitized and distributed via the Internet. They also point to the mind-set of the old compromise which tried to be an attractive shop-front as well as a well-stocked warehouse and often failed to succeed well on either count. Now, as in the case of music CDs, software and books, a Web site can offer superior information, huge stocks and quick response times without having to invest in warehousing or expensive town centre shop fronts.

Many other products and services will soon be available in the same way. Although still in its infancy supermarket purchases via the Internet are in experimental or pilot mode at many places around the world. At the moment they are generally run by the traditional retailers who, with their understanding of the complex supply chain of perishable products, may be able to retain control of this particular kind of cyber-shopping. But, as shown below in the case of *Encyclopaedia Britannica* (EB), the attractions of cheap richness with a wide reach to new entrants to markets should not be underestimated by even the most successful of current businesses models.

*Gnawing away at the value chain*

There is always a part of the value chain that the new breed of digital entrepreneurs might have a pick at. Evans and Wurster [3] highlighted the near demise of EB to illuminate the spectacular way in which new competitors in alliance with IT can disrupt the conventional value propositions of a well-established business. Sales of EB had plummeted from 350 000 hard copies per year in 1993 to only 25 000 by 1997 as much cheaper CD-ROM products like Microsoft's *Encarta* seemed to come from nowhere to threaten the serious hard-copy encyclopaedia business. The economics are devastating. Encarta sells for around $50 but is also often bundled in free with the purchase of a computer while EB sells for around $2200. EB was a high-quality product with a worldwide reputation while Encarta's content was licensed from the Funk and Wagnalls encyclopedia, a cheap and cheerful product that was often sold in supermarkets. In the past parents had paid for EB, often on credit, because despite its high cost it seemed the 'right thing' to have in the house for their children. When an apparently similar offering came free with a computer, which was easier to search, required no shelf space, was spruced up with a few movie clips and seemed to offer the same kind of information as EB parents felt happy that they had done two right things for the price of one. They had provided a computer (the new 'right' thing to do) and an encyclopaedia (the old 'right' thing to do).

The market for encyclopaedias, despite protestations from EB about the poorer quality of these other offerings, turned out to be more about doing the right thing than securing top-quality information validated by a highly-respected brand name. Although highlighting to some extent the general dangers of complacency in rapidly changing markets the EB story is also a warning about how quickly and profoundly the new economics of information can change the rules of competition. Traditional sources of competitive advantage, such as a first-class sales force, a supreme brand, excellent content, well-established marketing and extensive distribution facilities, can all crumble in the face of new production techniques and new ways of reaching customers. When the threat became really obvious EB did develop a CD-ROM version of the encyclopaedia. Initially, to avoid undercutting the sales force, the company included it free with the printed version or charged $1000 to anyone buying it by itself. Such a compromise was to little avail however as the rot had already set in and revenues continued to decline. Eventually EB's owners, a trust owned by the University of Chicago, sold out and the new owners, having dispensed with their entire sales force in early 1998, are attempting to rebuild the EB's business around a CD-ROM version that can be supplemented by information from the Internet. Surprisingly the editorial content of EB represented only 5 per cent of its costs. Its vulnerability was derived principally from 'its dependence on the economics of a different kind of information, the economics of personal selling' [3] which represented the bulk of its costs, a factor which is clearly pertinent to many other businesses, e.g. car sales, insurance, real estate, toys, travel and clothes.

While the digitized address list based on the zip codes and post-codes used by modern postal services has been one of the most potent marketing tools of the 1990s, the delivery of digital images, explanations, and updates on products and services to virtual addresses on the Internet looks like being the 'killer' marketing tool of the new century, particularly if it can be accessed via a digital television with interactive facilities. Connecting with the customer now seems more up for grabs than ever before as new entrepreneurs roam cyberspace looking for likely targets. They are on the lookout for the plum bits of a company's value chain to deconstruct. By peeling off the critical bits and leaving the original provider holding expensive physical assets (once so necessary to build up the business and construct barriers to entry) and offering the selected bits to customers as their whole business they hope for bigger margins at much reduced cost. All big companies face the possibility of such cherry picking. The coincidence of uncertain events, technology, de-regulation and a growing desire by customers to have direct access to key information suggests that the time of the broker, the middleman and the agent is over unless they can offer their customers something else of value, like comparative data to help them choose between particular products or services.

## Reuters awake!

During 1998 Reuters, a world leader in the $5.8 billion financial information business with some 40 per cent of the industry's revenues, was accused of stealing information from Bloomberg, its main rival. Reuters' revenues though substantial have depended largely on its trading floor business where dealers use its systems to price securities and currencies. As investment banks merge the number of traders and thus the number of screens needed is falling and this looks like the wrong sort of business to be dominating. The growth area is on the buying side among money managers and big institutional investors who want to know if, say, a particular bond would be a useful addition to their portfolios and Bloomberg has cornered this market. It provides terminals that come with a range of analytical tools which as well as giving bond prices also gives price histories and past performance compared with other investments. Reuters has only recently entered the 'complete with tools' market with its Reuters' 3000 but the tools came from a company, Reuters' Analytics, which is alleged to have hired a company founded by a former Bloomberg employee to steal information about Bloomberg's analytical software.

Coincident with these allegations is the introduction of the single European currency which will reduce greatly the scope for foreign exchange dealing. Reuters makes a large part of its earnings from supplying information to this declining market and the consolidation of European banks that is likely to result looks like more bad news in the pipeline.

Like many others involved in the manipulation of price-sensitive information money managers want to add their own whistles and bells to the consensus-driven capabilities offered by data providers and there are lots of software companies who will be only too willing to provide them with tailored solutions. The premium prices once paid for basic financial information has already fallen sharply (to almost zero in the US) and will fall further as such solutions become commonplace. Big players like Reuters who have made a good living from the fast delivery of 'simple' information will have to re-think seriously their strategies around more bespoke solutions if they are to survive.

## Particles and HOGs

Reaching out to customers has been a loud mantra of management commentators during the last quarter of the century. Although good at facilitating the collection of data and charting the preferences of existing customers, stand-alone computer databases have not been too insightful in guiding companies to new customers or in identifying the potential source of new competitors. What is coming to be called E-commerce, Net.Commerce or E-business (see Chapter 6) offers the potential, when used in association with software like IBM's 'Intelligent Miner', for a deeper analysis of the individual tastes, habits and preferences of both current and potential customers at the micro level rather than at the more scatter-gun level of the postcode or zip code. Such 'particle' marketing will supposedly facilitate the kind of follow-up that encourages us to feel special or unique in our relations with suppliers.

In a range of advertisements for its E-business in newspapers in the UK during 1998 IBM showcased the kind of benefits that some of its customers had gained from using its software in conjunction with the Internet. It reported that KLM discovered that many passengers flew economy to the US from Europe but business class back home to cope better with jet lag, so the airline put together a 'mixed' package to cater for them. Safeway supermarkets, having analysed the buying habits of eight million customers, were able to ensure that vegetarians were not sent junk mail on meat promotions and that only people who bought children's products received information on new children's videos. French power utility Électricité de France was able to analyse 10 000 press articles in a few hours to identify a marked shift in attitudes towards the idea of an electric car. Formerly promoted as a gimmick they realized that it could now be promoted as a viable second car.

Such possibilities are undoubtedly valuable in the war to gain a competitive edge and no doubt our electronic mail boxes will become the doormats on which some very personalized junk mail will fall. But until every household has a simple-to-use electronic doormat this will be as well as, rather than instead of, the paper-based promotions that we already receive. Depending on our ability to read the signs on the envelope before we chuck it, it will have the same kind of success rate. Thus 'reach' will invariably increase and be very cost-effective but the anticipated 'richness', however skilfully put together, may be exaggerated especially in relation to serious purchases well above the low-cost item and 'special offer' level. Above this level making contact with existing and potential customers in real space, i.e. orchestrating 'rich' experiences, rather than electronically via a computer screen or a printout, will remain important as customer choice multiplies and cost and qualitative differences look marginal.

The 90-year-old Harley Davidson Company of Milwaukee was written off in the 1980s as a casualty of Japanese superiority in motorcycle engineering. Quality had begun to decline dramatically with customers complaining of leaking oil, missing parts and serious vibration problems as AMF, who owned the company, tripled production over a short four-year

period in a rush to get more motorcycles out of the door. As a consequence their market share fell from 40 per cent in 1979 to 23 per cent in
1983. A buyout of AMF in 1981 by Harley executives was followed by an
audit to kick-start a 10-year plan, something the company had never done
before. The audit revealed the importance of quality in every aspect of
bike production leading to the creation of employee-based work teams
managing their own quality control and inventory at every level. As part
of this programme Harley managers began sponsoring and participating in
weekend Harley rallies where the managers listened to what Harley riders had to say and then fed this information back into ideas for engine and
styling improvements. Later Harley employees started the Harley Owners'
Groups, more popularly known as HOGs which fortuitously corresponds
to the affectionate generic name that owners give to their Harleys. HOGs
began sponsoring motorcycle events almost every week-end somewhere
in the US and more than 100 000 HOG members participate in nationally
advertized events, frequently held to support charitable causes. Good management and customer loyalty paid off and by 1993 Harley had taken over
60 per cent of the US big bike market. All Harley owners can join a HOG
to get a pin, patch, membership card and six issues of the club's official
publication *Hog Tales*. Staying close to the customer, finding out what
makes Harley riders tick and providing a community as well as a product
has become the hallmark of this company's connecting policy, helping it
to improve both quality and home sales. Harley has even overcome initial
European objections to their weight and 'agricultural' engines to become
a major exporter to the EU.

## Turning Japanese

As a tribute to the growing cultural diversity of their customers many
western organizations now go to considerable trouble to educate their
staff about the communication habits of other cultures, especially in Asia.
These efforts often include such niceties as remembering to use both
hands to present and receive business cards in Japan and paying close and
obvious attention to those cards that you receive rather than pocketing
them straight away as you might do at home. During difficult negotiations
with Chinese people executives are urged always to leave some room
for a face-saving escape so that no one is pushed into saying an outright
'No!' Western managers are also urged always to take a gift – something

expensive in Japan but in other parts of Asia something modest is more polite as outside Japan it is the thought, rather than the value, that counts and too expensive a gift might put pressure on the recipient to respond in kind. Also beware that certain gifts might symbolize something unhelpful to your cause. In China carnations suggest mourning and clocks are associated with dying. Be prepared for plenty of male chauvinism in Asia and avoid physical contact. Hugging or back-slapping chumminess to celebrate the consummation of a deal is generally not appreciated in Asia and touching someone's head (the dwelling place of the soul) is definitely out, as is presenting your host with the soles of your feet. When offering a Chinese client a hotel with room be careful to note that number four is out (bad luck), but that seven is OK (good luck).

The continuing need for such preparations belies the culturally sterilized image that the purveyors of a globally homogenized business world often present to us. Every big city in the world may have access to the same fast food but they eat it differently. Similarly although the bright young people of Japan study the same MBAs as their counterparts in the US, often at the same colleges, it is unusual for a chief executive of a US firm to be Japanese or vice versa. The Scottish-born head of Mazda, put in place by Mazda's partner Ford to help them out of trouble, is still a rare exception and it will be interesting to see if this kind of cultural exchange in the executive world will accelerate much after 2000. I suspect that it will but as a trickle rather than a flood.

## Regulating for the customer

The regulation of commerce and trade comes in many guises. It is a topic of considerable currency given the avalanche of privatizations that is still sweeping Western Europe and that is about to engulf some of the industrialized nations of eastern Asia. Many of the industries most affected by regulation are in the connecting business: airlines, telecommunications, post-offices, or PTTs as they are known in Europe, the media and highway provision. Regulation, give or take a few cultural differences, aims to ensure that markets are monitored to ensure fair competition, the prevention of monopolies that create barriers to entry for new competitors and that customers of once public-owned monopolies get a fair deal from their operation in the private domain. Connecting with regulators, anti-trust agencies and monopoly commissions of one type or another is the price organizations pay for the de-regulation and privatization of the business environment. Most regulation, as Rupert Murdoch found in China with his Star TV global satellite business, is still controlled by the nation state. The EU is busy putting in place regulatory regimes that will cover all of its members and so in Europe the harmonization of regulation across national borders will eventually transcend those borders, but it is a slow and tortuous process. Regulators have the unenviable role of representing citizens and customers. They have to try to balance those movements and fluctuations in the market which are a normal part of competitive commerce against those which, by design or by default, throw up seemingly incontestable or impenetrable positions for certain firms. Standard Oil, IBM and AT&T have all been broken up, in the public interest, as a result of regulatory interference. More recently Microsoft has had to face the glare of an anti-trust action promoted by the US Department of Justice and the telecommunications industry throughout the world is in a melting pot of privatization and regulatory activity.

## 2.   Connecting with employees

A regular feature of a company's re-structuring, re-engineering or re-anything is a fresh look at internal communications. Inevitably it finds that they are not working, that the communication channels put in place during the last re-something have become silted up and need to be re-visited. The usual discovery is that old habits have returned, the top-down approach has crept back in and there is a need to shift things around again to facilitate more upward and horizontal communication flows. Despite the popularity of flatter management structures, the growth of human resource units and more employee-oriented approaches to organizing work, any discussion with any group of workers about the strengths and weaknesses of their organization will inevitably centre on the issue of poor communication. They will often cite examples of information about mergers, take-overs, downsizing, lay-offs, re-structuring, changes to pay rates, etc. as areas where they have been kept in the dark for too long before being told. Because of the direct impact on workers of such issues they often get a 'constructed' version of the story first via the 'grapevine' which, however valuable it may be as part of an internal communication network, often breeds bad news faster than good. Nervous employees are always more receptive to rumours and although constant interaction between the different actors in organizations is impossible the rumour mill, handy as it can be to prepare people for some changes, is not the way to hear about a merger or impending redundancies.

> Of the 30 000 managers, professionals, and clerical personnel surveyed by Opinion Research Corporation over a four-year period, 60 per cent felt that their organizations were not doing a good job of keeping them informed about company matters. Moreover, fewer than 30 per cent felt that their companies were willing to listen to their problems. [4]

'No one tells us anything' or 'we only get to know when it's too late or all over' must be two of the most common responses from workers to questions about the effectiveness of communications within organizations, large or small, public or private, for profit or not-for-profit. In interviews with 350 managers and staff at UK organizations employing in excess of 1000 people in late 1998 Mori [5] discovered that less than 10 per cent felt that their views were valued by their organization and only 15 per cent 'strongly agreed' that they have confidence in their organization's leadership. Kevin Thomson, chairman of the Marketing and Communications Agency that commissioned the survey noted that:

> The study's findings illustrate that UK organizations are not nourishing their intellectual and emotional capital by cultivating commitment and understanding in their employees. This is a dangerous scenario on the eve of a global recession. [6]

He also suggested that a lack of communication between employers and employees is a key factor leading to negative attitudes among staff.

## Managing curiosity

One of the obstacles to effective internal communication is that organizations are generally not built to facilitate it. Indeed the very nature of building up an organization around 'compartments' of skills to deliver its objectives successfully tends to inhibit, and at its worst deny, good internal communication. As organizations grow, whatever technology they have available and however flat their management structure, internal communications inevitably get worse. The multi-disciplinary teams that operate in many organizations today often owe their genesis to communication failures of one kind or another. Such teams are seen as a powerful antidote to information retention by small groups whose status was defined by specialist knowledge and who had no incentive to share it until pressed by calamity. At such times the group would be at pains to explain how, despite the walls and barbed wire, everyone surely knew what they knew and that they shouldn't be held solely responsible! The multi-disciplinary team however hasn't really penetrated the mystery of compartments; rather it is generally used in an ad hoc way to address particular challenges which when fixed find employees releasing huge sighs of relief as they flee back over Hadrian's Wall to the less stressful management of mono-thinking. This happy rush back to the known, the understood and the comfortable is something with which all of us who have worked on multi-disciplinary projects can identify. It's not that we didn't enjoy new challenges or the triumph of mixing our skills with those of others, it is the relief at being able to give our curiosity a rest for a time and to re-charge our batteries among the familiar ornaments of our own discipline.

But such a respite is not an option in many of the fast-moving markets of the modern world. It is often mooted that the future economics and success of the firm, the enterprise and the global corporation will largely depend on it using and mobilizing the knowledge, imagination, curiosity and talent of its employees – all of the time. Tom Peters' questions: 'What if we could learn to tap the wonderful, rich differences among people? Wouldn't a corporation that could exploit the uniqueness of each of its 1000 employees (or 10 or 10 000) be phenomenally powerful? Put negatively, isn't a corporation that doesn't figure out how to use the special curiosities of each of its people headed for trouble?' [7] capture the spirit of the times even if no one has quite worked out how to answer them. In the same work Peters, inspired by Albert Einstein's famous 'curiosity is more important than knowledge', takes issue with Peter Drucker's equally famous 'knowledge worker' and suggests that a bigger and more important idea than the 'knowledge worker' would be 'curiosity worker'. Although naturally curious humans have learnt that discovering more in the work-place is often associated with being given more to do, often without any additional reward or recognition. So they often save their curiosity for out-of-work experiences, which to them are often much more fulfilling, perhaps developing just the kind of 'unique' expertise that Peters wants to see brought back and shared in the workplace.

This challenge of 'curiosity-transfer' has often been set out but rarely met. Indeed the sharing of knowledge developed by individuals at work in a fluid and dynamic way around the organization is still something that most organizations strive for but have not achieved to the extent they would want. 'The Power of Knowledge', a 1998 report from KPMG Management Consulting in the UK, suggests that knowledge management is still a largely misunderstood issue within many organizations. They suggest that even simple questions like 'do you know who your customers are? still often remain unanswered. They make a number of suggestions to help, e.g. staff meetings to discuss ideas (see *Show Time* below) and an appraisal system that rewards staff known to share expertise actively. They emphasize (unsurprisingly) that knowledge management is about making the best use of the experience within a company, sharing that experience with others, supporting innovation and making sure that IT is properly harnessed to the business strategy. They note that poor knowledge management can create large discrepancies between the performances of different divisions carrying out very different tasks and could, if for instance a company ever lost its senior technical team to a competitor, result in untrained juniors with precious little know-how being left to make mission-critical decisions.

## Barriers and barbarians

Volumes of material have been written about the importance of good internal communications in organizations for maintaining morale, generating higher levels of motivation and job satisfaction, all of which in turn help achieve better individual and organizational performance. Yet the old barriers to good communications are still thriving 50 years after people-conscious management started its journey into the pages of management books and journals. They include:

- status-conscious hierarchies
- too many organizational levels
- Closed functional compartments seeking to protect the mystery of their specialization against the barbarians who would misuse their secrets (the Hadrian's Wall Effect)

- The continuing status allocated to the holders of secrets rather than to those who celebrate openness and sharing
- Information overload, too much organizational 'noise' squeezing out the important signals
- Interpersonal conflict arising from plain old dislike or widely differing perceptions of similar issues
- Poor listening and poor attention span
- The imprecise use of language and fuzzy vocabulary that skirts around the precision required for dealing with difficult interpersonal relations
- A failure to frame messages in ways that different groups can comprehend and assimilate.

There are other more general reasons for failure. One is simply the amount of time it takes to communicate effectively. In a world increasingly impatient and unwilling to spend time on anything which does not seem directly related to the bottom line effective internal communication is often left to sort itself out. Poor connectivity between employees for any of the above reasons might well impact on the bottom line as it builds up over time but it usually takes a dramatic example, e.g. a shipwreck, an oil spillage, a near miss above an airport or the near melt-down of a nuclear power station, to prove it. Yet another reason may be cultural; for example in the UK we have inherited a minimalist 'need to know' philosophy which inevitably creates both conscious and unconscious sins of omission. In Japan the cultural card, for all the sharing done among small quality teams, is likely to manifest itself in secrecy bred out of respect for authority, i.e. though you know you don't say because you're not supposed to. In Germany hard factual information is usually communicated well through the proper channels but the softer more fuzzy stuff is given less chance to surface. In southern Europe the bigger picture might always seem more important than getting bogged down with communicating a lot of complicated detail.

We also have to face the reality that some individuals, whatever culture they belong to, will never be able to communicate well however many tools and instruments we provide to help break down the barriers. I once returned to my office in a university to meet a colleague who brushed past me in the doorway. He said nothing but had left a note on my desk saying that he would like a word with me. There was no dispute, we had good relations and he only wanted to talk about routine things, but the note had to come first, however close we got while passing in a doorway. He was a man who found it difficult to communicate with anyone and, given that his job as a lecturer involved communicating with a wide range of people every day, he would probably have been happier in another occupation. Many academics, for all the theatre involved in their daily presentations, find open communication within their host organizations difficult. They invent committees on a daily basis to avoid effective communication and, like some other occupational groups, e.g. doctors, positively revel in obfuscation. It should not surprise us therefore that many populations of workers in other less presentational occupations have problems communicating.

## Show time

Paradoxically the formal orchestration of policy meetings, committee meetings and so on, although an obvious recognition of the need to provide settings for people to exchange information and influence one another, often produces little or nothing in the way of key decisions. All organizations invest a tremendous amount of time in setting up formal mechanisms for the group deliberation of problems and challenges which, on close examination of the correlation between group decisions and subsequent action, often prove to be nearly empty displays. We have come to know that the real negotiations go on within much smaller groups either before or after the meeting that is supposed to consider them. We have also grown adept at using language in ways that imply openness and transparency during these public displays while knowing that in reality something else has been agreed or that something else is going to happen. It is not unusual for groups to retire from meetings believing that certain policies or practices have been adopted only to receive some later communication, from the chief officer or whoever, explaining why this will now not be possible and that the following changes have had to be made. Such actions are often justified by declaring that 'new information has come to light' that was not available previously. Sometimes a rebellion of 'members' seeks a further meeting (an expensive and troublesome outcome) but often the tacit understanding that this is the way things really work (i.e. inertia) triumphs and the new decisions are allowed to go forward. We have grown to accept that many displays of group activity only imply the opportunity for communication and negotiation and we seem happy to collude in this. Those who don't collude are seen to be 'rocking the boat' and the British response to this is usually 'can it really be worth all this trouble and aggravation?'

This illusion value of the instruments of participation trickles down into all levels of organizational life. Hours and hours of work time are spent on showpiece gatherings while everyone knows that substance and reality lie somewhere else. The concomitant of all this experience should be that we openly and vigorously re-assess the fora that we use for negotiation and discussion and start building new channels. If 'the show' rather than the outcome is the thing we can perhaps use networking technology to provide an outlet for it. We won't have to spend our time at dull events, we will have more time to formulate our contributions and we will have access to precisely what was said (lack of precision being a particularly potent form of decision manipulation). Cut the 'shows' by 50 per cent and we seriously reduce the frustration and angst that knowing the real score always causes because we will have removed the theatre of irritating pretence that we have to sit through. 'But some of us want the theatre', I hear you cry. It's important, it's symbolic, it helps bonding and sometimes our voice is heard and we change things. No problem. Review all the 'shows', analyse those that seem to have had the most effective outcomes over a year or so and then just cut those that don't meet a minimum level of real participation as measured by changed agendas.

Most of my scepticism about the role of 'show' meetings in organizations derives from the lack of analysis between value (as in time spent), outcome (as in real decisions taken) and need (as in just how necessary is it to take 20 people away from the core business to do this). This last point is particularly true with regard to time available for customers versus time used up in meetings. I have lost count of the number of times that I have made enquiries of various service providers only to be told that the supervisor or relevant person is 'away at a meeting' and no decision can be taken without them. Such experiences also suggest that the pushing downward of decision-taking to those nearer the customer, so heralded in the management literature, may still have some way to go as an organizational norm. Where the value of meetings is regularly reviewed and doesn't preclude or inhibit the 'closing down' of old established groups, assemblies and rituals, then the 'show' can come to have some real meaning, not least in monitoring the quality of the decision being made by the executive branch of the organization.

## Email, aggression and Health Warnings

Communicating with each other via Email over vast distances has brought many benefits and creative possibilities. Fixing up a speaker for a conference who would otherwise be 'protected' by a phalanx of agitated gatekeepers, maintaining links with friends and colleagues all over the world and the 'almost' guarantee that the recipient will get your message some time, have made Email the Internet's most popular facility. However our increasing use of Email over short distances – room-to-room and building-to-building – is leading to a decline in face-to-face contact and this carries with it some serious social disadvantages. There is a great deal of anecdotal evidence to suggest that internal Email is often used in a thoughtless or aggressive way. During June 1997 Novell published the results of a survey of 1000 regular Email users that added a slice of hard evidence to the many stories of muddle and hurt that excessive Email use has caused. It revealed that over half of the respondents had received abusive Emails that had seriously affected working relationships. These impacts were serious enough for a third of this group to have stopped communicating with a colleague for a significant time, while some were so upset enough by these 'flame' mails that they actually left their jobs. In this survey 46 per cent of the respondents declared that Email had reduced face-to-face communication, and many others were convinced that it impaired co-operation, generated greater internal conflict, caused more bullying, reduced productivity and generated an unpleasant working atmosphere.

Overdosing on Email inside organizations reduces the physical signals and tonal clues that we value so much when garnering meaning and that so naturally grease the rails during the to-and-fro of face-to-face communication. Encouraged by a culture of brevity, short sharp sentences that are meant to be grasped quickly, the lack of care which can characterize this kind of communication can often result in messages that are impetuous, ill thought out and virulent. The Novell research also showed that most anti-social Emails were sent from managers to their subordinates with one in six of the respondents reporting that they had been officially disciplined by a manager via Email. Needless to say such Emails were five time more likely to have been sent by men than women.

Managers in the UK can have a reputation for being fuzzy when dealing with difficult issues, particularly personnel issues. This is particularly true within academic institutions where Email is well established and where some of those higher up the managerial ladder owe their position more to doffing caps and lying low than to speaking their minds. It is not surprising then that they often fail to say what they mean face-to-face either out of sheer gutlessness or an inability to command a suitable vocabulary to cope with difficult interpersonal situations. Such people are likely to seize on Email as a salvation. No need to face the person, not yet at any rate, just press 'send' to squirt out the words that they wouldn't dream of using otherwise and all with no danger of seeing or hearing the recipient's immediate response.

Used in such ways Email becomes a coward's charter rather than a valuable adjunct to intra-organizational communication. Nonetheless we can expect this form of communication to increase because it is easier and involves less stress for the sender. Concomitantly we can expect face-to-face communication within and around buildings to decrease. Some mitigation might come from the potential advocacy of the 'printer' in creating a record that rarely exists during real-space conversations. Perhaps a 'health warning' printed at the top of each Email application reminding those moved to do a bit of bullying this way that 'what you are about to send may be printed out and archived via a paper record' might help curb the worst excesses.

*Face time*

Given the growing ubiquity of electronic rather than face-to-face contact it is not surprising that some encounters in organizations are now so rare that, when achieved, they earn a much higher recognition factor than they ever did. As everyone who wants to influence events through a president, corporate linch-pin, government minister or vice-chancellor knows it is proximity to the 'body' that brings respect, power and patronage. Press reports call it 'someone close to', envious academics call it 'corridor-creeping', White House staff call it face time and all of us set enough store by it to take some trouble to get our own share of face time whenever we can. At work we may fall back on Email or group-sharing networks like Lotus Notes for day-to-day exchanges with colleagues but when it comes to serious stuff, our salary, our continued employment, the discomfort of a re-structuring, etc., we want some face time with the body responsible. This is where we see, hear and feel the responses to our worries, questions and ideas and we feel cheated if we don't get any. Seeing is not only believing; it also confers status. An Email or an internal memo from the boss proves that we are in touch with a higher being but to be able to report a meeting or several meetings with him or her puts us in another league vis-a-vis our work colleagues. As the opportunity for face time decreases so our status increases when we are granted some.

Scarcity always inflates value and as chief executives become rarer so the value of even the most trivial face time increases in the eyes of beholders. This poses a problem for the leaders of organizations. They know that face time is important but increasingly they have less of it to give so on whom should they bestow it on? They have external affairs to deal with, finance to handle, the changing boundaries of the organization to patrol, protect and influence and so such one-on-ones, many of which will be uncomfortably grounded in individual struggles and differences, have to be carefully rationed. However putting off serious interpersonal stuff for another day inevitably means having to find a much bigger window of time to sort it out later when it reaches the catastrophe level. The early and effective identification of human resource problems needs face time and the executive who uses all of his or her senses to identify and action such problems promptly will use far less of their time than if they allow the problems to grow and fester.

## 'Ask HR'

Big companies with staff scattered all over the globe are beginning to accept that face time, particularly with regard to dealing with routine personnel issues, is going to be in even shorter supply. One approach is for a company to put its employment and management handbooks on its Intranet so that for instance someone interested in applying for maternity leave can access a handy checklist and Email the personnel department for additional information pertaining to her own circumstances. Information on grievance procedures, promotion policy, pensions, annual leave, sick pay, etc. can be made accessible in this way to all employees wherever they are allowing for out-of-office-hours consultation, easy updating and, most important, consistency in all the information provided. In really big concerns an internal call centre manned by staff who can handle different levels of enquiry can back up the information held on the Intranet. Lloyds TSB in the UK launched its national call centre in 1997 to advise managers and personnel advisers, rather than general staff, with the aim of sharing management burdens, ensuring consistency and tracking the issues which seem to cause the most problems.

IBM's much more ambitious 'Ask HR' employs 70 staff who can serve all the company's 92 000 employees worldwide from one multilingual point of contact. The centre offers advice at different levels of complexity but around 80 per cent of its enquiries are straightforward and can be answered on the spot. The more complicated ones are handled by more experienced personnel who aim to produce a reply within two days. As in many other companies IBM employees used to take their routine queries to their manager who then went to their local personnel advisor. This was all very time-consuming and not always satisfactory when the manager or advisor were tied up with other business.

Such a central call centre backed up by detailed Intranet checklists should free the Human Resources (HR) department to concentrate on addressing strategic issues such as appropriate salary levels, staff turnover and the changing skills and resources needed as the company's environment changes. Managers should also have more time to discuss career roles and salary prospects with staff, having been relieved of the more routine stuff. Separating the operational from the strategic parts of the HR function allows the operational side of HR (always perceived as a cost) to be more effective while the strategic part of HR can be seen to be actually adding value. No one approach offers a panacea in the HR domain but an intelligent appraisal of the kinds of encounter that require face time versus those which can be handled satisfactorily by easily accessible alternative sources of information can at least bring some logic to one of the most important parts of the internal communications process.

## Constructing urgency: who started it?

Senior managers are hampered in their desire (if they have one) to walk successfully the tightrope of balancing face time with their other responsibilities by the tyranny of the many forms of portable communication that they are now expected to carry around and to which they are obliged to respond. The mobile phone, the bleeping pager, accessing Email from whatever location – all these use up time on the hoof which might have been better spared for the refreshment of those parts that will be needed to deal with people rather than devices. This is not an easy trick to turn.

Seeking people on the move can become a habit. We have the technology so why not use it? Such a cavalier approach to connecting with people wherever they are has given rise to a 'cry wolf' kind of urgency where the trivial and the important merge in a stressful avalanche of calls and messages. If not filtered in some way this can render the recipient confused, stifling and impeding action rather than accelerating it as hoped.

The premium now so often given to face time may derive, in part at least, from the kind of constructed urgency touched on in Chapter 2. Surrounded by all the apparatus of networking, Email and paper correspondence that dominates communications in organizations it is easy to see that priorities constructed out of interaction with computer systems can seem more important than dealing with individuals in real space. Status consciousness among managers may be absent from the *Harvard Business Review* but it is alive and well in many large organizations and with it can come some precious definitions of urgency that inevitably give second place to troublesome humans. It is easy to fall in with habits of 'vital definition' where what is important emerges (if the truth were known) as a messy mix of preferences and responsibilities. At such times we hope that no one notices when we use our position to define and act on our preferences while using the language of responsibility to portray it as urgent.

This is not to suggest that all the urgent requests or demands made on us stem from whimsy but it warns us to beware of the growing cult of 'everything is urgent'. Such awareness might encourage us to step back at times of workplace stress and perhaps dare to ask (a bit like Oliver Twist without the bowl) why something has to be done overnight or within the next 24 hours. The line back to the original source may be long but the perpetrator closest to you may choose to give up rather than to explain that this particular urgency has been constructed by someone four moves back who has failed to deliver their own part of the job on time. Or, just as likely, they have built in a massive margin for error so that they can relax within a big time envelope while you give yourself a heart attack struggling to work with a small one. It's always worth asking the question.

## Local rationalities

As noted above a considerable part of organizational life is dedicated to not connecting. At many levels within large organizations avoiding making connections comes about simply as a result of how individuals seek to cope with bigness. One way, sometimes unconscious but always powerful, is the way that we create a web of local rationalities for what we do. This will encompass how we behave, the little codes and rituals we use, the secrets we keep within our group and the community spirit that we engender in the compartments in which we 'live' – the creation of a village football team in the big city. Mission statements and the 'big picture' may be disseminated, talked about, promoted and even acted on but it is the local rationality of units and departments that will ultimately determine which changes will or will not be implemented effectively.

The interface between big and small rationalities can often produce outcomes that surprise and shock all concerned. A residential college that takes senior managers in for three-week intensive courses sought to develop a culture where the students stay on over the weekends to do syndicate work, to bond and to use the resources of the library. Mature students with families are notoriously difficult to keep away from home and hearth, and it is well known that given half a chance they will slip off back to their home comforts especially if home is not too far away. At this particular residential college all the tutors regularly reinforced the 'stay-on-campus' culture and so all should have been well. The catering chef however, working on a tightly controlled procurement budget, needs to know precisely how many meals to prepare and being a realist he knows that dinner on Friday evening could be something of a moveable feast. So he posts up a big notice in the canteen asking people to sign up if they are going to stay on for weekend meals. It's a small chink in the armour of the main mission by suggesting that it could still be optional whether one stayed on over the weekend or not. It might also suggest that staying on just gives the kitchen staff more problems and it would be a relief for them to have fewer people to cater for. The intersection between the two rationalities creates enough ambiguity for some students to feel relaxed about bunking off home.

A manager with a large office of administrative staff under her control is trying to rationalize the practice of carrying several days' holiday over into the next year. Some staff have been carrying ten or more days over and this is making the cover for some duties unmanageable. She asks the office supervisor to explain to everyone that the practice of carrying any more than three days' holiday over into another year is to cease and that in future the norm will be that all staff use all their holidays in the year in which they fall due. The supervisor sends a note round to the staff asking them to let her know how many days holiday they would like to carry over into the new year. The upshot is a concentration on current entitlements rather than on change which, as a conscious or unconscious side-effect, ensures a hostile reception to the new policy.

Managers trying to abandon or modify flexi-time arrangements often have a similar experience. The occasional move to inter-disciplinary teams mentioned earlier is one way to break down some of the bad habits of rabbit-hole living. But the comfortable rabbit hole is still the norm and in seeking to understand communications within organizations it is important to recognize that the negative forces at work within compartments can be strong. They can be all about not connecting across a wide range of issues, the sum of which can represent a significant holding back of a company's plans. It is at times of great external change when the organization needs to re-think what it does and how it does it that the compartment can turn in on itself and become a secret society dedicated to opposition. Knowing the power of local rationalities managers can adapt the way that they connect with them, perhaps taking time to frame changes in a way that fits a number of small cultures rather than relying on all-purpose decrees. After all these compartments deliver what the organization wants most of the time because they are comfortable collections of like minds who have honed their particular functions to a high order. Taking a bit of time to anticipate their particular concerns and positing change in ways with which they can identify is worth the trouble. Assuming that all groups in organizations operate and react in the same way to proposed changes or that all groups buy into the same organizational culture is to ignore the power of local rationality and will inevitably prolong the introduction of change and the effective achievement of wider goals.

## Fair process

During 1997 International Survey Research (ISR), a leading consultant whose employee opinion surveys cover 450 companies in 18 countries every year, placed the UK second from bottom after Hungary in its latest survey of employee satisfaction. ISR has recorded a year-on-year collapse in morale of the UK workforce since 1990 despite the kind of general economic recovery that should have brought improvement in worker–management relations rather than deterioration. The ISR survey published at the end of 1995 revealed that UK workers' attitudes had suffered 'the most precipitate decline' of any European country over the previous decade. Motivation and commitment were even lower than in the strife-torn days of the mid-1970s. Coincidentally the 1995 survey was the first conducted after the notorious annual general meeting of British Gas. During this meeting British Gas' big institutional investors sanctioned a much-increased pay package for CEO Cedric Brown at a time when profits were substantially below their level in 1990, customer service was deteriorating and employees were being shed in large numbers. Further 'fat-cat' pay awards followed thick and fast in the context of similar circumstances – poor or unremarkable results + big worker lay-offs = big pay rises for senior managers.

The escalating pay and share option privileges of managers in the UK's privatized utilities proved to be a particularly pointed scandal given the monopoly position still held by most of these businesses. A donkey just standing still and facing in the right direction would have had trouble not making money in areas like gas, electricity and water supply even if they are regulated. After years of downsizing, de-layering and re-engineering the British work-force has been rewarded with ever widening pay differences between shop-floor and senior managers and the kind of approach to industrial relations that was characterized by British Airways threatening sanctions against its employees during its industrial dispute of July 1997.

The standard rhetoric about 'empowered' employees being vital corporate assets increasingly rings hollow against such a background and UK business seems to have a greater problem with legitimacy than companies in 'stakeholder' nations such as Norway and The Netherlands. Any contract that views the employee as both an asset (in good times) and a cost (in bad times) will always have an innate tension between 'fair' and unfair' processes. In order to develop theories that seem to be based on something economists have often made assumptions about the human condition, particularly about what motivates us, which they have to set in concrete for a suitable term, in order that the rest of the edifice might seem credibly robust. Attributing a set of basic motives to workers is a plank on which many economic theories have been built. One such theory assumes that people are always maximizers of utility driven principally by rational calculations of their own self-interest, i.e. that people are concerned first and foremost with successful outcomes.

That we are all motivated in part by successful outcomes or final destinations is reasonable enough but it is the 'part' that is important. The other just as important component in motivation is being involved in what we perceive as a 'fair process'. A magistrate immediately ruling that one has a case against an unfair prosecution after only ten minutes in court frustrates us because, although pleased with the outcome, we didn't have the chance to explain our side of the argument. As well as a result we also wanted to 'have our say', to be able to convince others of the strength of our argument and to experience the joys of successful persuasion. When push comes to shove we will happily seize on a successful outcome in lieu of the *obiter dictum* but we find it so much more satisfying to have also had a successful journey.

Management literature is replete with stories of successful firms who engaged in 'fair process' during the management of big changes and of the equally unsuccessful firms who, even when delivering acceptable rewards, forgot or simply misunderstood the need to engage in it. Fair process is not a deeply profound idea – it just responds to a basic human need. Whenever we feel part of systems and processes that are fair, comprehensible and just we are more willing to accept contrary views and decisions. Under such conditions we will bring the invaluable good will and active co-operation to effecting change that will make all the difference to the execution of the well-laid plan! The good-will factor is not an easy quality to measure or to use but its undoubted value in executing change behoves managers to spend more time understanding what fuels it and having fuelled it to study how they might put it to good use.

We all want to be valued as human beings not just as human assets or a personnel roll number. We want some respect for our intelligence, we want our ideas to be taken seriously even if not always accepted, we want to understand the rationale behind specific decisions and we want someone to take the time to explain them to us. Despite propaganda to the contrary we are ultra-sensitive to the signals conveyed through an organization's decision-making process. They reveal all kinds of soft information about the management's approach, e.g. whether they are willing to trust people, whether they mean what they say, whether or not they are confident, whether or not the organization is willing to change in the face of good information. These last two are particularly easy signals to pick up. Managers who regularly hide behind hierarchy and intricate protocol often give out signals about lack of confidence; they are seen to use the 'slowing down' of decision-making that is the inevitable result of such protocol abuse because they are frightened of taking a decision. We know that they hope that at least some of the problem will have gone away before it makes its way over the last hurdle of a purposely-intricate regime. Many organizations invest heavily in information technology in order to bring timely and relevant information to support their various levels of decision-making. Despite our reasonable expectancy that there should be a strong link between information and behaviour in enterprise many employees, often those closest to the action, still observe an organization's stubborn refusal to change its behaviour in the face of good information, bringing to mind T.H. Huxley's comment that 'there is no sadder sight than an ugly fact slaying a beautiful hypothesis'.

## 3.   Connecting with 'The Others'

It is a strange paradox that in most democracies taxpayers and ratepayers generally get less feedback about how their mandatory taxes have been invested by local and national governments than do shareholders, who goodness knows get little enough information from the companies in which they freely invest. In Chapter 4 we saw how BT and MCI failed to keep in touch with their shareholders during the sensitive re-negotiation of their (eventually failed) merger in August 1997 and there have been many similar examples of 'the children don't need to now yet' behaviour by large corporations. Discovering the real attitude of company director's to issues like pollution is still often confused by the language they must use because of the law and what they would like to hide. This is because the high cost of the remedy might adversely affect profits. The managing director of a carpet works, where a great deal of chemical waste is created, once explained to me that the firm would have avoided investing in most of the processes needed to neutralize this waste if it had not been for the severe penalties imposed on those discovered polluting rivers and streams. He was candid enough to make it clear that without such penalties shareholders would not have sanctioned the filtering processes necessary just for the public good.

We noted above how 'show time' in an organizational context is often a necessary evil that executives have to plod through as part of the pretence that power is shared and not just exercised arbitrarily, but there can also be big downsides to their sewing everything up in private. Chief executives of local authorities, hospitals, companies and vice-chancellors of universities, etc. may enjoy the easy ride given them by 'show time' for a while but the media are now much more apt to amplify cases of corruption or financial incompetence when they eventually surface. Many such examples have surfaced in the UK: vice-chancellors' incompetence in management and high finance, inflated pay packages for the inheritors of privatized public utilities, the mismanagement of big computer projects and the covering up of pollution scandals. In the UK, a normally passive 'show time' culture, there has been much recent public discussion about accountability in the face of the obviously casual interpretation of their role by some of those selected for the governance of our institutions. There is no doubt that citizens all over Europe and the US have lost faith in the way that their public institutions are managed. The stake-holding public, urged on by more and more investigative reporting, no longer accepts the inviolable legitimacy, although it still often has to accept the consequences, of unaccountable priesthoods. Better education, including higher education, must take credit for helping to create a less deferential age in which authority is challenged and individuals' rights are asserted. Unfortunately most of these action-based challenges, e.g. the poll tax demonstrations in the UK and the long-term public demonstrations against apartheid, tend to find their most vigorous outlet in single-issue causes. Public concern about the 'big picture' of the kind instituted by the students in Indonesia which brought down President Suharto have not been seen in Europe since 1968.

## All hail the whistleblower

Although uncomfortable for those used to the immunity of office some criticism is becoming more open and the Internet is playing an increasing role as an effective conduit for questioning the 'truth' as handed down via the discredited processes of many institutions. A symptom of this change is the rise of the 'whistleblower' or insider who breaks the casing of the organizational womb to tell the world about wrongdoing. Recent statutory protection for whistleblowers in the UK has followed similar legislation in the US. This explicit recognition of the need to give individuals who 'know' some protection from intimidation reflects the growth of public distrust in the integrity of self regulation and the need for alternative avenues of communication to help monitor their doings. The culprits defy classification and reinforce the view that lying and cover-ups are endemic in the organizational cultures of both public and private organizations.

The famous case of the sinking of the Belgrano during the Falklands war of 1984 exposed levels of official mendacity that seriously damaged the UK government's credibility. Allegations in 1998 about the exaggeration of the progress and properties of a new drug being developed by the UK firm British Biotech left shareholders stunned and severely harmed the company. The allegations of an employee that the US government had been overcharged by $20 million by a company, which later became part of Tube Investments Ltd., supplying wing slot seals to the US airforce between 1984 and 1990 eventually prompted Tube Investments to pay back $12.4 million to the US government in an out-of-court settlement in 1998. Late in 1998 Blondel Cluff dared to question the effectiveness of the UK's Commission for Racial Equality (CRE) in a comprehensive dossier (she had just finished a two-year term as a Commissioner) and as a result was subjected to a personalized and vitriolic attack by the officers of the CRE confirming, if any confirmation was necessary, that this was an organization in dire need of reform.

In 1998, and confirming that the whistleblower is now an accepted and necessary link in the chain of public awareness, *THES*, the weekly journal covering higher education in the UK, began including a weekly 'whistleblower' section. This feature provided a platform for the anonymous 'outing' of malpractice and mismanagement among the once quiet and secret groves of academe. The previous eight years had seen a considerable growth in the number of chief executives leaving universities and colleges after the exposure of various indiscretions that were largely enabled by the new independence given to these institutions by the British government. Portsmouth University, Swansea College of Higher Education, Thames Valley University and Huddersfield University have all been investigated for one thing or another. Some universities and colleges in the UK have even been accused of being 'creative' with their admission statistics in order to secure the grant aid that follows student numbers, and some university vice chancellors have been discovered sewing up generous severance packages just before being asked to leave in disgrace.

Previously many of those 'found out' had been under the control of local authorities whose audit function had been somewhat keener than the new business-based governors who now sought to control them. The business acumen, so often touted as necessary to give higher education a new lease of life, of these 'new' governors was largely derived from past experience as many of them had long since finished with gainful employment. Loosely regulated by articles that they had created they also favoured filling vacant seats via a variety of secret or closed behaviours. The upshot of the 'new' regime has been a collapse of public confidence in the governance of colleges and universities in the UK and in the way that they manage public funds.

In some places whistleblowing can get you locked up or, as in the case of Alexander Nitkin, under city arrest in St. Petersburg, an eternity spent in a Kafkaesque nightmare where the courts keep returning the case to the prosecutor for further investigation. Nitkin's crime is that he warned the world of the dangers posed by 90 of Russia's retired and rotting nuclear northern submarine fleet. Though his research on accidents aboard soviet nuclear submarines for the Oslo-based Bellona Foundation was based solely on public and authorized sources he is five years into a legal case which the Russian security service keeps framing in such an ambiguous way that it cannot be refuted in legal terms. Over that time the charges against him have been sent back to the secret police eight times to be re-tailored and brought up again, confirming that the old ways of persecuting dissidents in post-Soviet Russia are alive, well and potentially dangerous to the rest of us. Nitkin claims that there is no money to decommission the northern submarines properly leaving them rusting and leaking away in a kind of slow-motion Chernobyl that could instigate a disaster at any time. These submarines, together with the mountainous stores of spent nuclear fuel in Russia's north pose one of the world's biggest environmental threats. All this doubt about Russia's inability to deal with its huge stocks of nuclear waste allied with the as yet unanswered allegations that Russia is dropping nuclear waste into the Sea of Japan confirms our need for the brave Nitkins of this world.

Of course some whistleblowers will be malicious or disappointed employees whose exposures will need checking against other evidence. But the last decade has seen an explosion of information from these sources that, once the stone has been turned over, has clearly proved that many organizations harbour components that regularly commit illegal acts or, where still legal, often act in a manner contrary to their mission and work against the public interest. Such a weight of evidence clearly demonstrates that the conscience of individuals is still one of our most valuable resources. The conscience of the 'official' organization has too often been shown to be temporary, blown hither and thither by the winds of expediency, public relations and the fear that owning up to faults can only harm or disable them. This issue of public confidence in the information put out by governments and public and private organizations is one of the greatest challenges facing us as we enter the new millennium. Given the growing interdependence of citizens, states and institutions and the complex links that now bind them together, e.g. the relations between scientists, farmers, the meat industry, public opinion and politicians during the UK's BSE crisis, the need for independent, uninhibited and, if necessary, brave agents of conscience is more necessary than ever.

## Relationships: the invisible prefix

The concept of 'the organization' as an institution layered with certainties may be collapsing faster than new entities are growing up to replace it. In particular the idea of what now constitutes a successful relationship both within organizations and between them and their host environment is becoming more complex. The word 'relationship' has had a long shelf life but it is one from which we now expect too much, having loaded it with an excess of meanings and connecting opportunities. At a personal level having or not having a 'relationship' is often associated with a successful life spent with one or a number of partners and having a band of reliable and trusted friends. For a statistician it is more likely to mean a link, possibly a causal one, between two or more phenomena. In business it often refers to other people outside our own organization whom we deal with, or selling to people you know as in 'relationship marketing'. Developing a 'good relationship' is often a capricious and uncertain affair drawing on the mysteries of 'chemistry' or empathy or both.

Despite all our experience of forging them we are still not sure how these qualities coalesce to form deep, sturdy relationships that we feel confident will stand the test of time. Because solving this mystery is not a universal endowment among peoples many individuals go through life suspicious of the consequences and ignorant of the pleasures of such close relationships. The annual reports of many organizations often take great pains to draw our attention to the good relationships that they have with their employees, suppliers, customers and shareholders. Such a report tells us a story about the slow build-up of links via trust, mutual respect and straightforward dealing. Much of this story will be true but we have also seen enough evidence to know that it will not all be as it is reported. Our confidence in the relationships forged by the 'connecting organization' at all its levels needs a boost. We have more access to information about organizations, we have those whose conscience guides them to expose corruption and mendacity and, working as part of an organization ourselves, we can change it for the better if we choose to use our energy in that way. If the word 'relationship' has been overloaded to the point of reducing the value of its coinage we might consider reassessing how we use it. By endowing it with less intensity and less depth we might give it a new lease of life. Accepting the invisible prefix 'temporary' when it is used by organizations and institutions might be one way to live with it. It will nearly always be nearer the mark, their failures will disappoint us less and we will be happily surprised if they turn out to have meant it in its non-qualified state.

# References

1.  Handy, C. (1997) *The hungry spirit: beyond capitalism a quest for purpose in the modern world.* London: Hutchinson

2.  Tom Peters quoted in Micklethwait, J. and Wooldridge, A. (1996) *The Witch Doctors: what the management gurus are saying and how to make sense of it.* London: William Heinemann

3.  Evans, P.B. and Wurster, T.S. (1997) 'Strategy and the new economics of information. *Harvard Business Review*, Sept/Oct 1997, p.71–82

4.  Goodard, R.W. (1989) 'Communicate: The Power of One-on-One'. In *Communication for Management and Business* 5th edn. Sigloand, N.B. and Bell, A.B. New York: Scott Foreman & Co

5.  Mori (1998) *The buy-in benchmark.* London: Marketing and Communications Agency

6.  *Management Consultancy*, October 1998, p.4

7.  Peters, T. (1994) *The Pursuit of Wow: every person's guide to topsy-turvy times.* New York: Vintage Original, pp.65–66

# CHAPTER EIGHT

# Six stories

'It's not the voice that commands the story: it is the ear.'

Italo Calvino, 1972

## Squeezing those patterns

Storytelling has always been one of the most potent ways to connect with and share past experience. Many of the stories handed down to us mix fact, fiction and entertainment with instruction about how we should behave towards our fellows or to illuminate how success might be achieved and failure avoided if only we would learn this or that lesson. But we don't learn lessons: we learn patterns. Mark Twain noted that 'the past does not repeat itself but it rhymes' and we face the problems and challenges of life by matching the conditions we find against our pattern (rhyme) store. If something looks familiar we call up the knowledge and experience we have gained in coping with a similar pattern and test it on the current problem. Because the patterns from our store sometimes do not fit what we find we try to squeeze a 'close' pattern to fit. By concentrating on squeezing one of our old patterns to fit a set of particular circumstances we often lose sight of the fact that something completely new is happening, something that, however hard we squeeze, won't fit our repertoire of patterns to match against it. Under such circumstances if a 'squeezed' pattern just manages to fit OK, we make contact and solve the problem; at other times our intellect, all used up in squeezing, fails to recognize the unique features of the problem facing us and we make mistakes. Having failed we turn our minds to dealing with the consequences of failure which, in our time, is often about formulating credible excuses rather than learning new ways of approaching problem solving. The following 'stories', or short essays on fame, false economy, knowledge creation in special spaces and the uncritical acceptance of IT, all involve pattern recognition of one sort or another and are meant to arouse an interest in revitalizing all of our connecting senses.

In connecting with each other in real or virtual space we handle increasingly complex media, transport and communications technology. One challenge for us in a world of constructed urgency is the time that we give to reflecting on and understanding the things in which we get involved. Although we don't need to understand how everything works we might suffer from less stress if we invested a bit more thought at the front-end of our connecting activities. Giving a little time to say how the media construct news, how important calendars are to electronic devices or what airport we are supposed to land at can improve the quality of our experiences and may save us much more time later. Our relationship with fame has been a story that has moved over time from passive wonder to active involvement in all its ingredients. Enjoying vicarious adventures with celebrities in our private fantasies or swooning over them in the context where they became known to us e.g. the cinema, the theatre, the football field, the palace or the seat of government is now not enough. Now we want to see the underside, the backside and the all the other sides of fame that were once safely tucked away in the private bit of a public life. More, we want to connect with the famous, we want to see, right up close, just how different they really are.

## Kariba Dam

Once, together with a group of conference attendees in a restaurant, I helped to create a game. Everyone at the table was awarded points from 1–5 if they could report having been close to someone famous or knew someone who had been close to someone famous. We called it Kariba Dam after someone claimed that they had met the designer of this worthy African project and we gave them zero: a valuable work for society but no great shakes in the hall of 'fame'. We only gave high scores to those who had actually been in contact with the famous, e.g. had helped Joan Collins pack her sack in a supermarket, had shaken hands with Queen Elizabeth or met Al Gore at a party. The point of this nonsense was to confirm that we, the groundlings, could meet such people up close and gain a moment's celebrity for ourselves. At the time none of us stopped to examine why we all wanted to be able to declare this 'association' but I do remember that my having seen Norman Wisdom outside a theatre in the Haymarket and saying hello to Micky Dollense in a London park received poor scores.

Where once the famous were celebrated for having sprung out of our ordinariness we are now more entranced when we glean some affirmation that their anxieties, hopes and weaknesses are much like our own. Our hunger for signs of fallibility among our heroes and heroines has seemed more ardent at the end of the century than it was at the beginning. As fame so often surfaces as the result of success in the superior accomplishment of something, an attainment of standards to which most of us could only aspire, some signs of human frailty sneakily relieve us. Building up and then destroying our illusions has become an industry with which we conspire as part of a see-saw of self-flagellation, now adoring, now despising, that requires daily feeding on one side or the other. Given the slightest whiff of a big audience all the apparatus of our modern communications industry is only too happy to gratify us with all the background information we might need to see-saw back and forth. Indeed without the media creating 'fame', building it up pixel by pixel, story by story, chronicling every twist in its rise and fall before moving on to new themes, our see-saw would be starved of its fulcrum.

Our addiction to fame may be harmless most of the time but addictions tend to exclude other experiences and may even construct such a powerful false world that it damages our connections with the real one. The UK's royal family was designed to be distant. Up until the time of George V they cultivated a world of aristocratic separateness where royals married royals (pretty simple pattern recognition) and everybody involved knew the rules, and the rest of us watched their weddings and funerals from a carefully orchestrated distance. A 'royal' life came with leisured privilege, servants on call, transportation always close at hand, palaces and splendid gardens, freedom to be as eccentric as you liked in private and total insulation from the struggles of a brutish world. The price: some public duties and obligations, the patronage of a few charities and an assumed dignity and detachment in public. The price also included, in varying degrees, the sacrifice of any personal desires that did not fit in with society's expectations as mediated by those at the centre of the 'royal' system and the loss of that freedom of movement that the rest of us take for granted, the latter being a cost that most of us, however fairy-tale our fantasies, probably would not want to pay.

## The Princess' tale

'Are you wearing that hat for a bet?'

> Princess Diana to a journalist covering one of her public engagements.

### Giving an inch

In 1917 Russian villages just a few hundred kilometres from Moscow had to wait two or three weeks to hear about the Russian revolution and the killing of Czar Alexis and his family. Eighty years later in 1997 the death of a young English princess in Paris reached the remotest Russian villages within minutes of her last breath. The widespread interest in Diana's short life and tragic death was a testament to the way her fame had been constructed and disseminated by fast-moving media with global reach. But she also owed her access to fame from a decision made by a dull King 74 years earlier. In 1923 George V approved the marriage of his son, the then Duke of York, to a commoner, Elizabeth Bowes-Lyon, rather than a royal princess. He acquiesced in this for two main reasons: one – the usual suppliers, the decimated crowned heads of Europe, were running short of eligible royal women; and two – because the Duke was a second son who was unlikely to become King. Although a break in the pattern from the tradition of a strictly 'insiders only' royal family, it hardly looked revolutionary; Elizabeth was after all the daughter of an Earl and she definitely looked the part.

But to those who observed these matters closely the thin end of a small wedge had been placed in the palace door and it was one that became decidedly more firmly positioned after the unexpected abdication of Edward VIII. The Duchess of York suddenly found herself being declared Queen [1]. During the Second World War King George VI and his 'commoner' wife appeared in newsreels walking among the debris of the London Blitz, showing solidarity with the pain and grief of their war-torn and long-suffering subjects. The images of the royal couple walking among the ruins of east and central London were reported widely in cinemas and newspapers. As warm and compassionate as the commentators made it look, the tone of the message was still one of regal, almost divine figures coming out to walk around to see at first-hand the trials of ordinary folk. However these images were unusual in the degree to which they showed ordinary people connecting with the gods, softening them up a bit and emphasizing shared troubles at a time when national sentiment ran high and improving the morale of the population was a legitimate war aim. Much of the high standing of the British Royal family after the war can be traced back to George VI's decision to stay on in London, close to the bombing and occasionally connecting with his people, rather than high-tailing it to some safer spot in the country. As a contingency lorry-loads of tinned spam had been delivered to Madresfield Court in Worcestershire just in case things got too hairy in London.

In October 1952, on being presented with the unanimous view of the British Cabinet that her coronation should not be televised the bold daughter of that king, the young Elizabeth II, overruled their objections and the TV cameras entered the sacred confines of Westminster Abbey. They were to record an event that had, up until that time, only been witnessed by a small coterie of aristocrats and the elite of government. Her decision was momentous. From that time on it was taken for granted that all 'big' royal events would be covered by television.

The 'small' events, i.e. how they lived, what they did with themselves in their spare time, their disagreements, the kind of games they played, were all very still very much out-of-bounds. But connecting with moving pictures of the Royal family going about their visits and ship-launchings in our homes would soon be commonplace via television. Learning more about their personalities and their private lives was not a sport encouraged by the still obsequious media proprietors, be they in newspapers or television. As it was with the 1936 abdication of Edward VIII, it was the 'moral high ground'; who claims it and whether it's worth claiming that began the substitution of 'small' for 'big'.

This is because moral behaviour is made up of all the small human details that make our relationships with each other so fascinating, something about which we all hold opinions and which royal families had always managed to keep well hidden. It was Princess Margaret, the Queen's younger sister, who swung open the doors to further change when her love for a dashing, war-hero divorcee prompted a dramatic escalation in press and media attention, offering us the chance to see that these details could be just like ours. Her later marriage to a fashion photographer was the first royal wedding to be televised and her sub-sequent divorce was the stuff of many tabloid front pages, as was her flirtation with an 'other' man on an exotic island in the Caribbean. She had seen to it that the way the media, and thus the wide mass of people, connected with the Royal family would never be the same again. The Queen herself tried to break with some old traditions in seeking to educate her children in the real world rather than via tutors locked away in royal apartments. It was a modernization programme that had very mixed results.

> It has meant that her children are a hybrid generation, enjoying a taste of freedom but anchored to the world of castles and royal protocol. Their actions, particularly of the Prince of Wales, demon-strate the particular perils of allowing future sovereigns to breathe, even for a short time, the air of freedom. Unlike his predecessors, doubt, uncertainty and questioning have been added to his inherited faith in and acceptance of royal traditions. [2]

While social attitudes to the Royal family, their private lives, their relationships and their opinions changed gradually over decades the tech-nology that could open up all these mysteries was changing much faster. As in the more general challenge of regulating telephony and television at a national level, these developments in technology were racing ahead of the protocols and rules that usually governed relationships between the Royal family and the media. What was possible could not now be held back by antique claims to privacy. They had opted to live more in the public eye, we had glimpsed some of the detail, and we wanted more. Also there was now an increasing number of younger members of the family whose private lives were difficult to control and their doings seemed fair game for the faster films, longer lenses and rapid digital transmission available to the servants of the media. Communication technology, by constantly re-defining what was possible, encouraged media managers to be more adventurous. Because they could capture a reasonable (in newspaper terms anyway) image of a young female member of the Royal family doing private things on a yacht 200 yards away then they did. Once the gold standard had been set by one newspaper then the rest, according to their definition of what we all wanted to see and read about, had to follow. Technology allowed the effective invasion of privacy from a distance and Royal families, having given out some tit-bits to hold back the dam, were now facing its total collapse. Long-standing symbols of decent, clean-living family life, close associations with the established church, charity work and 'proper behaviour', their every move was now being digitized and, if they didn't live up to this impossible construction of themselves, every digit would be enlarged until the pips squeaked.

## Global Diana

Diana Princess of Wales was the most potent symbol of the triangular intersection of the 'hybrid generation', decomposing protocols and fast news. Her life within and without the Royal family became a drama that Princess Margaret, in a spirit of *deja vu*, must have sighed over many times. Diana's death in a car crash in Paris at the end of August 1997 was relayed around the world in minutes by satellite technology and every television station in the world stopped what they were doing to report it and to repeat the story at regular intervals. But old technologies also rose to the occasion. Using 600-year-old paper printing technology the tabloids began a campaign to prod the stodgy, protocol-bound British Royal family into action over the symbolic lowering of flags and revising the arrangements for Diana's funeral. The even older technology of public assembly, with its raw human emotion, street-bonding and just wanting to be part of a big event, brought thousands of people with flowers and poems to London. Over a million people waited on London streets to witness her last journey while over 30 million in the UK, and an estimated 1.5 billion world-wide, joined them in watching it on television.

Diana had been brought to the people of the world by highly visual and rapidly disseminated media that captured her glamour, her anxieties, her fallibilities and her humanity. They may also, in their voracious appetite for images of her to relay to us, have contributed something to the circumstances of her death. The various microprocessors that manipulated all those sought-after pictures were impassively doing their uncomplaining job of turning them into clinical 0s and 1s, but the defining moments were felt in millions of houses and on the streets of towns and cities around the world. If ever there was a story of a desire to connect with many via the world's media without understanding the uncontrollable levels of fascination and intrusion that such a contract inevitably brings, this was it.

People can only be famous if people know about them and Lady Diana Spencer, a plump and shy nanny until she was kissed by a prince in 1981, was unknown. She became famous because she married a prince who was the heir to the British throne. Later her fame rested on being a glowing princess who had to cope with a strange husband and his dysfunctional family. Later still her fame rested on stories of her alleged unhappy incarceration within this family and her battles to escape its claustrophobic clutches. Even later still her fame rested on all these plus her glamorous persona, her support of AIDS and children's charities and her campaign for land mine clearance. Andrew Morton (subsequently the author of *Monica's story*) boarding a plane to meet his publisher to consider an 'in her own words' version of his earlier book about Diana just hours after her death may look distasteful, but he was no more guilty than the rest of us in wanting something from her fame. 'Was there ever a story of such woe as this of Juliet and her Romeo?' Diana was a media creation during the latter part of her life and she was by turns both manipulator and manipulated. If the media was at times her 'Romeo', carrying agreeable images and propaganda which she needed to help her in her struggles with a suffocating establishment that now found her an embarrassment, it was also a poison on which she overdosed.

Since her death many aspects of her life have been dissected and the profusion of publications about her suggests that we still cannot get enough of the iconography that sets down stories and myths about beauty, goodness and damaged lives. Her death created a prism through which people began to view everything from the lack of spiritual purpose in their lives to the length of hemlines.

Those on whom we bestow fame and who die young are blessed never to age and are mourned for what they never became, to say nothing of what they never were. Marilyn Monroe, James Dean, Jim Morrison, Buddy Holly, River Phoenix and Che Guevara all occupy a place in the pantheon of fame that might well have been denied them had we grown accustomed to their wrinkles. Tragedy and death always re-boot and then sustain iconographic status just as diminishing happiness makes us love our live heroes and heroines more. Great wealth had freed Diana from the grinding domestic worries that make most women's lives earth-bound and ungenerous and prevent many of them from having the kind of vocation that she was able to create for herself. As a side issue 'Dianology' high-lighted an interesting challenge for contemporary, rational, enlightened feminism, i.e. how to find ways to empathize with the power of myth on the collective imagination which allows for the importance of politically incorrect fantasies such as the beautiful princess in the psyches of both sexes. Without the support of a central organization the death of a glam-orous, apolitical member of the British aristocracy brought more ordinary people on to the streets of Britain than any other populist political cause in recent history.

Something of a 'cultural studies' industry has grown up around this enigma and, if in her life the media fed well on her, academe has not been slow to claim the carcass and pick over the bones. Her death preserved her unique position, at the intersection of crown and commoner, princess and outcast, victimized and virtuous, at a moment of tantalizing mystery when her future was wide open to speculation. Such a vivid example has provided ideal teaching material for classes in media studies, feminism, psychology and sociology while at a higher level academics have been busy arranging conferences and seminars to discuss how and why Diana's death touched as many people as it did.

The public response in the UK and around the world was incred-ible but other deaths, some vividly captured on film, have moved people in a similar way and public outpourings of grief, particularly at the funerals of the famous, is not unusual even among the normally reserved people of England. George IV's only daughter (who lived a rather secluded life) Princess Charlotte dying in childbirth in 1817 aged only 21 produced a great outburst of public grief expressed by the school-book jingle 'Never was sorrow more sincere than that which flowed round Charlotte's bier.' The funerals of Nelson and Wellington attracted huge crowds for the time while President Kennedy's assassination and funeral moved a nation and the world as much because of what had happened to the 'office' as for grief over a young man cut down in his prime. In 1856 thousands of people lined the railway tracks in silence and more than 7 million people viewed Abraham Lincoln's coffin at the many stops made by his funeral train on its 1700-mile trip from Washington to Springfield, Illinois. Churchill's lying in state in Westminster Hall in 1965 was attended by a non-stop stream of ordinary people seeking to connect with the memory of someone who had inspired them throughout the dark days of the Second World War. Vincent Mulchrone in the *Daily Mail* likened the long queues waiting to pay their last respects to a river:

> Two rivers run silently through London tonight, and one is made of people. Dark and quiet as the night-time Thames itself, it flows through Westminster Hall, eddying about the foot of the rock called Churchill.

Other great events have excited and silenced people on the streets. Wellington and Blucher's victory at Waterloo in 1815 was read aloud from broadsheets in London to crowds who were both excited and silent. Chamberlain's message, 'I have to tell you that no such assurance having been received we are now at war with Germany', was received in silence by a nation huddled over the crackling Bakelite boxes that would later carry Churchill's exhortations to secure victory at all costs. On these occasions many British people were deeply moved and often over-whelmed with emotion. It was a normal response. They did not need official permission to grieve or for the media to say 'we all feel like this don't we?'

## 'The hour of gold, the hour of lead'*

The media technologies of each age have carried messages and reports of and from the famous but Diana represented a new mix. The coincidence of our obsession with the details behind fame, the inherent shallowness of her claim to fame and the instant responses that our communications technology now facilitates lie at the root of our fascina-tion with Diana. Perhaps our new obsessions arose out of the details that the new fast-reacting media could provide or perhaps the media did, as they often claim, only respond to our demands for more. Whichever came first, never until our time was a single human being seen almost daily by millions of people all over the world who had never met her. The regular comparison of her life to that of a television 'soap opera' was a reason-able one. By appearing twice or three times a week the characters in soap

---

\*      The title of one of Anne Morrow Lindbergh's autobiographical books published in 1973.

operas constantly refresh their image with the audience, and like Diana was, they are nearly always embroiled in domestic upheavals of one sort or another. The world's longest running TV soap opera, Coronation Street in Britain, has been running for 40 years and has always provided the backdrop for rumbustuous family disputes and trauma as well as some serious social comment.

> Their [soap opera's] particular brand of heightened reality – real life with the boring bits left out – has proved a potent mix. It enables them to secure the viewers' identity with some very individual destinies while at the same time suggesting that they are somehow typical. There can be no doubt that the modern soap opera has become a vehicle for enabling agendas and stimulating everyday discussion about issues that other media have much more difficulty addressing. . . . The escape promise of weekly drama has thus become a major source of hard information for many people who would not regard themselves as particularly well informed. [3]

Politicians, seeking to identify with the mainstream of popular culture, often have their photographs taken with soap opera stars, join them on the production set and occasionally feature in cameo roles. News items on Princess Diana were awaited with the same 'next episode' expectation that greeted the television serial. By being everywhere on TV and on the covers of popular journals Diana's image closely resembled the kind of religious icon that many people used to hang on their walls. Now they hang images of the sacred island strewn with flowers and, on the anniversary of her death, no doubt share in the spiritual renewal they believe she symbolizes.

The kind of contact with fame on which we now insist is more difficult for famous women to cope with. Women are expected to be different from men but the same as each other. By insisting on a more precise self-definition of themselves women have to face the consequences that come from throwing off this ancient expectation. As photographic technology has become more sophisticated and its handlers more intrusive the famous of both genders have started to become more ambivalent about fame. The privileges bestowed by fame are now coupled with regular encounters with invasive media, stalkers, the impossibility of finding privacy anywhere and a constant fear of being 'discovered' committing the kind of indiscretion or minor offence that the rest of us would shrug off lightly.

Celebrities now employ armies of bodyguards, live behind high security walls and spend a lot of time in rehabilitation clinics of one sort or another.

Being famous has always tested the human constitution and seemed incomplete without an addiction or two. Now the inner crises faced by celebrities are paraded daily before a public desperate to hear the worst. In response the famous have been moved to spawn a culture of confession in an effort to pre-empt uncontrolled publication and to put the best spin on things. Molly Dineen's 1999 documentary about former Spice Girl Geri Halliwell highlighted the troubled nature of one person's inability to recover from being famous. We might be happy to see Geri slip away quietly and live off her millions. Despite seeking the occasional oasis of anonymity though, she is addicted to fame. Her struggle to find a role that would make use of her old fame while keeping her famous now and in the future, was a torture to witness and sad to contemplate. Spawning is particularly frantic in the US, where celebrities feel moved to re-cast and share with the world the wildly narcissistic misjudgements in their lives as courageous battles with inner demons. When a lone flyer landed his *The Spirit of St Louis* in France in 1927 adulatory crowds across Europe and the US chanted his name, presidents and ambassadors jockeyed for position to shake his hand and camera flash guns became his constant companion. For Charles A. Lindbergh fame was something that truly happened overnight and, with the aid of the movie camera, this precise, plodding, calculating man ('I would rather have extra gasoline than an extra man') became the first global superstar. His fame grew even greater after his baby son was kidnapped and assumed murdered in 1931. A natural isolationist he campaigned against US intervention in the Second World War and was branded an anti-Semite and a traitor through the rest of that conflict even while flying allied combat missions in the Pacific. A great achievement, followed by a terrible family tragedy, followed by personal ignominy and stigmatization – Lindbergh and the movie camera, the people and the cinema, a personal life in the spotlight, good deeds turned to bad: the re-definition of what fame was going to be had begun.

## The bug's tale

As we approach the year 2000 (or as some purists would have it 2001), we might reflect on the terrors and portents that greeted the year 1000.

Many Europeans, alerted as ever by the calendar-conscious Catholic church, were convinced that all sorts of things were going to happen to them at midnight on December 31st 999. Rarely optimistic about it they assumed that the new millennium would bring a string of bad omens, storms, comets, dark skies and the like and all foretelling the coming of some kind of judgement. Believing that God worked to tidier timetables than the rest of us, and that this would be a neat 10 centuries after the birth of his son and that things probably hadn't gone quite as the family had planned, it was natural to assume some sort of come-uppance. The memory of those fears has long faded other than where the digits remain as a response to tragedy as in the three numbers that we dial in the UK for emergencies but a thousand years on we don't seem to have grown any more optimistic about the endings and beginnings we construct on calendars. The new 'judgement' (pulpit portents offer few terrors for us now) is that all our computers will start doing horrible things to us as the 'millennium bug' begins its ominous journey through millions of slivers of silicon.

## A few digits short

Strictly speaking it is not a 'bug'. It's more a legacy of conscious 'cancelling' of the millennium due to shortage of funds. Programmers working in the late 1970s and early 1980s often worked to tight budgets and, although they knew that the year 2000 would eventually dawn, they ignored it. Technology was far more expensive and less highly prioritized during that time and shortening the date codes by two digits was a good way of keeping costs down and saving on storage space. Thus computer engineers cheerfully programmed the year into the system as say 78 rather than 1978, leaving the computer to assume that all dates (forever) began with the digits 19. Thus when it comes to the year 2000 a politically incorrect computer will assume that it is 1900. The problem has been compounded by the software and hardware hanging around in systems much longer than expected. The 'cancellation' problem thus has to be addressed if it is not to lay waste the data in our bank, gas, electricity and credit card accounts, health records, property registers, missile systems and income tax returns – indeed everywhere where the ubiquitous computer, together with its inscrutable inner clocks and calendars, holds information about us and our connection with the wider world.

More real than the omens that beset the world in 999, the IT industry should at least be happy. The 'bug' has done very well for it, pumping hundreds of millions of pounds into fixes or, as with the Abbey National bank in the UK, a near total re-build of computer systems, creating employment for thousands of programmers, consultants and systems trouble-shooters as well as giving us all something to be pessimistic about. In the UK the cost to 'fix' the FTSE 100 companies is conservatively estimated to be around £5 billion and this could be much higher when all the associated costs are included. The problems are not so much technical as logistic because every machine has to be examined and then scoured to see what mischief might be lurking there. Supermarket retailer Sainsbury's in the UK estimates that 14 000 separate programs on its systems will have to be checked.

Also, when found, working out the language in which the code was written adds a further challenge. Much of the computer code that has to be amended was written in computer languages hardly ever used today and many software firms, flying in the face of their usual ageist personnel policies, have hired older persons in the shape of retired software technicians to help tackle the problem. ICL in the UK did not have enough space to accommodate the 'wrinklies' that it hired to fix some of its old software and so it persuaded over half of them to work from home using teleworking. An interesting irony: older staff recalled from retirement, working from home on old code, over new networks to solve a problem brought about by their having to cut costs 20 years ago. Others, like Safeway in the UK, have farmed the work out to India where there are many talented and relatively low-paid software engineers. An opportunity, perhaps, for them to bump up their prices and realize their true market value, for a couple of years at least.

### Embedded and expensive

Scouring the intricacies of the programmes living in many embedded systems, e.g. process control equipment and associated field instrumentation, is a particularly specialized challenge often requiring, as Allied Domecq have realized, the skills of specialized electrical consultants. The problem with the embedded chip challenge is that chips are made by one firm, assembled into components by another firm and then these components are assembled into a car, lift, aeroplane or hospital resuscitator by the final supplier of the product. The line is long and no one can remember just how many chips got put into various components and whether or not someone added a calendar chip to the mix just in case the component ever needed one. Whatever explorations need to be made during 1999 delaying them will inevitably prove to be more expensive as consultants continue to put up fees as the millennium draws near. At the start of 1998 a conservative estimate suggested that 30 per cent of small firms in the UK would not have tackled the millennium problem by 2000. Many of these small firms supply big ones so the confusion will not be ring-fenced in any way. Many small firms are being quizzed by their customers, auditors and insurers as to how they plan to cope with the problem. The pressure to get something done, something which they will not know has been properly solved until 1 January 2000, makes small firms easy prey to cowboy programmers and quick-fix artists.

No one really knows what will happen after 2000. Will microwave cookers burn out? Will elevators leave thousands of office workers stranded between floors? Will we record even more of the wrong programmes off TV? Will trains get de-railed? Will aircraft drop from the sky? The more questions you ask, the more and more it sounds like a medieval doomsday scenario. Insurance companies have started asking the questions early as they will be second (I am assuming that we will all be first) in the firing line when the bug starts spluttering away in all the household gadgets in which it lives. Some insurance companies in the UK wrote to their policyholders during 1998 to clarify their position on the year 2000 problem. For example the Prudential's household policy now states that your policy does not cover:

> damage to, or loss of, any electrical equipment, computer program or computer information as a result of any computer program, computer, data processing equipment, microchip, integrated circuit or similar device failing correctly to recognize any date as its true calendar date.

British insurers maintain that new clauses like this are all right and proper because insurance is about insuring against the unforeseen and the onset of the millennium is a totally foreseen risk. The irony that every insurance company in the UK is having to pay out hundreds of thousands of pounds in order to make its own systems year 2000-compliant – a 'totally foreseen risk' – is clearly lost on them.

The telecommunications companies face some particular tricky problems of compliance. They were all urged by the International Telecommunications Union to have all the tests on the soundness of their international links completed by the end of 1998 in order that international calls can terminate in, or transit through, all the countries of the world after 2000. Given the great variance of resources available to some countries, particularly in sub-Saharan Africa, they may have needed a lot of help to make the deadline which, given the shortage of expertise in the developed world was unlikely to be given. Although telephone bills charging for calls made since the beginning of the twentieth century and pension cheques due at the start of 2000 being cancelled as the computers decide that the claimant has not been born yet seem too crazy to be likely it is wise to remember that computers don't understand, they just do. Computers in hospitals, handling life-critical missions across a whole range of activities, while looking like a high priority, may not get fixed due to the shortage of necessary resources to ensure their compliance. Lawyers, a group for whom computer failure has provided a completely new canon of liability law, will be circling these and other potential failures as the prospect of institutional liability arising from accidents that 'could' be attributable to the bug increases. Telecommunication companies have been busy recruiting armies of lawyers both to sue suppliers who have sold them non-compliant equipment and to handle the incoming lawsuits when a telephone system collapses.

## Empty seats

Those responsible for carrying us in bulk over time and space have some of the heaviest responsibilities. Railtrack, responsible for all the stations, signalling and track on UK railways, hopes to have all of its work completed by June 1999 but it cannot test the systems until Christmas Day 1999 because that is the only day that the network is closed. That is just seven days away from the deadline. Like many other companies, armies and police forces it has cancelled leave for key staff over Christmas and the New Year 1999 and ordered them to be on standby on January 1st 2000 to provide manual back-up in case anything fails. British Airways and KLM have said that they will not fly to countries that are not year 2000-compliant, however that is to be proved. UK charter airline Britannia Airlines has decided to avoid putting its aeroplanes in the air from seven hours before the start of 1st January 2000 until seven hours after. They claim that no one, including their own staff would want to be in the air at that time anyway! Air travel on January 1st 2000 promises to be a lonely affair as many people will avoid flying on that day and during the early weeks of the year. The empty seats will result from a mix of AD 999 superstition and the worry that as so many bits of a modern jet (there are 6 million parts in a new Boeing 747) are operated by computers it would be very easy for one to slip through the checker's net.

IBM has not helped. In early 1998 the company warned the UK Civil Aviation Authority that six older IBM machines that make up Britain's core air traffic management systems will require extensive work, or total replacement, to be made year 2000-compliant. At the same time it also warned that 40 of its model 3083 mainframe computers, used at 20 Air Route Traffic Control Centres, which handle long-distance traffic passing to, from and across the US cannot be debugged before 2000. No one was sure quite how these old machines, the last of which was sold in 1987, would go wrong, just that 'they would not work correctly'. A simulated switchover from 1999 to 2000 had caused the air traffic screens to which they were linked to go blank. Airline pilots from over 90 countries expressed some serious concerns over the progress of computer fixes in aeroplanes, airports and the systems that monitor air traffic control corridors at the International Federation of Airline Pilots conference in January 1998. They declared that they would not fly to those airports that could not guarantee that their systems were completely fixed. It is a surprise to me, as it must be to airline pilots, that so many of these safety-critical computer systems are as old as they are. We must assume that software updates have just been written over the basic programmes leaving the underlying 'calendar' code in place.

## Pope and Emperor still inside

But that's not all: Julius Caesar and Pope Gregory XIII both live on in computer clocks. Julius Caesar introduced leap years in 46 BC to cope with the earth taking c. 365.25 days around the sun and in 1582 Pope Gregory XIII firmed this up to 365.2422. He also ordered that 10 days be taken off the Julian calendar, and that leap years should only be observed in years divisible by four, except those centenary years like 1900 whose numbers are not divisible by 400. As the year 2000 is a leap year

260    *Only Connect: Shaping Networks and Knowledge*

not all software packages will know to add a day to their calendars at the end of February e.g. packages only expecting 365 days in the year 2000 might be fooled into thinking that December 31st 2000, is January 1st 2001. In the US the Federal Aviation Authority (FAA) which logs thousands of flight plans each day, admits that 400 of its computers cannot enter flight information for February 29th 2000. Leap years have fooled computers in the past. On December 31st, 1996 the Tiwai Point smelting plant in New Zealand went into emergency shutdown causing almost £1 million of damage because the software failed to recognize the 366th day of the year. Without the computers to regulate internal temperature five of the pot cells overheated and were damaged beyond repair.

While on clocks, dates and times we should spare a thought for Unix systems. They provide the backbone for electronic networks including the Internet and have a built-in 'expiry' date for the year 2038. They store time in seconds in a 32-bit binary code from a start date of January 1st 1970. In 2038 the 32-bit chips will be full up and the computers will cease to function. In theory this should be a minor problem, as most of these computers should have been replaced long before 2038, but then that is what we thought about the 'save two digits' software created in the 1970s and 1980s. It seems that we do like to get our money's worth out of technology and many Unix systems might just zimmer-frame their way through noughts and ones well beyond their sell-by date and 2038 could see interesting times.

## What to learn?

It has often been the boast of the computer industry that if cars had advanced as quickly as the memory and processing power of computers over the past 25 years they would now travel at supersonic speed and cost just a few dollars. Many computer users see it another way. Prone to frequent and inexplicable breakdowns, hugely demanding of both time to read the handbooks that explain how to get the machine up and running and skill in manipulating the information that is presented via icons and hierarchical lists, many see today's PC as more like an unpredictable 1920s motorcar. Most of us can drive someone else's car, as in borrowing a friend's or hiring from Avis, without having to read a 100-page manual but we would rarely contemplate borrowing someone else's computer, and companies offering computers for short-term hire are pretty thin on the ground. For those already frustrated by poor performance and poor reliability from computers the great millennium bug disaster will just reinforce their cynicism. For novices it will seem like a costly absurdity from an industry that they assumed should be at the forefront of contingency planning. It has damaged people's faith in computers and it will make them suspicious of all future claims that might be made for them. We have learnt that although icebergs might be clearly identified on the charts the captains of computer technology are just as capable of ignoring them as was the captain of the *Titanic* in 1912.

Computer technologists continue to have had difficulty in shaking off their reputation for arrogance and this self-inflicted wound has done nothing to help us love them. Yet there is a recent message of technical humility in the face of catastrophe out there if any of them were looking. Intel, the world's largest producer of microchips, turned human after it hit a similar, if much smaller, iceberg in 1994 when it released millions of flawed Pentium chips. The problem was small (an integral routing glitch that caused a mathematical error) and infrequent but the instant media coverage threatened to swamp the firm's reputation. After some sleepless nights Andrew Grove, the head of Intel, agreed to spend $475 million dollars to replace the flawed chip and to offer an in-home fix if necessary. All the publicity, good and bad, generated more awareness of Intel's name and the firm's promise to replace all faulty chips at its own expense gained it recognition for being committed to putting its house in order. Indeed fixing the 'flaw' signified just how important the microchip was to the processing power of a PC and later prompted the company to use the 'Intel inside' logo on the front of PCs and in TV advertisements. Responding quickly to fix a media-exaggerated mistake led to something most marketeers would never have dreamed of, the promotion of a microchip as if it were an end product.

Technology has the fallibility of humans built into it. We, and the machines that we make to build other machines, put it together and we can make mistakes. We stand on the threshold of accessing a new generation of easy-to-use computer-based devices. These will include fixed-screen Web phones, networked computers, smart mobile devices, handheld computers and intelligent TV set-top boxes all using common communication standards, generous bandwidth and, eventually, all responding to normal language speech commands. These devices will revise, and probably re-name, what we now call computing. As with the PC and mainframe computer we will come to rely on them and begin to believe in their infallibility. One lesson we can learn from the Bug's tale is that it would be sensible, where we use them for critical activity, always to have a non-computer-based alternative solution on hand to cope with any failure. A second lesson to learn is that by the time we reach the middle years of the second millennium all PCs, or their equivalents, should carry a logo declaring 'Don't worry. Year 3000 clock already inside'.

## The Formula One tale

In October 1997 the promoters of Formula One (F1) Racing told the new Labour government in the UK that a ban on tobacco sponsorship within the sport would put 50 000 jobs at risk within the UK motor sports industry. They also threatened to re-locate F1 racing outside Europe in the event of an early EU tobacco sponsorship ban. Later revelations that the Labour Party had received a donation of £1 million from Bernie Ecclestone, the world-wide promoter of F1, prior to the UK general election of May 1997 and that he had offered to make further donations to the Labour Party after the election of Tony Blair's government further complicated the relationship between cronyism and legitimate lobbying. The Labour government responded by declaring that they would support F1 racing being exempted from the EU ban despite having made quite a high-profile manifesto pledge to ban ALL tobacco advertising before the election. They also quickly returned the £1 million donation. The F1 lobbyists won the day, gaining nearly a decade in which to find substitutes for the £100 million currently injected into the industry by the tobacco industry. UK ministers were, at one time during the negotiations, fighting hard within the EU for F1 to be exempted permanently from the ban on tobacco advertising. Notwithstanding that this 'exemption' looked a little too cosy for comfort (the classic calling in of 'favours' typical of UK Conservative and all US politics), the decision appeared hasty and the case made by the lobbyists seemed to have been accepted without any corroboration from an independent body. The claim made by the F1 lobbyists that thousands of UK jobs would be put at risk by a transfer overseas of a 'flagship' UK industry was declared to have been an overriding factor in the UK government's pleas in Brussels for F1 to be treated as a special case with regard to cigarette advertising.

## The benefits of study

Eight weeks later in December 1997 a team of UK-based economic geographers from the universities of Southampton and Birmingham, who had spent 18 months investigating the UK motor sport industry, published their report to the Economic and Social Research Council (ESRC) [4]. The researchers, unlike the lobbyists, had carried out in-depth talks with all but one of the UK-based F1 teams as well as many other companies active within the industry. They found a completely different picture from that painted by the F1 lobbyists. They discovered that the integration of engineering and other specialist knowledge within what had come to be called 'motor sport valley', a 100-mile crescent across southern England, could not be re-created elsewhere in an acceptable time-frame and that all the F1 managements were very much aware of this. The ESRC report made it clear that the UK's dominance of world motor sport – it produces three-quarters of the world's single-seater racing cars and houses the majority of F1 teams – 'lies in its features as a geographically concentrated knowledge community', built up and refreshed in the UK over many years. The report went on to emphasize the importance of just 'being there':

> motor sport valley is a knowledge pool, a centre of world-class excellence that is on a constant learning trajectory. To be outside of the valley is to risk your position within the knowledge community.

This highly successful sector of British industry had evolved over 40 years into a 'truly global industry with finance, sponsorship, drivers, engineers, parts and expertise coming from all over the world'. All this thrived principally because of close interaction in a small area within a deeply entrenched motor sport culture that embraced nearly 400 companies, only a minority of which had direct connections with F1.

In yet another clue to the importance, and cost, of 'knowledge valleys' the South Cambridgeshire District Council in England has begun to restrict the development of science parks. This action is due to the supposed detrimental effect on the quality of life (congestion, inflated house prices and pollution) by the inward migration of businesses and people to Cambridge and the surrounding areas. The lure of 'being there' has helped Cambridgeshire to become one of Europe's greatest concentrations of high-technology firms with nearly 900 companies locating there, employing around 28 000 people in the IT, electronics and health sciences sectors. They account for around 19 per cent of the county's GDP in 1991, a figure that is expected to rise to over 24 per cent by the year 2000. However, local planners and residents want greater use of the digital technologies, which are the *raison d'être* of many of these firms, to enable sophisticated trading and communication at a distance. They want to see the companies using digital technology to expand their activities, using services like tele-working, tele-learning and tele-medicine, rather than by moving more people into the area [5].

## Knowledge rubbing

The planners and residents may have a point but they are unlikely to stem the tide. University cities everywhere are busy building up partnerships between industry and academe that all governments like to see by developing science and business parks to attract the high-knowledge end of IT work and development. The industries attracted to these parks will use ICTs to keep in touch with their bases in other countries and with other research centres, but the reason the people need to be there is to rub up against other experts on a daily basis in real space. A growing number of such centres is springing up around the globe creating physical 'knowledge-rubbing' nodes that facilitate the kind of high-quality knowledge exchange that cannot be replicated by long-distance communication. If we then imagine each of these centres linked by an electronic network we can easily see where the 'global knowledge' factory idea comes from. These are hi-tech clearings in the forest linked by electronic footpaths and each clearing will stand or fall on the quality of its distinct or unique knowledge base, the conviviality of its 'rubbing' space and how good it is at refreshing that space with new blood.

Bill Gates' Microsoft, a company capable if any is of using electronic networking to share knowledge, chose Cambridge as the location for its European research facility. The reasons for this are obvious. Some universities have gained the kind of 'first mover advantage', mentioned in Chapter 6 in relation to technology, in knowledge fermentation. The advantage in Cambridge's case dates back to some students and teachers who escaped the riots and intolerance of Oxford around 1209. Europe's great universities developed environments where ideas could flourish by building monastic-like retreats, creating libraries and defending their right to tolerate diverse ideas and ideologies. Not for nothing are universities the first places to be closed down by oppressive governments. Monastic to foster reflection they also took advantage of the worldly progress of communications infrastructures with their scholars being among the first great travellers and sharers of information, a quality that their modern counterparts are only too happy to emulate. Such environments are constantly refreshed by new ideas often inspired, but not limited by, the shades of those great thinkers who also passed that way. Such atmospheres are not easy to replicate quickly; they are firmly fixed in real space and only pale imitations can be created in virtual worlds.

Paradoxically another reason for the growth of real-space clustering is the existence of a first-rate electronic network infrastructure. Dialog, a leading provider of online information and search software with its main headquarters in London, England, decided in 1998 to locate its US headquarters at Cary in North Carolina. Keeping its 200-strong technology team in Silicon Valley it decided to concentrate its marketing, finance and administrative functions in North Carolina's Research Triangle Park area. Here a state-supported initiative embracing universities and telecommunications companies has created a high-speed, big bandwidth network known as the North Carolina GigaPop. Along with other companies Dialog hopes to utilize the connective capabilities of the GigaPop in conjunction with its own network to offer customers faster and more secure communications. The two coasts, east and west, offer different and distinctive knowledge environments that cannot be replicated in one place. The two geographical 'hotbeds' are 'hot' for different reasons and Dialog's dual location aims to squeeze the best out of both. Many corporations now operate in a similar way using electronic networks to maximize, rather than replace, the distinctive knowledge growth that has become the *raison d'être* of particular locations.

## Knowledge compost

Although they do not always understand all the ingredients that make it work corporations and research institutes understand that 'knowledge rubbing' in real space delivers a different kind of value and richness of result that justifies the sometimes high costs of 'being there'. And that cost can be high. Not everyone is a millionaire in California's Silicon Valley and the high cost of property there has meant that many company employees have to live some distance away and use tele-working for most of their time, only commuting to the company's offices every month or so. It might take them two or more years to raise the cash to come up with the downpayment for a house in the Valley proper and during that time they know that they operate at a disadvantage. They know that a lot of critical stuff will be going on during that all important 'face time' and that what is conveyed over lunch is not the same as in Email. Even less easy to distil and explain is the impact of particular cultures on knowledge congregations.

> . . . culture is both the repository of all past information growth and also the slowly maturing 'compost' wherein the loosely arranged ingredients of new information moments potentially reside. When we say that information is 'culturally dependent' we are simply recog-nizing that we operate within a particular kind of social structure, and that information and knowledge transmitted to individuals within it carry strong reinforcing signals about the values, beliefs and roles that underwrite and sustain one kind of social structure rather than 'another.' [3]

Much of the connectivity that we hear about nowadays emphasizes just how unimportant is cultural space to the distillation of ideas. Individuals interested in developing ideas and theories within a particular knowledge domain, though scattered around the globe, can now develop cyber-communities that facilitate multi-person contact at whatever level of discussion and exchange they wish to explore. Each brings their own culture of 'loosely arranged ingredients' to such a knowledge nervous system and the totality of the osmosis that they generate, having been through so many sieves, is assumed to have been culturally sanitized. But how inescapable are the attachments of one's culture to the ideas we generate? Why have knowledge stereotypes hung around for so long? – Germans and Swedes as engineers, Italians as designers, Americans as producers of movies and software, the Japanese as designers of manu-facturing systems? Could we imagine Hollywood, Microsoft and Silicon Valley being anywhere other than in America? Is it just an accident that Bangalore has become the programming centre of India? The silicon explo-sion in the US had its roots in 1970s California because it was a milieu where established patterns of behaviour, both social and industrial, had been customarily disregarded. Paradoxically it was also a place where the liberation spirit of 1960s youth movements fed comfortably into the free-wheeling and buccaneering spirit of the material, computer world and these values accelerated the speed and through constant feedback multiplied the scope of the rapidly diversifying technological innovations.

It may seem a contradiction in terms that a sixties hippie culture could snuggle down so comfortably with mammon but the nature of the snuggling, in the beginning at least, holds the key. Small groups, drinking coca cola, doing their own thing, unsupervised, creative and in loose assemblies of like minds can be seen in retrospect as no more than a commune which eventually gets to pay its bills.

In recognizing 'knowledge communities' we are witnessing to some extent the accidental convergence of some physical, social and educational characteristics that may get lost over time as the characteristics needed to fuel a knowledge community in its early phases may not be so important to it once it becomes established. But the continuing importance of knowledge communities emphasizes just how much cultural strengths and weaknesses operate in the physical universe; they are personal, rich in the sediment of human experience, a little bit mysterious and they cannot be replicated across impersonal electronic networks.

In the old days the US film companies moved out to Hollywood to get constant sunshine and more space. Modern movie-makers create their own sunshine and the world is full of big spaces but the movie business still makes many of its connections in Hollywood. The bond between the past, present and the future of knowledge communities may be less easy to identify as time goes on but look under the surface and it will be there. Many Japanese live in small spaces where dogs and cats are forbidden and so animal lovers often have to be satisfied with small pets like hamsters and goldfish; they also like tiny gadgets so was born the small, gadgety, electronic pet of the Tamagotchi. Is it any surprise that the world's premier network security company Check Point Software Technologies started its life in Israel where security and defence have preoccupied the Israelis since 1948.

# A tale of two flights and one aircraft carrier

## The DC 9's tale

On 11 May 1996 ValuJet Flight 592 left Miami bound for Atlanta with 110 people on board, luggage and a few tyres (the only hazardous substance that ValuJet was licensed to carry) plus some boxes of oxygen generators removed from another aircraft some time before. A child of de-regulation ValuJet had been growing very fast and was something of a 'virtual' airline, outsourcing to subcontractors everything from training to routine mainten-ance and repairs and they often communicated with the contractors over distance, e.g. issuing engineering instructions on paper, rather than in face-to-face encounters. The average age of ValuJet's fleet of DC9s was 26 years old (American Airlines' average is 8 years) so they needed a lot of maintenance. Earlier in 1996 the Inspector General at the Department of Transportation, a kind of 'who guards the guards' watchdog whose job it was to watch over other watchdogs including the US FAA, had researched the history of ValuJet. In February 1996 it sent a team to talk to the FAA office in Atlanta to discuss their concerns about ValuJet's recent record of mishaps and to ask the FAA what they were doing about it. An engine explosion on the Atlanta runway in 1995 caused by a fault in an engine bought from a Turkish airline, undercarriages failing to drop and fumes in the cabin on one flight all added up to an incident rate 14 times greater than the average for the bigger airlines. The FAA response was cool although the local officers did send a note about the visit to the FAA's head office in Washington prompting an FAA officer, based in the Office of Aviation Flight Standards, to do some research on the ValuJet data and prepare a report. He did and it was damning. His report dated 14 February 1996 noted 58 recent violations, 43 of which involved main-tenance problems, and recommended grounding ValueJet until it had sorted out its problems. A senior manager received this report but decided to put it on hold.

The FAA is a strange watchdog, part regulator and part promoter, of aviation. To ground such a high-profile airline as ValuJet the FAA would have to admit that there was something wrong with their own oversight of the airline and this would have shown them as failing in some way. The FAA's critics complain that it really needs to do just one job well, i.e. airline safety, and to the exclusion of all others so that it is never tempted to compromise airline safety in its role as business partner. Flight 592 plunged into the Florida Everglades killing all 110 people on board. The oxygen generators stored in the hold should have been deactivated by inserting a small yellow cap over their firing mechanism but these had not been available to the sub-contractors who removed the generators from the other aeroplane. The general view is that the generators got hot, caused a fire and then fuelled it with their own oxygen despite having been labelled empty on the manifest. The FAA was in the middle of a 120-day review of ValuJet at the time. This type of review allowed the airline to keep flying while their systems and procedures were examined. As at early 1999 the families of the victims are still awaiting compensation as no one party has been willing to claim responsibility for the disaster. As far as safety is concerned we believe that all airlines are 'run' by governments who conduct comprehensive safety checks on our behalf and refuse permission for doubtful airlines to fly. Rapid growth following de-regulation, cheaper operators offering a no frills service, the outsourcing of vital functions, poor communication between the carrier and subcontractors and a schizophrenic role for the key regulator all look like a recipe for disaster. The FAA is currently re-assessing its role including the way it approves and monitors airline sub-contractors. ValuJet did get its certificate to fly a reduced number of aeroplanes back from the FAA after the Everglades disaster but it later merged with another carrier to form AirTran. Few lessons seem to have been learned from this accident. In 1990 US air personnel discovered undeclared hazardous materials on 63 occasions, usually because it leaked or emitted a smell; by 1997 this number had increased five-fold to 349. Shippers are still not required to disclose to air carriers the contents of their parcels or crates – not even if they contain hazardous materials [6].

## The DC10's tale

The ValuJet tragedy arose from human error as a result of poor communications between the various parties involved in handling dangerous components. Fortunately less tragic situations can sometimes look humorous, in retrospect at least. Such occasions highlight the indomitable quirkishness of the human interface with IT; they throw a chastening light on the continuing challenges that we face in getting the mix right and remind us of the unpredictable way that humans can behave when engaging with even the most sophisticated of technologies. One of my favourites is the 1995 story of the two pilots happily landing their DC10 at Brussels when they were scheduled to fly to Frankfurt. The passengers sat silently watching a representation of their flight, clearly landing at Brussels, on a graphic display conveniently provided by the airline. They expected to see Frankfurt but they stayed dumb: out of courtesy, good manners or confused disbelief. The cabin staff were also watching the aeroplane's progress on the same graphic display but chose to remain silent as they moved to and fro getting on with preparations for landing. They thought that there had been a secret hijack and that the best thing to do was behave as if nothing had happened. After the aeroplane landed the pilots were suspended, the passengers were one city and one country removed from where they wanted to be and the cabin crew felt some satisfaction from the success of their 'don't panic' training.

This is not a story from the early days of flight. A tremendous amount of communication technology was wrapped around this flying cigar but in the end the constructed beliefs and social conditioning of the humans involved proved just too much for it. As the electronic revolution in communications and representation of our world unfolds and the revolutionaries proclaim the new utopias we must ensure that we don't lose the confidence that comes from using all of our senses, including 'common sense'. The screens might often have it right, the pilots (whoever they are) may have got it wrong, there may be no need to panic but whenever we feel that what is happening to us looks strange or intuitively wrong we must resist the temptation to stay dumb!

## The aircraft carrier's tale

The US navy is equipped with some of the most advanced communications technology in the world. But the spirit of the Titanic – 'I am big so icebergs please get out of my way', lives on even in this hi-tech navy. This 1998 exchange between the Canadian authorities and a US warship off the coast of Newfoundland illuminates that arrogance that can still come from being big, powerful and wrong. It helps to imagine the growing irritation and grumpiness of the captain on the US warship to enjoy this excerpt to the full.

US ship:     'Please divert your course 15 degrees north to avoid collision.'
Canadians: 'Suggest you divert your course 15 degrees to the south to avoid collision'.
US ship:     'This is the captain of a US Navy ship. I say again divert your course.'
Canadians: 'No I say again, you divert.'

US ship:    'This is the aircraft carrier *USS Missouri*. We are a very large
            warship of the US Navy. Divert your course now!'
Canadians: 'This is a lighthouse. Your call.'

One cannot help but be entertained as well as amazed by the scene. All that data whirling around on those green screens with all those highly trained marine engineers watching over them and yet somehow they still mistook a lighthouse for a sea-going vessel. No harm was done on this occasion, other than to the captain's pride, but over-confidence in the correctness of computer technology is now regarded as a major factor in aircraft (both military and civil) and maritime accidents. Automatic navigation systems have reached a high level of technical reliability, so high in fact that recourse to other sources of navigational data is not always checked.

## Rubbish in, rubbish out

Focusing on using the technology to the exclusion of all other senses can have the same effect as a child brought up to do its mathematics on a calculator. It fails to recognize a ridiculous answer because it doesn't have even a rough idea of what the answer should be. This insensitivity to false data entry can mean life and death in some situations. Nursing involves quite a lot of measuring and simple calculation but most candidates for nursing courses admit to being bad at, if not terrified of, maths. Indeed being 'bad at maths' in the UK (exceptionally for a European country) is almost a badge to be worn with pride. Many students entering higher education in the UK actually find comfort in the discovery that this is a state which they share with the majority of their new colleagues. A university mathematics teacher quoted in an article about the extremely poor maths performance of adults and students in the UK doesn't see any sign of change:

> I don't want my life ever to depend on software written by my undergraduates. I don't want them to have designed the autopilot of the plane I get into . . . All software is wrong now. The whole style of software writing is not 'Get it right.' It's get it roughly right, try it and then patch it. . . . It is serious because of students' sense of what is correct and what is not. Numbers now control our lives – but decimal points don't mean anything to someone who has grown up with a calculator. Whether you're a car mechanic, banker,

teacher or software developer, you need a robust sense of how numbers behave – to the point where it almost hurts physically to get it wrong. [7]

Donald MacKenzie [8] has noted how accidents caused by failure in the interaction between human beings and a computer system are 'messier' because isolating the cause of failure (i.e. who to blame) inevitably becomes a contentious tussle between the operator and the designer of a computer system. His examples of such failures: underdosing patients in isocentric radiotherapy at a UK hospital between 1982 and 1991; the failure of the US frigate *Stark*'s computer systems to recognize two incoming Exocet missiles in the Persian Gulf in 1987; the shooting down of an Iranian passenger airliner by the *USS Vincennes* in 1988; and the shooting down of a Korean airliner over Soviet air space in 1983 all exhibit 'messy' characteristics. A simple, undetected mistake seems to have doomed the Korean airliner. The autopilot had been connected to the aeroplane's compass rather than to its inertial navigation system. The aircraft therefore followed a constant magnetic heading throughout its flight rather than the intended flight plan. Interestingly in the 1988 Iranian airliner incident '. . . it was the highly computerized *Vincennes* that misidentified the radio contact, while its technologically more primitive sister ship, the *Sides*, correctly identified the Iranian aircraft [as climbing] and thus no threat.' [8]

## Reclaiming all of our senses

If there is a common theme among these six stories it is that we need to show a little more humility in the face of complexity. Possibly a more profound lesson is that 'information overwhelm' sourced by electronic devices has sapped our inquisitive senses to the point where we have little or no energy left to run a test or two using our own natural sensory devices. Humans have come a long way by 'sensing' the stimuli in their environment. However some now have to operate in environments, e.g. airline pilots and air traffic controllers, where they have to put most of their trust in the flawless functioning of computerized systems. In these arenas there is little or no opportunity for them to check out the information derived from electronic systems against other sources. However, although most of us don't work in these high-speed-screen-only environments, we seem to have drawn a lazy inference from them and transferred similar belief systems over to the less constrained arenas in which we operate. We are succumbing to the sensory poverty that comes from a belief that we have gained complete control over our environment through technology and so there is less and less need to hone or keep active our natural sensory apparatus. Such a situation, overwhelmed by one kind of information and yet deprived of stimulus from another, suggests that although one kind of information overload is real and stressful the part of our psyche that has surrendered us to it has decided to run down our other sensory periscopes. It is as if we have declared that operating computers leaves no margin for randomness or surprise so we no longer hone our capacity to deal with these. Instead we concentrate and focus our energies on the purely rational, purely conscious, computer-friendly sides of our sensory apparatus. Whereas in pre-computer times we were hospitable to a whole gamut of information about our surroundings, nowadays we willingly submit to an electronic drip feed of information in lieu of the real thing.

The real culprit in all this sensory deprivation is not computers or databases or the Internet but consciousness itself. Because we've virtually expunged hunches, intuition and the subconscious from our problem solving in favour of binary-based conscious thought we have reduced the world's gloriously complex reality to a cognitively simplistic model that Tor Norretrander calls the 'The user illusion' [9]. Norretrander uses artificial intelligence as proof of his main contention that we need to celebrate more of our old intuitive canniness and put human consciousness back in the frame as just one of the range of ways, rather than the only way, to approach problems and process the information that we pull in from all around us. An intelligent device that mimics consciousness alone does not actually come anywhere near being human because humans function mainly through non-conscious thought. Computers and electronic networks are a consequence of our own thought paradigm and it is therefore up to us to re-assert the complexity of both the world and the individual when we construct our information processing environments.

An unmanned computer-operated lighthouse on the seashore may keep the lamp flashing at the correct rate but it does not see the red signal rocket fired out on the horizon. Another part of our challenge is the too narrow, too focused and sometimes too arrogant professional. Educated and trained to recognize old patterns, and perhaps acknowledge the potential for one or two new ones, it is they who take charge of the many critical systems on which we now rely. It is they who fly and maintain the aircraft, captain the ferries, secure our computers and telephone lines at critical periods in our lives and ensure that princesses and governments receive accurate and timely advice. They study these matters closely but they are often too sharply focused, they don't get much encouragement to look from side to side. Although the idea that technology is neutral, driven by an autonomous, non-social internal dynamic of its own has been widely discredited, this kind of technological determinism

> . . . still informs the way technology is thought about and discussed in society at large, especially where modern high technologies are concerned. The idea that technological change is just 'progress' and that certain technologies triumph simply because they are the best or the most efficient is still widespread. A weaker but more sophisticated version of technological determinism – the idea that there are 'natural trajectories' of technological change – remain popular among economists who study technology. [9]

## Improving but still too slow

In earlier chapters we have seen how humans, both as individuals and as part of companies and despite their growing obsessions with urgency, have often still been very slow at solving problems critical to their success. Many companies have been slow to save themselves thousands of pounds by using the Internet rather than analogue fax machines, Microsoft was taken by surprise at the success and growth of the Internet and Barnes and Nobel were caught off guard by Amazon.com. As recently as 1987 car ferry companies were fatally slow to see the dangers of speeding above the 17-knot threshold with their bow doors open, or indeed even to put failsafe devices in place to ensure that their bow doors were closed when setting sail. The UK's place at the top of the single parent league mocks the thirty-odd years that the pill and other methods of birth control have been widely available. Despite the proliferation of research information available to governments and corporations they still make decisions, as we saw from the Formula One story, using the thinnest of 'thin' knowledge. There are at least three lessons for us here. Firstly we routinely over-estimate the quality of information available to the highest level of decision-makers in a system, be it governmental or corporate. Secondly, good information (remember the Titanic and the ice-flow warnings) does not translate unproblematically into good solutions. Thirdly, however skilled someone is at programming a computer they can still enter a mistake which can go unnoticed for years before a critical moment forces its exposure. Human error and human preference cannot be mechanized out of existence.

## References

1.  'This Life'. *The Sunday Times* News Review, 1 February 1998

2.  Morton, A. (1997) *Diana her true story – in her own words*. London: Michael O'Mara Books Limited, p. 204

3.  Haywood, T. (1995) *Info-Rich – Info-Poor: access and exchange in the global information society*. London: Bowker Saur, p. 157

4.  *The Financial Times*, 15 December 1997 pp. 1 and 18

5.  *THES*, 12 June 1998, p. 4

6.  'No Safe Harbour'. *Time*, 14 September 1998, pp. 50–51

7.  'Maths Problem'. *Mail On Sunday* Night & Day, 25 October 1998, p. 27

8.  MacKennzie, D. (1996) *Knowing machines: essays on technical change*. London: The MIT Press

9.  Norretranders, T. (1998) *The user illusion*. London: Penguin

# CHAPTER NINE

# Epilogue: some final thoughts

'If you lived here you would be home by now'
> A sign on a new housing development on the main
> road north out of New Orleans.

## More information, less faith

Faith makes the world go round and it forms the basis for every connection we ever make. Every day we invest in it to reveal truths and to support us in our progress through life. Pressing a light switch, turning on the kettle, believing in a promise made by a friend or a car mechanic, dialling up an Internet service provider or waiting for a bus all represent an almost unconscious belief in things working as well today as they did yesterday. When we invest faith in the spiritual sense we have different expectations. This faith, the belief in an awesome power that we cannot explain rationally but we feel sufficiently moved and inspired to offer our prayers both to honour it and to solicit help or guidance, is less precise in its anticipation. We sacrifice time and energy in worship and in following a particular way of life and we expect something in return, usually a different quality of post-mortem opportunity than that which unbelievers can expect. Sincere believers bounce back when this kind of faith lets them down in this world as part of their belief accepts that they are but a small part of a much greater scheme of things and that all gods move in mysterious ways.

But faith is also something that we build up rationally based on information that we collect and patterns that we recognize. This is the kind of faith that we have in each other, in the institutions that our societies have constructed, in technology and in what we might call the daily apparatus that enables us to live fruitful and peaceful lives. We are less tolerant when our faith in institutions and technology proves to have been misplaced since we have refined the logic and intelligence on which these are now based over two thousand years and we expect a high hit rate. When they start showing some cracks, as our faith in democracy is doing, or we fail to incorporate a key date change in our electronic devices, we look back at our long evolution and ask ourselves why haven't we got this right by now?

We have suffered a severe crisis in sustaining the foundations of both kinds of faith during the last half of the twentieth century. Spiritual faith has been demonized by its organization and management into distinct compartments whose strictures often deny the sanctity or value of other kinds of faith. Institutionalized religion comes in many forms but, despite the recent rhetoric of ecumenicalism, they all still have great difficulty sharing their faith with each other, agreeing on complimentary approaches to the deity or in tolerating each other in their places of worship. The managerial structures required to channel resources, instigate missions and maintain ceremony and elaborate infrastructures within established churches have made them look secular, hypocritical and overtly concerned with protecting material structures. The other kind of faith, the faith we have in the codes and institutions we have constructed to live by, has also been dented as our confidence in their veracity has been undermined by the many failures of which increased knowledge and familiarity have made us aware. Religious faith, not requiring hard information as proof of the existence of a deity, has suffered more from its enthusiastic adoption of secular organizational models than from the scientific knowledge that renders big issues like the creation, resurrection or miracles less credible. A faith built on ideas developed from ancient writings is difficult to expose as being fraudulent or of failing to meet its obligations to people. Its failings are thus much less susceptible to exposure than say the liberal ideals of justice, freedom of speech, equality and liberty that require continual bursts of evidence and comparative information to reassure us of their continuing value.

The end of the twentieth century has seen ordinary citizens withdraw their once easily assumed loyalty to institutions that have, sometimes ruthlessly, confirmed their short-term and often indifferent or uncaring relationship with them. We are much more sceptical of politicians, businessmen, journalists and academics as we enter the new millennium than we were in 1901, principally because we know more about them. This knowledge has not only undone their one-time mystery but also shown too many of them to be morally flawed and unworthy of retaining their traditional status as mentor and role model. Blind faith in religion and in a natural human hierarchy kept the ignorant in their place up until the end of the fifteenth century. After that each century facilitated access to more ideas, more roads on which to travel, more literacy, more information and more discontent with prescribed faiths. The new millennium will also offer more people greater access to once closed knowledge and information. If the same patterns unfold in the future we can expect to see even less confidence in the received wisdom as handed out by conventional institutions.

Lack of faith is already encouraging people to fragment into more single-cause groups, more new-age religions, artificial cyber villages and fan clubs for the long-term and temporarily famous. Our growing desire to be part of the fame, to be a player, to be both commentator and audience, has also left us unsure of the roles that we play in relation to others. So many of the contracts written and unwritten that legitimized our roles over what we perceived to be reasonable lengths of time are now framed in the language of ambiguity and transience. Uncritical pedestal worship in worlds of limited options caught, used and secured our faith in the stones of parliaments, revolutions and cathedrals. Access to information and its multi-option bedfellow choice shrinks such a faith and the resigned feelings of security that it often bestowed.

The urge to siphon off public funds to feed personal greed, always rampant in dictatorships and closed societies, has not been dulled by liberal institutions. Examples could be taken from any country and any region of the world. Some of the most recent include members of the International Olympic Committee taking bribes, EU Commissioners being accused of corruption and mismanagement, Swiss banks shamelessly profiting from the holocaust for 40 years before being forced to own up and Belgian political parties accepting donations from companies who later picked up rich military contracts. The noise of exposed corruption and greed at the end of our century has been deafening. Authority has disappointed us so often that we can no longer summon up any awe for it, civic life has shrunk to a shadow of its former self and our enthusiasm for democracy as we live it now has been dulled by over-familiarity with its key actors.

   This is not a plea for a return to a Dark Age of mystery and servitude or for more ignorance and the ostensible bliss that it bestows but the prelude to a serious question. How do we turn access to greater knowledge about the workings of the institutions we construct into a positive rather than a negative part of our lives? One solution is to find the energy and sense of purpose to resurrect our connections with our neighbours and our communities in real space and to raise our visibility above that of house-bound consumers. This would require us to spend some time taking what we learn out on to the streets, exchanging and debating it with others and resurrecting our connections with each other as actors as well as watchers. As western homes become machines for living in with more and more information and entertainment pouring out of holes in our walls the temptation to stay in the warm and watch an issue develop, rather than brave a cold night to attend a meeting to help solve it, will be even worse than it is now.

   Electronic networks offer the opportunity for individuals to locate themselves in manageable communities of like minds who can each provide leadership via their individual contribution without the need for hierarchy or edifice. They can help and support each other in a pleasant micro-world of their own making which can be satisfying on many levels including the spiritual level and the value of this to individuals is not to be sniffed at. But this kind of connectivity also needs to feed and be fed by a parallel world of rich engagement with others in real space. Assuming that the specialized intelligence generated by cyber-communities is a substitute for restoring our faith in the wider arenas of citizenship and community action is naïve and, if promoted as replacing the need for citizens to act out their dreams in real space, possibly dangerous.

   Despite all its frailties humanity engages best in real space. It is in real, rather than remote communities, that the solutions to the great issues of war, famine, inequality, plague, poverty, justice and intolerance will be found. It is in real space where we need to refresh our faith in ourselves to construct institutions and technology that truly serve all citizens rather than just those elites whose economic power gives them access to brokering our futures. A machine for living in may be a comfortable place to hide from a world of neighbours or to grumble about a self-serving authority but it is not a place from which we can launch the kind of movements that stimulate real change. The end of communism and the end of apartheid came to pass as a result of action on the streets. Changing governments, stopping oppression, attacking pollution and forcing a re-think on policies such as the closure of hospitals, the release of prisoners of conscience or securing fair treatment for racial minorities require more than an Internet round-robin to be effective.

Reclaiming the faith we need to connect with each other as we once did before we started retiring to our bunkers will not be easy as many agents have a stake in reinforcing a stay-at-home, plugged-in life-style. Single-cause activists have, sometimes violently, filled the vacuum left by an indolent citizenry but win or lose they tend to retire back into small bunkers of their own and often have little or no interest in harnessing the same energy to address wider issues of justice or governance. A world covered in electronic networks has done little to mitigate the decomposition of the values that, however tentatively, once held communities together under a common umbrella of shared experience. Corruption at all levels of democratic government, ostentatious greed amongst corporate leaders, sub-cultures that perceive little or no meaningful stake in the world around them and day-to-day transactions that often lack confidence and sincerity are now the hallmark of the so-called developed world.

Those old established excesses, motivated by greed or a desire to exert unearned and undue influence over others, are now made easier to embrace by the loss of faith in the ideas of community and monitoring that once exposed, punished and outlawed them. The changing nature of the spatial link between voters and their representatives in democracies is making things worse. Otto von Habsburg, MEP and son of the last Austrian Emperor, has noted that as time goes on fewer and fewer Europeans have experienced life under a dictatorship. The temptations of totalitarianism, as a solver of economic and social ills, can look attractive to those who have not seen at first hand what happens when a nation tries to solve its problems in that manner. He suggests that the great danger to democrats

> . . . comes from perfectionists who don't see democracy as a political system whose greatest goal it is to guarantee freedom and legal order. They give it a theological function and it becomes more and more abstract as a result. But when you make something abstract people lose interest in it. Slowly but surely, we are heading for a

proportional representation system in which candidates are selected by the leader of a party alone. Consequently people no longer know who they voted for and politicians no longer know who voted for them. And as the link between parliamentarians and constituents vanishes, democracy will disappear. [1]

In order to give smaller parties a chance to derive some meaningful influence from the votes cast for them proportional representation (PR) has become the norm for parliamentary elections in Europe and soon British MEPs will be elected in a similar manner. The downside is that the link between those who vote and those who represent them is much weaker. PR increases party dependency, cronyism and sometimes an arrogant detachment from the community. The issues specific to a particular space, a space with human dimensions that is comprehensible to voters, are shared among a 'list' of representatives and although big economic issues are addressed individual voters feel that their influence declines in direct proportion to the growth in the size of constituencies. Italy has always had difficulty forming governments that last for more than a few months – it has had 56 since the end of the Second World War. During April 1999 Italians voted in a referendum on scrapping the rule whereby 25 per cent of the seats in parliament should continue to be assigned by proportional representation. The hope of the reformers was to reduce the smaller parties ability to use their seven or nine per cent of the popular vote to continue to wreck governments. Unfortunately and like the Portuguese referendum on abortion (see Chapter 1), the 49.6 per cent of registered voters who turned out to vote was just 0.4 per cent short of the number needed to give effect to the vote, even though 90 per cent of those that did vote demanded reform. The Italians have had 31 referenda since 1990 and despite some other low turnouts, have come to see them as perhaps the only way to effect change on some big issues (to legalize divorce in 1974 and abortion in 1981). Unfortunately apathy, particularly in the poorer south of the country, rather than reform was the winner on this occasion; a moment that could have reduced the need for serial referenda in the future.

Increasingly divorced from the electoral system the 'democratic' community is being replaced by collections of numerically coded consumers who have little or no interest in those who don't have the means to consume or whose bunkers will never be wired up. We may make many more connections after 2000 but without some restoration of our faith in the value of connecting and in the integrity of the language we use to connect we will continue to feel less rather than more influential.

## Faith in words

Our overwhelming desire to be part of societies that are led by groups in which we can have faith won't go away and a great part of that faith was, in the past, secured by the words our leaders used to persuade us of their authority to act on our behalf. Unfortunately faith in words isn't going to help us much in understanding just what it is our politicians mean any more. Now politicians give us a 'performance' rather than an understanding of the meaning or consequences of words. A good performance inspires our confidence and, having gained our confidence, the implications of what was said or meant can be explored privately later when all the savoury and unsavoury consequences can be sorted out. Given many recent events we could be forgiven for thinking that the words we use to describe the moral weight of a given nation's crisis is in inverse proportion to its wealth and power. Thus the US in its opulence gets docu-porn in the Starr Report at its darkest moment of a year while Rwanda gets its rivers clogged with corpses, Kosovo its murdered families and Bangladesh floods and famine. Somewhere along the way, probably encouraged by the media's limited dictionary of drama, we have sanitized the words we use about crises, Starr equals genocide, equals murder, equals famine.

But this Humpty Dumpty world of word management is also a world of consequences, some of which can be tragic in the real meaning of that word. In 1994 the Clinton administration, embarrassed by its earlier and poorly prepared involvement in Somalia, was desperate to stay out of the terrible violence going on in Rwanda. It used a semantic quibble in debates at the UN about the meaning of the word 'genocide' to avoid US involvement while millions of Rwandans died ignorant of the word play that left them to their plight. The same kind of Jesuitical parsing of meaning surfaced later in the US about what constitutes 'sexual relations' when uttered under oath by a naughty President. The Justice Department's case against Microsoft may well turn on similar Clintonesque semantics: 'It depends on what you mean by monopoly' or 'Is a 90 per cent monopoly just a slightly bigger than normal market share?'

We rely on the veracity of words to support our faith in our trans-actions with one another. They were our first connecting facilitators enabling us to describe experiences, explain our feelings and share mentally constructed perceptions of our physical world. The brevity of Email communication, the fast scanning of information prompted by constructed urgency, the vocabulary of wriggling now so common among our politicians and the decline of attention span in the face of information-overload are all coinciding to damage our faith in this the oldest of our connecting technologies. Our response to this might be 'So what, it has ever been so'. Lloyd George, Aneurin Bevan, Hitler and Mussolini all relied on an orchestrated 'performance' to secure support and everyone knows that you've never been able to trust politicians. Another response might be that today's politicians are elected by an electorate that is far better educated than that which voted before the 1950s, and making some progress in the veracity and integrity of our politics is important enough to figure as a serious agenda item for the future as the evidence suggests that it is getting worse rather than better.

## Guerrilla country

In the preface to his 1969 book *The age of discontinuity: guidelines to our changing society* Peter Drucker noted that:

> The future is, of course, always 'guerrilla country' in which the unsus-pected and apparently insignificant derails the massive and seemingly invincible trends of today. [2]

The derailing of massive and seemingly invincible trends by un-suspected and apparently insignificant factors is just the kind of David and Goliath story that, unless we're a Goliath or employed by a Goliath, we all like to hear about. There is always a tension between the comfort of the conventional wisdom that helps us to recognize familiar patterns and navigate our way through our day and our desire to see it punctured by revelations that show that it was always wrong or at best just a temporary fix. In the world of electronic networking the hills are alive with guerrillas in the shape of those who put their knowledge to work solving the challenges of replicating intelligence in computer and network systems.

Linus Torvalds, a 21-year-old Finnish student at the University of Helsinki created the Linux version of UNIX in 1991; he made it freely available on the Internet and encouraged other programmers to download, test and modify it as they saw fit. The Linux community grew and grew very much like a successful band of guerrillas but friendlier. Basing themselves out there in the cyberhills somewhere, they added new features to Linux, fixed bugs and transformed it into something which 'conventional' organizations began to desire and seek to appropriate. Unlike conventional guerrillas they were happy to see their ideas appropriated by anyone, as their victory was one of an internalized triumph over convention rather than via certificates of corporate recognition.

Such groups will undoubtedly populate new worlds where some software development is accomplished in this way alongside the more conventional 'let's work on this project' company approach. Although a revolution of sorts commercially valuable ideas such as this one rarely remain in the 'hills' for long. To the chagrin of Internet idealists such innovations still need the respectability of a 'responsible' entity to develop them and to guarantee their future if they are to gain wide acceptance. This generally results in the guerrillas, their ideas or both being bought up by a big corporation, or like the founders of Yahoo, they join with a venture capitalist to form their own corporation. Unlike the old industrial economies in which economies of scale led to relatively stable oligopolies the information economy is populated by monopolies seeking a long life in a temporary world. They try and secure this by locking their customers into their technology and aggressively fighting off or buying the alternative technologies that might offer them some competition.

This is the 'long–short', 'temporary–permanent' dilemma facing regulators attempting to even out the playing fields in the new arenas being carved out by communications technology. Many of the combinations of technologies being introduced into the market are still too new to bring any one of them to trial for unfairly dominating it. The PC operating system is not so new, being nearly 20 years old, and Microsoft has clearly sought to 'dominate' this market via some unsavoury behaviour, but future PCs may not be PCs, let alone use an operating system in the way that we differentiate them today. For regulators their uncomfortable challenge is to assess just how temporary a monopoly is likely to be and the extent to which it is being maintained or extended by anticompetitive means. It is Microsoft's very awareness of the probably temporary nature of its Windows monopoly that makes it such an aggressive player, both in its defence and the attempts it makes to replicate it in new markets. It is probably too early to say just how contestable such monopolies are or will be or how effective the Internet guerrillas might be in aiding their fall.

Although there are many contradictions inherent in assessing how electronic networks will change work and employment patterns over the next 20 years I suspect that workplaces for the majority of us will look more or less the same. Bands of guerrillas will move into and out of the corporate machine much as they are beginning to do now – sometimes long-term, sometimes short term, sometimes, as life in the hills gets more precarious, they will sell out altogether. The truth is that although the next 20 years is not so hard to predict, beyond that the balance between guerrilla and corporate economics is not easy to see.

## More state, less state

The drives of corporations like Microsoft, Intel, News International, Disney, Yahoo, Oracle, Cisco and Sun involve a not very profound mix of gradualism (to keep the installed base) and opportunism (to buy up quickly new ideas and keep them in the family). The drives of states, to keep the best of their culture and their traditions while bending a little to assimilate new social, economic and technological trends, look similar and their adaptability, and tenacity in retaining a large measure of influence over their citizens, should not be underestimated. Like some futuristic views of the city the death of the nation state has been greatly exaggerated.

Those commentators who see a millennium dominated by corporations who know no boundaries and who occasionally issue global manifestos are often those who also see a world of independent screen-watchers selling their intelligence to the highest bidder wherever they are. A world full of independent cyber-guerrillas *and* a world where state boundaries have been replaced by over-mighty corporations seems something of a contradiction. Our faith in the political systems of states may be in crisis and in need of radical change but independent workers such as these need the support of a state as much as anyone else. They need it to regulate their environment, to provide roads, to protect them, to

manage their areas of natural beauty, to regulate the over-mighty corporation, to give them some cultural identity and to give them some rights
of citizenship rather than just an option to buy some electricity.

The oft-discussed demise of the state ignores the unique part that
it plays in the network of global interconnectivity. The market needs a
political framework. The state needs societal legitimacy. Societal legitimacy requires economic productivity and both wealth and power require
science and technology. Excising one part inevitably threatens the whole.
There can be no doubt that all states face the challenge of powerful market
forces that in media headlines seem to reduce all individual–society relations to no more than restrictive contracts. It is also true that many of
the identity-based social movements that we now see around the world
have grown up as protests against the powers of the state. We see this
in the militia and patriot groups in the US, the Basque separatist movement in Spain, and the ongoing struggle by the Quebeçois to set
themselves up as an independent entity within Canada.

Contrarily other groups have also arisen as defensive movements
mobilized by fear of state impotence in defending its citizens from what
they regard as the worst effects of racial dilution, trans-national consumerism and the informationalized capitalism that feeds it. We have also
seen an explosion in nationalism, partly as protest against the nation state
as it was defined in the nineteenth century. The explicit goal of the new
nationalist movements has been to create an entity, a new state, based
on perceived identity rather than historical heritage or territorial control.
This narrow definition of statehood, i.e. the principle that the right to self-
rule resides solely in ethno-linguistic credentials, while sitting uneasily
alongside the liberal ideal of the multi-racial state, has been the driving
force among many of the countries that emerged after the fall of communism. During all this upheaval the notion that people can reconcile more
than one cultural identity with their individual selves has been surrendered
to the more exclusive and simple notions of the jihad variety which always
need an enemy on whom to focus their rage.

In a replay of the struggles that characterized post-colonial Africa's
rejection of the map-making constructions of their colonial masters these
new movements challenge the concept of the state which emerged as a
result of historical alliances, old treaties signed at gunpoint or convenient
border drawing. The atrocities of ethnic cleansing that we have seen in
the Balkans have shown this definition of statehood to be as intolerant

and as impoverished as the policies of those oppressors who once ruled them as part of old and corrupt empires. In the UK nationalist movements in Ireland, Wales and Scotland, seizing on the devolution opportunities offered by the new UK government, have increased their profile and sense of identity. The 'English' meanwhile are beginning a struggle to understand just where they fit in a jigsaw where the smaller pieces seem to own more certainties about themselves.

The vibrant regionalism that we see around the world, in the UK, Canada, Spain and in South West region of China, and the growth of economic regions such as the EU, ASEAN and NAFTA both stand in stark contrast to the rhetoric of globalization and harmonization that has long commandeered the high ground of debate about trade, finance and economics. The emergence of the nation state, the industrial revolution, the persistence of conflict and optimistic expansion overseas – these were the drivers that transformed Europe's role from a regional power to a global one. Now ecology, planetary environment, identity, knowledge, capital, population, sovereignty and military power feature at the centre of the new forces that will dominate the start of the new millennium.

Despite the continuing influence of the US on all corners of the globe we are also seeing something of a shift from a world dominated by the west to one where the west's influence is felt more as a set of 'westernistic' ideas. A vast penumbra of peoples and cultures has been influenced by western ideas. The new millennium will see the end of a long period of direct western dominance and the start of a new period where western nations are more *primus inter pares* than *primus*. So many cultures have been so heavily penetrated by western ideas, many of which are crucial to the generation of wealth and power, that it is a safe bet that, albeit in a more multi-centred and multi-cultural form, they will continue to have important social and economic consequences. Not the least of these will be the continuing influence of western nations in the creative elements of all the ICTs.

## Growing up with the net

In 2010 those babies born in the sunny mid-sixties of reasonably well-to-do parents in developed economies, who will have grown up with computers, Email, computer games and CD encyclopaedias to help with their homework, will be in their mid-forties and occupying leadership roles in business and government. In their teens when IBM launched the first PC, using electronic devices to 'connect' will be second nature to them. However they will find no tranquillity in being able to access everything from everywhere. They will come to know that fast access to more and more information as well as helping them to solve the problems of their day will also create as many challenges and contradictions.

- They will have to accept less personal ownership of knowledge because of all the knowledge that will be signalled to exist.
- They will have to accept less certainty as they are exposed to an explosion of options and counter-strategies as facts and expertise become more disputable and as less and less knowledge is derived from their own senses.
- They will suffer more anxieties as the complexities of life become more visible but no more comprehensible.
- Instead of inhabiting a personal world of greater certainty their confidence will always be qualified by the anxious suspicion of incompleteness.

As well as these personal challenges they will also know that unless a larger population than that for which the workings of free markets allow, are drawn into the networking club:

- Competitive advantage and economic growth will reside with those nations who have developed educational and training systems that offer all citizens the opportunity to understand both the limitations and possibilities of electronic networks and advanced IT.
- A sizeable sub-culture of the disaffected will be created who are not able to access the basic tools of a modern society either at work or at play and whose frustration could become manifest in social unrest.

These last two issues are important because, as well as connecting them to like minds enjoying like lifestyles without leaving their homes or their desks, the electronic nervous systems will also make it easier for them to ignore events going on in the parallel physical world. Poverty and the reality of inner city life is much easier to ignore while cruising cyberspace – indeed poverty, in the techno-global economy, becomes almost invisible while illusory but satisfying constructions of a happy, healthy world are made much easier.

The majority of the babies born in Africa, South America and much of Asia during the mid-sixties will not have grown up in a world of computers and networks. Rather than information overload or an excess of consumer options their anxieties are likely to have more to do with avoiding violence and gaining access to clean water, basic education and medicine for some time to come. It is chastening to remind ourselves that 100 years after the invention of the telephone the majority of people in Africa and Asia have yet to make their first telephone call. At the moment, and despite the migration of many of them to overcrowded cities, most of them connect with each other in small communities and travel over distances that can be covered on foot and in a day much as we did in the early fifteenth century. The easy dispersal of communicating technologies to these peoples, so often accepted as inevitable in the 1960s and 1970s, has not happened. Even with the support of wireless and satellite technology their circumstances suggest that for a long time yet access to the kind of 'liberation technology' that we now celebrate in the west looks set to crawl rather than romp through their lives. Good permanent roads followed by a reliable and cheap bus service is the kind of communications technology that many of them still crave.

## Fax and figures

Paul Krugman, the contrary economist at MIT, typifies the confusion that abounds concerning the impact of IT on employment. On the one hand he argues that technological change will cut the demand for unskilled workers while creating more graduate-level jobs. On the other (noting the paradox that 'computers are very good at doing apparently difficult tasks like highly complicated mathematical calculations, but bad at the apparently simple ones like cleaning a house') he surmises that in consequence they [computers] are more of a threat to graduate-type jobs. In his book *The Accidental Theorist* he suggested that 'by 2005 or so it will become clear that the Internet's impact on the economy has been no greater than the fax machine' [3]. The Internet's impact on the broader economy will be much greater than that of the fax machine, significant though it has been. Most computers can already send faxes to multiple points across the Internet without the intermediate creation of a paper record and although the fax machine is often used to distribute sales information and even to confirm purchases it is not a vehicle around which whole new industries can be built. The Internet may get over-hyped by some and it is often tedious to use but its potential is vast and we are only at the 'childhood' stage.

Computers or computerized robots that clean houses with the kind of slick pattern recognition employed by your average human house-cleaner may well be a long time coming and they may not need to. One sure sign of the future is the great disparity that already exists in what we generically call 'the service industries'. This includes the rise of cheap servant labour to keep house, wash the cars, mow the lawns and do the shopping for all those graduates, too busy making money in knowledge-intensive (or curiosity) services, to do them themselves. If they all lose their jobs and have to return to house cleaning the staff of a lot of the new service industries could take to machine breaking in a big way.

Another sign of the future is the kind of jobs that graduates will be doing as employers continue to upgrade to graduate level jobs held until recently by people with sub-degree qualifications. A study published by consultants Business Strategies in the UK towards the end of 1998 showed that although the demand for graduates continues to rise, growing from around 13 per cent of UK employees in 1981 to 23 per cent in 1996, more and more of the jobs that they now do were traditionally done by less qualified people [4]. The computer will replace some medium and higher level occupations, particularly in those areas of the financial markets that can be reduced to formula and which have always had too many middle-persons just creaming juice off the top. The US has over 5 million private investors using the Internet to trade in shares and bonds (in the UK it is more like 6000), cutting out the person who picks up the phone or who makes contact with a market maker. These investors can now get the same kind of information on share movements at their desk as the big brokerage houses do and their buy and sell orders are executed as the order leaves their screen. Obviously the usual suspects, site-crashes and computer breakdowns, can cause havoc with the newly liberated private investor but systems will get more robust and financial loss as the result of the technology failure, although serious to those involved, is after all just a failure of one opportunity among many.

This kind of 'direct' customer access to the 'core' will increase across a wide range of financial services. The operation of all kinds of insurance, businesses that have relied on a large sales force, some retailing, the travel industry and business to business e-commerce will also 'let more people go' as their intelligence is transferred to zeros and ones on something akin to a Web service. The networked computer as a cutter of labour costs has a lot of potential but it has only recently been put to effective use in aiding the knowledge and curiosity of the world's more developed human capital. There is certainly a lot more to be wrung out of this human-plus-network relationship before the network takes over completely.

## Who's watching who?

Although the disturbing agenda of films like *The Net*, *The Truman show* and *Enemy of the State* feed off our paranoia to reveal glimpses of a sinister world in which we actually might be living, the latter suggesting for instance that governments have been in cahoots with the telecommunications companies since the 1940s to peer stealthily into our lives, privacy no longer seems to be the big issue that it once was. It has become sidelined as we have gradually given up many of those liberties that we once thought were important in order to secure information, to facilitate consumption and to secure a more orderly society. A fundamental part of western culture used to include a strong belief in personal privacy backed up by careful regulation of individual anonymity. Now the level of monitoring of us by 'others' is so great that we have lost the will to fight against it and, worse, we actively collude with the collectors by trading personal information, rarely questioning why a supplier must have it, in order to secure a product or service.

Medical information is particularly vulnerable, and valuable. At their Annual Meeting in 1996 the British Medical Association voted to oppose linking hospital databases to the national network until confidentiality can be guaranteed. The BMA's IT Committee heard evidence from a lawyer working at an AIDS clinic in Boston who reported that patients always go to see her first to find out what they can safely tell their doctor as the clinic's computer records could, quite legally, be accessed by assurance and health insurance companies. A US banker who also happened to sit on the board of an American health centre used information from its database quietly to call in the debts of cancer patients being treated there. Patient information in the UK is also known to have already changed hands insecurely.

Surprisingly these kinds of problems arise not because mischievous hackers on the outside are breaking into hospital computer systems but because people on the inside are tempted by the serious money that others are willing to pay for information about their clients. Encryption technology and secure and restricted areas of databases these help to reduce access to private material but they can often be by-passed and they cannot anticipate every kind of human error or the worst excesses of human nature.

David Brin [5], in an unusual proclamation of faith in human nature, suggests that the only way to overcome the Orwellian nightmare of constant surveillance is for all of us freely to expose all. The nightmare would simply vanish if we created a completely open society where no one could hide in the shadows to misuse or profit from information about others. He argues that we can regain our liberty without the need for strong privacy laws if only we would embrace what he calls a 'transparent society'. In such a society, he argues, we would not mind our anonymity being eroded because everyone, every government and every corporation would be under the same level of 'surveillance'. Such a blanket availability of personal information would protect us from its misuse as its ubiquity would destroy the value to others that its scarcity currently bestows.

It is an interesting idea but without a fundamental shift in the western psyche or in the faith we hold in our institutions any concept that suggests that the watchers will allow us all equal access to watch them is too rich in its utopianism for me. The reality is that a lot of detail about us is already collected by both invasive and non-invasive technologies during our day-to-day transactions and recorded in computers. Currently the connections between different databases are often poorly coordinated because they lack common standards that facilitate effective data exchange but, and the common protocols of the Internet will help here, it will get better. While data exchange strives to improve we are busy laying down a data trail and reinforcing digital effigies and brief biographies of ourselves which later other people in both private and public bureaucracies will be able to read, form opinions about and act upon. Such 'biographies', as well as being largely unauthorized, may also declare us to be unfit, unstable, unreliable and 'unusual' in the eyes of the opinion formers as disorganized and faulty records criss-cross a system that may be good on quick replication but useless at checking or re-validating the information with the primary source, i.e. us.

Despite our collusion with the gathering in of personal information most people still believe in their right to privacy and that privacy is still an important part of their civil liberties. When quizzed about the information that they give away about themselves many people seem surprised that they may be contributing to a large accumulation of personal data or at the potential dimension of its use. Somehow the act of giving it away in small chunks doesn't register as much of a threat. Perhaps we need one or two well-publicized cases of the damage that the agglomeration of 'chunks' can cause as it is traded around to wake more people up to its potential misuse.

As well as feeding our personal details across the Internet and into retail databases that we know are freely traded we are increasingly familiar with CCTV cameras watching us in streets, stores and car parks. Since CCTV was introduced more than 20 years ago the authorities in most developed countries have sought to increase the range of purposes for which it can be used. Using leading-edge neural and pattern recognition technologies originally developed for space and defence applications scientists are confident that it will soon be possible to police whole areas of the UK automatically and alert the authorities to criminal activity. The main barrier to its effective use is still the quality of the images generally produced by existing CCTV equipment. It is perfectly feasible now to develop software that can distinguish between certain actions but the quality of the image capture means that it is often difficult to see exactly what is going on. Most research in the UK, currently funded by the EU, is centred on fusing together information from several sources to present a more accurate report on what the CCTV camera has seen. So we can expect the next step to be the addition of other sensory devices such as microphones to pick up the sound of breaking glass and sensors that can detect the smell of particular substances and trigger an appropriate response [6]. A lot of police time can be wasted in investigating incidents and individuals which turn out to be entirely innocent and it is generally agreed that surveillance technology has proved to be better at protecting property than people, but that it is still not adequately regulated to protect privacy.

## Behaving badly

The availability of the Internet to PCs in workplaces and the growing use of this connectivity in ways that are not related to the core business have generated a parallel growth in desk-top surveillance in offices. Consequently an Internet filtering industry has grown up where companies like Omniquad supply software that allows supervisors to monitor PCs and re-play the way a PC has been used during the day or later at night. Other 'net nanny' software like Mind Sweeper blocks certain words or images from being accessed by a PC, while others allow third parties to read Emails and monitor telephone calls. The wall clocks with pinhole lenses linked directly to a CCTV system is already a reality in a number of corporate headquarters. Employers respond to allegations of 'Big Brother' behaviour by emphasizing that a workplace is after all a place of work and not play, and that, as well as wishing to maintain their credibility, they also have a liability to ensure that their systems are not used for unlawful purposes. The Ministry of Defence, the BBC and NatWest Markets are just three of the UK companies using 'net nanny' software to stop their employees accessing 'adult' material on the Internet. Employees in the UK, it seems, top the league for accessing pornography across the Internet when at work; perhaps it is something to do with sexual repression at home or the laddish 'sex is just a joke' culture that predominates among many twenty-something UK males.

Some case law is already building up around the kind of liability which can arise from misusing an Internet connection, e.g. defamatory Emails, libel, breach of confidence and company liability for virus transmission. Emails, some of them purporting to emanate from Bill Gates, disparaging other company's products played a big part in the US Justice Department's case against Microsoft. The casualization of more and more work inevitably results in less loyalty to companies, particularly among the lower paid part of the temporary spectrum, and a possible side-effect of this is less 'social' responsibility of employees prompting more monitoring by the employers who casualized the work in the first place. We have all seen the 'your conversation may be recorded for security or training purposes' in the literature of companies which use a lot of tele-ordering and the monitoring of the daily key stroke tally of tele-workers has been going on for some time. The boundaries between personal freedom, restriction and responsibility at work have always been fuzzy and access to new forms of connectivity pose challenges of moderation and common sense to both employers and employees. Workplace distractions have come a long way from a stand-alone PC screen suddenly changing from a colourful computer game to the work that it should be showing.

## War as fast politics: where next?

The downside of the survival of the state, although there is no evidence to suggest that a world divided by corporations would act any differently if they thought that their interests were threatened, is its propensity to use war as fast politics. Irrespective of financial crises, famine, floods or pressing social needs poor nations remain determined to spend large sums of money on 'defence' and many rich countries are still spending vast sums on it. During 1999 South Korea announced that it intended to spend £43 billion over five years on defence against the communist North while the US government announced in October 1998 that it was going to increase spending on 'defence' by 10 per cent to $280 billion including a doubling of spending on missile defence. The US increase is a response to government critics who felt that it was increasingly ill-prepared to meet the dangers posed by rogue states (e.g. North Korea, India, Pakistan, Iraq and Libya), weapon proliferation and rising instability in the cold war era. Of the extra money $2 billion will go to the CIA, NSA and other agencies to help repair their threadbare espionage networks. The US was surprised by the distance that North Korean missiles could travel when they were shown off in 1998 (they could hit Hawaii or Alaska), and caught completely off-guard when India conducted its nuclear test in May 1998.

The post-cold war Pentagon foresees a US that needs a minimum capacity to fight two wars simultaneously – one in the greater Middle East, and the other probably somewhere on the Korean peninsula. The concomitant of such a mindset requires sufficient combat divisions, aircraft carriers and fighter wings to handle two conventional wars which, given sufficient personnel and materials, logistical support and superior intelligence, the Pentagon believes the US could just about cope with. However in a study for the US Air Force (USAF) in mid-1998 the Rand Corporation (the Pentagon's favourite think tank) published a list of 'wild cards' for the USAF to consider as possible future sources of conflict [7]. These included:

- a plunge in the cost of sending satellites into earth orbit. If anyone can get them up there then they sure as hell have the technology to drop stuff from them;
- the perfection of sensor technologies that, by making oceans transparent, leave submarines with nowhere to hide;
- revolutionary collapse and disorder affecting friendly countries (e.g. Indonesia);
- lethal airborne viruses, either natural or man-made, which can kill millions of people;
- a Fascist coup in a nuclear-armed country
- An earthquake that devastates highly populated regions of California; and
- A new cold war along 'civilizational' lines between the west and the Islamic world.

Whatever one thinks of these predictions, and I would have included potential water shortages and the ease with which water supplies can be poisoned and polluted, none of them looks like it fits the 'we must be able to fight two wars at once' imagination. Riot troops to prevent looting, hordes of peacekeepers to keep order in far-off places and battalions capable of responding quickly to the impact of big natural disasters look more like the resources that would be needed. Most invasions come as a surprise (despite vast US and European expenditures on intelligence services to predict them) and outbreaks of peace, perhaps in the very war zones where the Pentagon anticipates trouble, are also just as surprising. Russia and China by virtue of their vast nuclear arsenals, access to space technology and sheer size ('strategic depth') are generally regarded as serious regional challengers to the US after 2020. The Rand study acknowledges this but accepts that serious trouble is only really likely if one or the other or both should fail economically.

However, richness and stability have never been an obstacle to bad behaviour. Islamic belligerence draws at least some of its confidence from wealth created by oil revenues and there is no reason to believe that a rich and confident Russia or China would be less likely to use their regional muscle than if they became economically stricken. Rich countries have never had a moratorium on securing more riches or even more confidence, nor on betraying and sacrificing their youth to get them.

Despite all the tools we now have at our disposal to connect with governments the individual citizen remains powerless to stop wars, although we have seen that citizen intervention, aided by media coverage of anti-war protests, to stop them once started has been effective. So much of what we value is destroyed by war that we can only will that the remorse felt by the sane at its continued vitality as a way of negotiating must one day seep into the consciousness of those minded to start them. Until then they will remain a blot on what we call our progress in every other domain. An old 1960s slogan went 'Please wash your hands before leaving the twentieth century'. After a century where violent rather than peaceful ways to connect with each other have been so ascendant a feast of global hand washing might be as good a symbolic thing to do as anything else in the last hour of the last day of 1999.

## Liberating ideas, saving energy

Pontius Pilate's own hand-washing contribution to the start of the first millennium was as the somewhat bemused representative of a great power astonished at the vehemence of the Sanhedrin religious leaders in Judaea in seeking to suppress an idea. Christ was an early 'information' criminal. He made no claim to territorial kingship or to any of Rome's possessions and like many politicians today Pilate's confirmation of his sentence was made on the grounds of political expediency, a desire for a quiet life, rather than any perceived threat to Rome's greatness. Indeed the Emperor Constantine later took up the idea and went on to make it the state religion of the Roman Empire in AD 324.

Christ's teaching was an idea that couldn't be suppressed then, thanks to a network of mobile messengers, and it is impossible to suppress many ideas for very long today. Now they race around the world in a maelstrom connecting and interconnecting in ways which make it difficult to identify the original idea let alone crucify someone for it. The speed with which we disseminate ideas is one of the features about the way we live now that we will bequeath as a 'starter pack' to the citizens of the new millennium. The first of those third millennium generations will look back on the twentieth century as a time when we accelerated the process of liberating ideas from the constraints of time, space, and the cabals of the few to let them flow unimpeded around a primitive global nervous system.

One great advantage they will have over us is that the precise filtering and sieving agents that we yearn for will be at their fingertips and, thus armed, they will more easily control the information-overwhelm that so often cripples us now. Another advantage they may have is that by further leaps in the growth in information transparency the relationship between knowledge and the decisions taken as a result of that knowledge may also be more transparent – a link that we have failed to establish. We are still in the 'bedazzled by communication' phase of the rapid changes going on in ICT, often confusing having more information with having more influence and participation than we really have. They will also see our time, perhaps in association with the faster flow of ideas, as one where we anxiously devoted ourselves to the process of continual re-invention; a time when nothing – childhood, work, old age, education, value or citizenship – was exempt from the imperative of continual revision and review. Depending on their own construction of changing social, economic and technological velocities they may be tempted to dub our time as the 'anxious century'.

However if they find themselves caught up in an even more frantic re-invention of everything they may look back at our slower tempo as a golden age of stability and consolidation. They will also inherit the knowledge that this was the time when we awoke to the reality that all connectivity, no matter how it is orchestrated, has an environmental cost. Their urges to connect are likely to consume even more resources than ours have done. Perhaps they will take forward our tentative experiments with renewable energy and plug in to infinite non-polluting energy sources. If not, and like the complex web of regulations that govern the number of cars on a Singaporean street, they may seek to limit energy use regulating all movement and energy use via ration-chips. Air and automobile travel might be rationed (that embedded microchip could record the number of journies one takes) while whatever passes for a PC/WebTV will automatically turn itself off after consuming its daily quota of energy.

Those first generations of the new millennium will no doubt both thank us and curse us for the connecting habits and behaviours that we leave them. While we may not get all of our legacy right we should at least make sure that we are not cursed for scattering a million and one devices around the world all secretly assuming that all dates begin with 20.

300 *Only Connect: Shaping Networks and Knowledge*

## References

1. von Habsburg, O. (1998) 'Voices, vision of Europe'. *Time* Special Issue, Winter 1998–1999, p.166

2. Drucker, P. (1969) *The age of discontinuity: guidelines to our changing society.* London: Heinman

3. Interview. *THES*, 4 September 1998, p. 23

4. *THES*, 11 December 1998

5. Brin, D. (1998) *The transparent society: will technology force us to choose between privacy and freedom?* London: Addison and Wesley

6. 'Connected', *Daily Telegraph*, 3 December 1998, p. 3

7. Rand Corporation (1998) Study for the US Air Force

# Bibliography

Ascherson, n. (1996) *Black Sea: the birthplace of civilisation and barbarism.* London: Vintage

Brin, D. (1998) *The transparent society: will technology force us to choose between privacy and freedom?* London: Addison and Wesley

Buzan, B. and Segal, G. (1998) *Anticipating the future: 20 millennia of human progress.* London: Simon and Schuster

Cairncross, F. (1997) *The death of distance: how the communications revolution will change our lives.* London: Orion Business

Castells, M. (1998) *The information age: economy, society and culture* (3 vols.), Vol. 1 *The rise of the network society*, Vol. 2 *The power of identity*, Vol. 3 *End of Millennium.* London: Blackwells

Chomsky, N. (1993) *Year 501: the conquest continues*, London: Verso

Critchfield, R. (1994) *The villagers: changed values, altered lives, the closing of the urban–rural gap.* London: Anchor

Cronin, B. (1996) (ed.), *Information, development and social intelligence.* London: Taylor Graham

Davies, N. (1996) *Europe—a history.* Oxford: Oxford University Press

Dicken, P. (1998) *Global shit: transforming the world economy.* London: Paul Chapman Publishing

Dunant, S. and Porter, R. (1996) (eds) *The age of anxiety* London: Virago

Gates, W., Myhrvold, N. and Rinearson, P. (1995) *The road ahead.* London: Viking

Grove, A.S. (1997) *Only the paranoid survive: how to exploit the crisis points that challenge every company and career.* London: Harper Collins

Haywood, T. (1995) *Info-Rich—Info-Poor: access and exchange in the global information society.* London: Bowker Saur

Jamieson, L. (1998) *Intimacy.* Edinburgh: Polity

Janoski, T. (1998) *Citizenship and civil society.* London: Cambridge University Press

Jones, A.G. (1996) *Holding up a mirror: how civilisations decline.* London: Century

Kay, J. (1996) *The business of economics.* London: Oxford University Press

Kelly, K. (1995) *Out of control: the new biology of machines.* London: Fourth Estate

Kelly, K. (1998) *New rules for the new economy: 10 radical strategies for a connected world.* London: Fourth Estate

Lasch, C. (1979) *The culture of narcissim: American life in an age of diminin-ishing expectations.* New York: W.W. Norton & Co

Lasch, C. (1995) *The revolt of the elites and the betrayal of democracy*. New York: W.W. Norton & Co

Loader, B.D. (1998) (ed.) *Cyberspace divide: equality, agency and policy in the information society*. London: Routledge

MacKenzie, D. (1996) *Knowing machines: essays on technical change*. London: MIT Press

McRae, H. (1994) *The world in 2020: power, culture and prosperity: a vision of the future*. London: Harper Collins

Mulgan, G. (1997) *Connexity: how to live in a connected world*. London: Chatto and Windus

Pahal, R. (1998) *Time for life: the surprising ways Americans use their time*. Penn State University Press

Shapiro, C. and Varian, H.R. (1998) *Information rules: a strategic guide to the network economy*. London: MacGraw-Hill

Standage, T. (1998) *The Victorian Internet: the remarkable story of the telegraph and the 19th century's online pioneers*. London: Weidenfeld and Nicolson

Vogelsang, I. and Mitchell, B.M. (1997) *Telecommunications competition: the last ten miles*. London: MIT Press and AEI

Wallace, J. (1997) *Overdrive: Bill Gates and the race to control cyberspace*. London: John Wiley

von Weizacker, E., Lovins, A.B. and Lovins, L.H. (1977) *Factor four: doubling wealth halving resource use*. The New Report To The Club Of Rome. London: Earthscan

Winston, B. (1998) *Media, technology and society: a history: from the telegraph to the internet*, London: Routledge

## Journals/newspapers

*Newsweek* and *Time* are both useful sources for on-going debates about the impact of 'globalization' and every aspect of connectivity, particularly in relation to the world of business and politics.

*The Economist* often produces valuable 'surveys' of the computer industry, Silicon Valley, electronic commerce etc., which are pithy, accurate and up-to-date. *The Financial Times* also produces regular supplements on information technology.

*The Daily Telegraph* produces its 'Connected' supplement on Tuesdays.

*The Times* produces 'Interface' each Wednesday.

*The Guardian* produces 'Guardian OnLine' on Wednesdays.

*Scientific American* and *New Scientist* often devote special sections or even whole issues to developments in computer and networking technology.

Other publications of interest include *The Harvard Business Review, Information, Communication and Society: An International Journal for the Information Age, THES, Investors Chronicle* and *The Independent.*

All these newspapers and journals have W3 pages, many of which are selectively archived.

# World Wide Web pages

As noted earlier the World Wide Web can be one of the most exciting and one of the most frustrating sources of information. It can provide you with information before any other form of publication and it can hold out-of-date information for months before someone chooses to change it. The breadth of its coverage is astonishing to anyone working in the area of connectivity, telecommunications, computing and communications. I note below a few of the sites I have found of interest while working on this book and, as is always the case with the Internet, these few will guide you to yet more pages that will guide you to yet more. My advice to help avoid the 'malice of cyberspace' is to choose carefully, be selective and as soon as you begin to feel intimidated by it all turn your computer off and take the dog for a walk. All the big telecommunications, computing and software companies have W3 sites which are easily found via the various search engines now available. They 'showcase' their latest offerings and often provide access to their latest press releases. The W3 is also one of the best ways to keep up-to-date with the litigation going on between the 'browser' warriors and the other controversies that always beset this fast moving industry.

http://www.cwc.com/main.html   Cable and Wireless's Web page often carries brief pieces on telecommunications issues by industry commentators as well as the usual self-adulation.

As you would expect all the new satellite mobile phone enterprises have W3 pages:

ICO Global Communications is at http://www.ico.com

Iridium is at http://www.iridium.com

Globalstar is at http://www.globalstar.com

http://netec.mcc.ac.uk/~adnetec/FAQ/EconFAQ.html is a goldmine about economic resources on the Internet which also provides links to other sites with a similar 'guiding' function. This site is organized by Bill Goffe at the Department of Economics and International Business, University of Southern Mississippi, Hattiesburg, MS 39406.

http://www.sims.berkeley.edu/resources/infoecon/Networks.html   is   a
fascinating guide to academic papers and other documents available on
the Internet collected under the broad heading 'Network Economics'. It
provides links to a wide range of economic and technical information about
networking including links to the pages of the main US telecommunications companies.

http://cism.bus.utexas.edu/   The   Centre   for   Research   in   Electronic
Commerce at the University of Texas at Austin offers a wide range of
information about academic activity in the area of electronic commerce
including the full text of a selection of recent scholarly articles and their
own 'EC World Online' electronic journal covering the emerging discipline of Electronic Commerce.

http://www.spy.org.uk/   'quis custodiet isto custodes'. Paranoid about
those cameras and who might be watching you? Then you will love this
Web site. The UK CCTV Surveillance Regulation Campaign believes that
there are too many CCTV cameras out there watching our every move.
They aim to open up debate about the extent to which powerful technologies such as linked CCTV camera systems, neural network facial
recognition, car number plate recognition, multimedia image databases,
etc. are being applied in the UK.

http://www.auburn.edu/tann   Teledemocracy   Action   News + Network
is the Web site of the Global Democracy Movement dedicated to
the creative use of electronic media in all forms that directly empower
citizens to have meaningful input into the political system. Run by the
Department of Political Science Auburn University, Alabama 36849, it
also seeks to 'rate' projects going on around the world in terms of
their potential for real 'empowerment' rather than just show. It uses
a lightning bolt icon to signify the worth of the projects it surveys, i.e.
1–2 lightning bolts is Reformist, 3–4 lightning bolts is Republican/
Transformational and a project that scores 5–6 lightning bolts is
Democratic/Transformational.

http://www.brunel.ac.uk/research/virtsoc is the Web site of the 'Virtual
Society' research programme funded by the UK ESRC at Brunel
University. This programme gets involved in the 'big' debates about

whether or not fundamental shifts are taking place in the way people behave and interact as a result of electronic technologies. Lots of news from the programme is given here including conference dates, seminar papers, etc. The site provides an overview of the Virtual Society research going on at Brunel and allows you to access information on the other 22 projects currently funded by the ESRC.

http://info.isoc.org/guest/zakon/Internet/History/HIT.html is the location for Robert H. Zakon's 'Hobbes' Internet Timeline, v3.3. Hosted by the Internet Society this is a valuable source of information about the history of the Internet from 1957 to date including graphs on Internet Hosts, Internet Networks and WWW Server Growth.

# Index